W9-BUM-983

Championship Swim Training

BILL SWEETENHAM

JOHN ATKINSON

HUMAN KINETICS

Library of Congress Cataloging-in-Publication Data

Sweetenham, Bill, 1950-
    Championship swim training / Bill Sweetenham, John Atkinson.
        p. cm.
    Includes bibliographical references and index.
        ISBN 0-7360-4543-0 (soft cover)
    1. Swimming--Training.   I. Atkinson, John, 1968 Jan. 16-   II. Title.
    GV837.7.S93 2003
    797.2--dc21

                                                    2003008457

ISBN: 0-7360-4543-0

Copyright © 2003 by William Sweetenham and John Atkinson

All rights reserved. Except for use in a review, the reproduction or utilization of this work in any form or by any electronic, mechanical, or other means, now known or hereafter invented, including xerography, photocopying, and recording, and in any information storage and retrieval system, is forbidden without the written permission of the publisher.

Notice: Permission to reproduce the following material is granted to instructors and agencies who have purchased *Championship Swim Training*: pp. 24, 27-29, 33, 36, 40-42, 44, 45, 47, 49, 51, 69-70, 83-84, 94-96, 107-108, 215, 281-288. The reproduction of other parts of this book is expressly forbidden by the above copyright notice. Persons or agencies who have not purchased *Championship Swim Training* may not reproduce any material.

Acquisitions Editor: Martin Barnard; **Developmental Editor:** Leigh LaHood; **Copyeditor:** Robert Replinger; **Proofreader:** Kim Thoren; **Indexer:** Betty Frizzéll; **Permission Manager:** Toni Harte; **Graphic Designer:** Robert Reuther; **Graphic Artist:** Sandra Meier; **Art and Photo Manager:** Dan Wendt; **Cover Designer:** Keith Blomberg; **Photographer (cover):** Empics/SportsChrome; **Photographer (interior):** Dan Wendt, unless otherwise noted; **Illustrator:** Roberto Sabas (line drawings) and Brian McElwain (graphs); **Printer:** Bang Printing

We thank the Urbana Aquatic Center in Urbana, Illinois, for assistance in providing the location for the photo shoot for this book.

Human Kinetics books are available at special discounts for bulk purchase. Special editions or book excerpts can also be created to specification. For details, contact the Special Sales Manager at Human Kinetics.

Printed in the United States of America

10   9   8   7   6   5   4   3   2   1

Human Kinetics
Web site: www.HumanKinetics.com

United States: Human Kinetics
P.O. Box 5076, Champaign, IL 61825-5076
800-747-4457
e-mail: humank@hkusa.com

Canada: Human Kinetics
475 Devonshire Road Unit 100, Windsor, ON N8Y 2L5
800-465-7301 (in Canada only)
e-mail: orders@hkcanada.com

Europe: Human Kinetics
107 Bradford Road, Stanningley, Leeds LS28 6AT, United Kingdom
+44 (0) 113 255 5665
e-mail: hk@hkeurope.com

Australia: Human Kinetics
57A Price Avenue, Lower Mitcham, South Australia 5062
08 8277 1555
e-mail: liahka@senet.com.au

New Zealand: Human Kinetics
P.O. Box 105-231, Auckland Central
09-523-3462
e-mail: hkp@ihug.co.nz

Championship Swim Training

Contents

Preface **vii** | *Acknowledgments* **x**

PART I

Technique Drills and Sets 1

CHAPTER 1   Training Systems 3

A look at the different types of training and how to individualize intensities within five training zones: aerobic, anaerobic threshold, high-performance endurance, anaerobic, and sprint.

CHAPTER 2   Benchmark Test Sets 17

Twelve test sets and testing progressions that can be used for evaluating certain types of training, making adjustments to stroke mechanics, or setting future training times.

CHAPTER 3   Drilling for Performance 55

The reasoning behind the use of stroke-efficiency progressions for the four main competition strokes and how they are linked to stroke improvement.

CHAPTER 4   Butterfly 61

Six progressions to improve the complex butterfly stroke, with emphasis on such aspects as timing, breathing, and kick development.

CHAPTER 5   Backstroke 73

Twelve progressions for the backstroke, focusing on trunk rotation and the early application of force in the catch.

CHAPTER 6   Breaststroke 85

Twelve progressions to work on the kick as well as the lower-leg and ankle rotation needed to perfect breaststroke technique.

CHAPTER 7   Freestyle 99

Ten progressions designed to develop a balanced freestyle technique, with emphasis on rotation.

CHAPTER 8   Individual Medley **113**

Drill progressions, planning tips, and specific sets for conditioning, improving individual medley, and switching between strokes during competition.

CHAPTER 9   Sculling **127**

Sculling drills for each stroke, as well as for improving core strength and feel for the water.

CHAPTER 10   Starts, Turns, Finishes, and Relay Takeovers **137**

Drills, progressions, and technique checklists for the starts, turns, and finishes of each stroke, along with a discussion on relay swimming.

CHAPTER 11   Kick and Pull Training **161**

Over 50 sample sets for the training of kick and pull as endurance, quality, and speed work.

PART II

Workouts and Programs . . . 169

CHAPTER 12   Program Planning **171**

Advice on how to create and implement long-term and short-term training plans, recommended macrocycles and microcycles for age-group, youth, senior, masters, and triathlete swimmers, and information on developing junior swimmers.

CHAPTER 13   Sets for Training Zones **213**

More than 170 sets for the five training zones, categorized according to emphasis and distance.

CHAPTER 14   Tapering for Competition **237**

Information on how to plan and individualize a taper, tips on what to include in specific taper weeks, and a checklist to help with preparing for competition.

CHAPTER 15   Dryland Conditioning **253**

Tests for core strength and flexibility and specific exercises to work leg muscles, abdominal muscles, and other areas needed for strength and flexibility.

CHAPTER 16   Program Evaluation **279**

Details and examples of the information and evaluation forms that should go into a swimmer's training log.

Glossary **289** | References **294** | Index **297** | About the Authors **301**

Preface

This handbook is intended to provide swimmers and coaches from all backgrounds with practical tips to enhance their swimming programs. To maximize an athlete's potential, the coach should consider Bill Sweetenham's five golden rules for competitive swimming:

1. Every hand and arm movement is slow to fast. The learning process must therefore be slow to fast. If the swimmer can't do it efficiently at low speed, he or she won't be able to do it efficiently at high speed.

2. The athlete must learn to feel the water and so he or she must spend time doing that rather than just swimming fast. Learning how to feel the water the wrong way in comparison with the right way can help athletes learn the correct feel of the water. The coach may ask swimmers to swim one lap freestyle pulling with the arms outside the body line, then one lap with the arms pulling under the body, and finally one lap with the arms pulling under the body with a narrow pull. The athletes will learn the feel of pulling in different ways. They discover the correct feel by first performing the wrong way.

Another example of this learning method can be used with streamlining. The coach can have the athlete push off the wall like a star fish, push off the wall with the hands and arms at shoulder-width, and then push off the wall in the hand-over-hand streamlined position.

Most children do things the wrong way first as part of the natural progression of learning. Then, if they get it right later, they appreciate the benefits. Most fail, however, before they succeed. Winners do not accept failure, and they move on to find success. Losers accept failure and find excuses.

3. The fingers pull first, no matter what stroke the athlete is swimming. The swimmer maintains stable wrist position when pulling.

4. The swimmer minimizes resistance by keeping the head down and the buttocks up. No matter what the athlete does in swimming, if the head comes up the buttocks go down. To maximize force on the water with minimal resistance, the athlete must keep the back flat, in what can be called the flat-spine position.

5. The hips should be high on butterfly and breaststroke before the outsweep of the hands and arms begins. If the hips are not elevated, the athlete will be pulling himself or herself to the surface of the water (upward) rather then pulling forward. In backstroke and freestyle the hips should rotate before the hands start the pulling action.

This book offers something to every swimmer, regardless of background—the age-group, youth, or senior competitive swimmer, as well as the masters swimmer wanting to improve his or her swimming. If triathlon is your sport the section for freestyle drills can improve your technique, and the program planning and sets will make your training program more varied, interesting, and challenging. The five golden rules apply to all swimmers, regardless of background. All the training sets, test sets, and drill progressions outlined in this book can be adjusted to suit the skill and maturation level of the swimmer performing them. The coach or swimmer should consider those factors before the swimmer completes any recommended set, test, or progression. Adjustments may also be necessary for performing the set, test, or progression in a long-course or short-course pool.

The book is divided into two parts. Part I, "Technique Drills and Sets," includes chapters on training zones and benchmark test sets. These chapters give the swimmer and coach an understanding of the zones in which the swimmer needs to work. The benchmark test sets offer a practical way of evaluating training and setting future training programs and targets.

Part I includes a series of drill progressions and checklists relevant to each stroke and the individual medley (IM). Part I also covers sculling, starts, turns, finishes, and kick and pull training. The drill progressions can be applied to squad training for technique enhancement. Swimmers and coaches need to have a stroke model for each stroke and apply it to their strokes and swimmers. Coaches need to analyze the technique of their swimmers and choose a way to correct any faults. Technique is important for all swimmers because speed is a result of efficiency. Coaches and swimmers should have a series of drill progressions that they can use in different situations to improve deficiencies in stroke technique. For every stroke fault, a drill or progression is available to correct it. To improve feel for the water, swimmers should learn to scull efficiently. Later, they perform drill progressions for each stroke that incorporate sculling, and they integrate those skills into full-stroke swimming.

The individual medley should be regarded as a whole event, not just a collection of four strokes. We therefore devote a full chapter to it. Individual medley preparation should serve as a model for developing junior and age-group swimmers. To help the coach develop the individual medley swimmer, planning and training-set design are covered in detail. Every individual medley swimmer should complete the strengths and weaknesses chart shown in chapter 2 to identify their specific training requirements.

Starts, turns, and finishes are crucial for all events. Chapter 10 offers drill progressions and tips for starts, turns, and finishes in all strokes. Checklists for all strokes and events give the swimmer and coach tips for both training and competition.

Part II, "Workouts and Programs," gives the swimmer and coach an understanding of how to plan training sets using training classifications. The appropriate application of training sets is essential to the long-term development of swimmers and to ensuring that they receive the correct mixture of training required by their main events. Chapter 12 deals with planning the program for all swimmers, from juniors through to masters. Chapter 13 gives sample training sets that the swimmer and coach can use or amend to suit the required level.

Having constructed the yearly program, the swimmer and coach need to understand how to fine-tune for competition (race preparation). Chapter 14 deals with the taper, the crucial final phase of the plan. Following the taper, of course, the competition occurs. At national open level, the swimmer will have to cope with a progression of heats, semifinals, and finals in most events. Training for this element of the competition is covered in detail.

Dryland conditioning can provide substantial benefit to the swimmer. Chapter 15 deals with specific dryland training for swimming and covers tests, warming up, core strength training, and stretching.

Chapter 16 provides information about how to conduct a practical evaluation of a training program. Of course, competitions are the final test for swimmers, and test sets can be used to gain information along the way.

All coaches should have a one-page statement of their coaching philosophy and model that covers the physical and mental preparation of their athletes. More important than what is in the model is the coach's daily dedication to the coaching task and his or her belief in the model. Both the coach and the swimmers in the program must have confidence in the model.

We feel that this book will help both the swimmer and coach perform better in their respective roles.

The great challenge for national governing bodies is converting swimmers who are involved in the sport to swimmers who are committed to the sport. This is done by bridging the gap between participation and performance and understanding the difference. The following progression for maturation-age athletes is crucial to their achieving success in competitive swimming.

Swimming 8 Hours a Week

This level offers participation, fun, involvement, and significant heath benefits, but it is not competition swimming and never produces a competitive result.

Swimming 10 to 12 Hours a Week

This amount of swimming is too much training to be fun but not enough to produce a competitive result. The swimmers in this middle ground never feel good, and in time they become frustrated. We call this the competitive swimming twilight zone.

Swimming 18 to 24 Hours a Week

This level can be termed competitive swimming. Athletes in this program are committed and gain satisfaction by attaining improved competitive results.

There is a place for the 8 hour-a-week swimmer. The job of the coach is to sell the dream to the athletes doing 10 to 12 hours a week and persuade them to commit to the 18 to 24 hours a week they need to become successful competitive swimmers.

Acknowledgments

In writing this book we began to realize the amount of time and effort that goes into producing such a publication.

We are grateful to Dr. Ralph Richards for his valuable input to the book throughout its many stages. His expertise was extremely useful. Ralph provided the initial underwater photographs and was responsible for the videotaping and editing of swim footage, which now appears throughout the book as illustrations.

A book such as this results from what we learned by coaching great athletes and working with many outstanding coaches along the way.

Technique Drills and Sets

Training Systems

Specific training will improve different aspects of the swimmer's fitness. This chapter will look at the different types of swimming training that swimmers need to reach the level of fitness that will produce their best performance in the approaching competitions. The training that swimmers perform can be classified into five training-zone categories:

Zone 1—aerobic (A1, A2, A3)

Zone 2—anaerobic threshold

Zone 3—high-performance endurance (critical speed, lactate removal, and $M\dot{V}O_2$)

Zone 4—anaerobic (race-pace training, lactic-acid accumulating)

Zone 5—sprint

Zones can contain more than one type of training, as shown in parentheses in the preceding list and discussed in more detail in this chapter. The training zones are based on the level of intensity and swimming velocity required when training within each of the zones.

Coaches should try to simplify their evaluation of workout practices. Table 1.1 shows the percentage of the total training volume that swimmers should complete in each type of work. Zone 1, the least intense training zone, includes a greater total volume of work than any other zone. Zones 2 and 3 are grouped together, and most swimmers perform the next largest block of work in these zones. Most swimmers do the smallest amount of training in zones 4 and 5.

Monitor training in all of the training zones, because what you expect and what you get are often very different.

The coach and swimmer should monitor training in all the training zones, because what the coach and swimmer expect and what they get are often very different. If the swimmer performed zone 1 training at excessive intensity, it would affect his or her ability to perform training at the required level in zones 2 and 3.

TABLE 1.1 PERCENTAGE OF TOTAL TRAINING VOLUME

Type of swimmer	Aerobic (zone 1)	Anaerobic threshold and high-performance endurance (zones 2 and 3)	Race pace and speed (zones 4 and 5)
Age-group and youth swimmers	70%	20%	10%
Male sprinters	80%	10%	10%
Reverse periodization sprinters	50%	20%	30%
Female endurance swimmers	60%	30%	10%
Senior swimmers (post-maturation, not male sprinters or female endurance swimmers)	70%	20%	10%
Masters	85%	10%	5%
Triathletes	65%	25%	10%

How to Individualize Training Zones

Individual heart-rate values may be used to define some of the training zones. Another method used to identify training zones is to relate swimming speed to personal best times plus a constant (Pyne 1999b). All swimmers should train at intensities appropriate to them. The swimmer and coach can use two methods to set appropriate training paces.

If two swimmers training in the same pool have different maximum heart rates, are performing a zone 1 training set, and have been told by the coach to work at 40 beats below their maximum heart rates, they are working at their own levels. That is, the training is specific for each even if they are working at different heart-rate levels. The first swimmer, with a maximum heart rate of 201, is working at 161 beats per minute, whereas the second swimmer, with a maximum heart rate of 181, is working at 141 beats per minute. Both are working at the same level, but the training has been individualized to suit them.

If the coach asked each swimmer to train at a prescribed heart-rate level of 160 beats per minute and called this a zone 1 training set, the training would have a different effect on the two swimmers. The first swimmer, with a maximum heart rate of 201, would be working at 160 beats per minute, which is 41 beats below his or her maximum heart rate. This would be a good zone 1 set for the swimmer. The second swimmer would be working at 21 beats below his or her maximum heart rate and would be completing the set at the wrong intensity. This swimmer would be working a zone 2 set, which would be an inappropriate training set for that swimmer. Continued exposure to training at this intensity could lead to overtraining and have a detrimental effect on competitive performance. When using heart rates to monitor training intensity, the swimmer should work at beats below maximum to individualize training requirements.

The second method uses information about the swimmer's personal best time to establish training repeat times. This method will also individualize the training by setting a training repeat time for each swimmer in the program.

Examples

Personal best time for 200 m freestyle = 2:00.00

Half of the 200 m time = 1:00.00 for 100 m, as a training time

1:00.00 + 20 seconds = aerobic 1 pace (zone 1)	target time = 1:20.00
1:00.00 + 15 to 20 seconds = aerobic 2 pace (zone 1)	target time = 1:15.00 to 1:20.00
1:00.00 + 10 to 15 seconds = aerobic 3 pace (zone 1)	target time = 1:10.00 to 1:15.00
1:00.00 + 7 to 10 seconds = anaerobic threshold pace (zone 2)	target time = 1:07.00 to 1:10.00
1:00.00 + 4 to 7 seconds = high-performance endurance (zone 3)	target time = 1:04.00 to 1:07.00

Personal best time for 200 m backstroke = 2:16.00

Half of the 200 m time = 1:08.00 for 100 m

1:08.00 + 20 seconds = aerobic 1 pace (zone 1)	target time = 1:28.00
1:08.00 + 15 to 20 seconds = aerobic 2 pace (zone 1)	target time = 1:23.00 to 1:28.00
1:08.00 + 10 to 15 seconds = aerobic 3 pace (zone 1)	target time = 1:18.00 to 1:23.00
1:08.00 + 7 to 10 seconds = anaerobic threshold pace (zone 2)	target time = 1:15.00 to 1:18.00
1:08.00 + 4 to 7 seconds = high-performance endurance (zone 3)	target time = 1:12.00 to 1:15.00

Zone 1—Aerobic

The aerobic training zone represents swimming intensity below the anaerobic threshold. The body and muscles can cope with the amount of lactic acid being produced because it does not accumulate in large quantities in the muscles. Swimmers will produce lactic acid as they swim, no matter what the training intensity. Low-intensity zone 1 swimming will produce low levels of lactic acid, whereas swimming at high intensity will produce high levels of lactic acid.

The three types of aerobic training—A1, A2, and A3—provide balance to the overall training and the range of aerobic development.

A1—recovery work (to complement anaerobic and sprint work)

A2—aerobic maintenance

A3—greater aerobic stimulus to increase aerobic capacity

We recommend that A1 training not be done with females, unless they are heavily built sprinters. A2 training is more important than A1 training for the high-recovering type of athlete (that is, females).

Aerobic 1 (A1)—Low Intensity

Swimmers should train at a heart rate 70 to 50 beats below maximum. The suggested pace is half of personal best 200 m time plus 20 seconds (Pyne 1999b). The repeat distances to use when training at this level are 200 m to 1500 m, with very short rest between swims. The rest interval should be 5 to 20 seconds between repeats. Training

Jim Baron/The Image Finders

Swimmers can use personal best time to set repeat times, thus individualizing their training zones.

repeat distances of over 1500 m may be appropriate for some middle distance and distance swimmers.

Aerobic 2 (A2) — Aerobic Maintenance

Swimmers should train at a heart rate 50 to 40 beats below maximum. The suggested pace is half of personal best 200 m time plus 15 to 20 seconds (Pyne 1999b). The individual checking speed of plus 15 (freestyle, backstroke, and butterfly) and plus 20 (breaststroke) fits into this training zone (Atkinson and Sweetenham 1999). The repeat distances to use when training in this category are 200 m to 1500 m. The rest interval should be 10 to 20 seconds. As with A1 training, some repeat distances of over 1500 m may be appropriate.

Aerobic 3 (A3) — Aerobic Development

Training should be at a heart rate 40 to 30 beats below maximum. The suggested pace is half of personal best 200 m time plus 10 to 15 seconds (Pyne 1999b). This pace may overlap slightly with the anaerobic-threshold training pace for some swimmers. The repeat distances to use for training in this category are 50 m to 400 m with a rest interval of 10 to 20 seconds.

Zone 2 — Anaerobic Threshold

The point at which the lactate accumulation begins to rise sharply is termed the anaerobic threshold (R. Richards 1999, personal communication; Pyne 1999a, 1999b; Carew and Pyne 1999; Sweetenham 1990).

Swimmers should train at a heart rate 30 to 20 beats below maximum. This type of training is best done on repeat distances of 50 to 400 m. Shorter repeat distances use shorter rest intervals.

Distance	Rest interval
50 m swims	10 seconds
100 or 200 m swims	10 to 20 seconds
200 or 400 m swims	10 to 20 seconds

Set length ranges from 1500 to 5000 m as follows:

Sprinters	2000 to 3000 m
Middle distance	3000 to 4500 m
Distance swimmers	5000 m or more

A timed 3000 m swim can be used to gauge the anaerobic threshold training paces for swimmers. The 2000 m test is probably better for age-group and sprint swimmers. Chapter 2 describes these sets. The suggested pace is half of personal best 200 m time plus 7 to 10 seconds (Pyne 1999a, 1999b).

Zone 3—High-Performance Endurance

In zone 3 the swimmer works at a high intensity that he or she can maintain for the duration of the set. The coach and swimmer must understand that the swimmer should not work too hard at the beginning of the training sets in this zone. The swimmer who reaches maximum heart rate in the early stages of the set is working at too much intensity and may not be able to sustain the effort through the total distance of the set. This circumstance will affect the quality of any speed training that the coach may have scheduled for the next day's training.

Critical Speed

Critical speed (CS) is sometimes referred to as heart-rate training. The heart rate should be 20 to 10 beats below maximum, and the duration of the set should be 30 minutes of swimming effort. The best repeat distances to use when training in this category are 50 to 200 m.

The work-to-rest ratio should be approximately 1.5:1. A sample set is 24 × 100 m freestyle on 1:45 with the swimmer holding a time of 65 seconds per 100 m repeat. The recommended set length is 1500 m to 3000 m, although this will vary according to the time taken to complete the amount of work on the set. For example, a swimmer with a critical speed of 60 seconds per 100 m repeat could do a set of 30 × 100 m on 1 minute 45 seconds and hold 60 seconds for each repeat, providing 30 minutes of work. A swimmer with a critical speed of 1:15 per 100 m repeat on breaststroke would need to do a set of 24 × 100 m breaststroke on 2:00 to achieve 30 minutes of work.

Establishing training paces for critical speed training sets can also be done by using the heart rate versus velocity graph from the 7 × 200 m step test, as outlined in chapter 2 (see page 21).

The 7 × 200 m step-test heart rate versus velocity curve should be extrapolated to the swimmer's maximum heart rate. This point will show the critical speed of the swimmer, which is the pace the swimmer should hold on these sets.

Critical speed is also the point at which the athlete first reaches maximum oxygen uptake. Note that the intensity of a 400 m swim in competition is 3 to 4 percent faster than the swimmer's critical speed, and the intensity of the 200 m swim in competition is 8 percent faster than the swimmer's critical speed.

When performing this type of training, the 3 × 200 m snapshot test (at third, fourth, and fifth 200 m speed from the 7 × 200 m step test) should be used in the warm-up of the training session so that the coach and swimmer can compare the current stage of fitness and fatigue against what the swimmer did in the 7 × 200 m step test. Chapter 2 explains this in more detail.

If the result from the 3 × 200 m snapshot test shows a shift to the right when drawn on the laminated heart-rate velocity curve, or the result is on the curve from the previous test, the coach and swimmer can expect a good heart-rate set in the training session. If the result from the 3 × 200 m snapshot test is somewhat to the left of the curve, they can expect a different outcome and revise the training repeat times for the set.

If the swimmer swims too fast early in the set, he will not attain the desired effect of the set. That is, if the swimmer attains maximum heart rate in the first section of the set, he will be working too hard.

Attaining maximum heart rate in these sets will produce a buildup of lactate in muscle fibers. Continuation at this level will not allow the removal of lactate to take place as quickly as its production does, which will inhibit the swimmer's ability to do fast "speed" work the next day.

Some race pace can be built into the set, but the set should contain enough critical speed work to ensure that swimmers do not achieve maximum heart rate, especially sprinters. The reasoning for this is that distance swimmers have a critical speed pace closer to their racing speed than sprint athletes do (B. Treffene 2002, personal communication).

The actual point of critical speed is at maximum heart rate and maximum oxygen uptake, but the training to improve CS is largely centered on 20 to 10 beats below maximum heart rate level (D. Pyne 2000, personal communication). A way to judge if the set has been completed at the right level is for swimmers to perform the final 100 m repeat of the set at maximum effort. If they swim the last 100 m repeat of the set faster than they do any of the other 100 m repeats throughout the set, they have performed the set at the right intensity. If they cannot do this, they have worked too hard throughout the set.

When coaching swimmers on heart-rate sets, the coach should not hesitate to amend the training repeats to ensure that swimmers attain the required pace on the set.

Loss of technique can be a sign of working above the required level, even if the swimmer is holding the times. If this is the case, the coach may back off the swimmer on the set and have him or her hold a slower pace, give the swimmer more rest per repeat, or change 100 m repeats to 75 m repeats and 75 m repeats to 50 m repeats.

The swimmer should train down to high-performance endurance sets. For example, the swimmer should achieve 45 × 100 m on 1:20 (making cycle, with heart-rate level not important) at any heart rate and then reduce to doing 30 × 100 m on 1:45 to 2:00 at a prescribed heart-rate level (Sweetenham 1999a). Refer to the high-performance endurance test-set progression in chapter 2.

Lactate Removal

Bill Sweetenham introduced this term in 2001 to describe training in which an athlete produces high levels of lactic acid from high-performance endurance training. The purpose is for the athlete to work through a training set with high levels of lactate, which requires the systems of the body to remove high levels of lactate to complete the set. This training will cause the body to make significant training adaptations.

For example, swimming a typical critical speed set over 24 × 100 m will cause the lactate level of the swimmer to build through the set. For males the set should be conducted at 15 to 20 beats below the maximum heart rate, and for females the set should be at 10 to 15 beats below the maximum heart rate.

After completing the final competitive performance in a midseason competition, the swimmer should go straight to the swim-down pool and perform a lactate-removal set. The coach and swimmer should understand that the swimmer is performing the set with very high postcompetition lactate and that the duration of the set need not be as long. The lactate at the start of the set would be considerably higher than it would be in a normal training environment. The recommended set lengths are as follows:

50 m and 100 m swimmers: 800 m set

200 m and 400 m swimmers: 1000 m set

800 m and 1000 m swimmers: 1200 m set

The training repeat distances could be made up of 150 m, 100 m, and 50 m repeats. This type of training can be reproduced in the home program by having the swimmers perform a dive-start timed maximum-effort repeat to commence the set, which leads straight into the training set described.

MV̇O$_2$

MV̇O$_2$ is swimming speed near maximum, at a heart rate 10 beats below maximum to maximum heart rate. Most swimmers will not reach MV̇O$_2$ until the last 100 m of a 300 m to 500 m repeat swim. Some athletes can reach MV̇O$_2$ in 60 seconds or a little more, which in a highly trained swimmer can be 100 m to 150 m.

Swims of 300 m to 500 m are best for this type of training. Work-to-rest ratios should approximate 1:1. But swimmers may not be able to sustain the necessary speed over a straight 300 m to 500 m repeat distance. They could do sets of 3 × 100 m near maximum speed on very short rest (that is, 3 × 100 m holding 1:05 or 1:10 with a 200 m swim-down every set). They could repeat this three to five times to achieve the desired training load.

The suggested pace for MV̇O$_2$ training is half of personal best 200 m time plus four to seven seconds (Pyne 1999b).

Zone 4—Anaerobic (Race-Pace Training)

Anaerobic zone training is commonly referred to as lactate training. This type of training should be conducted as race-pace specific training, which is also referred to as quality training. The anaerobic training zone consists of three types of lactate training: lactate production, lactate tolerance, and peak lactate. The swimmer and coach should have a predetermined goal time for the competition and know split times, stroke counts, and stroke rates. The length of the set in this zone is shorter than it is in the first three training zones due to the increased intensity of this type of work.

Race-pace training is crucial to developing performance in all events and devising individual race strategy for each swimmer. Race-pace training can be used in a variety of ways. Any set done at 400 m pace or faster is an anaerobic-based (quality) training set. The type of training that could include race-pace work is limited only by your imagination.

High-performance endurance zone, anaerobic zone, and sprint zone training can all be race-pace work. Over the past few years coaches have become adept at teaching swimmers to train at heart-rate levels, but in races we talk of pace, not heart rate. Recall the last time you as a coach asked a swimmer to swim the first 200 m in a competition at 40 beats or 30 beats below maximum heart rate and then to increase the heart rate to maximum over the second 200 m. We ask swimmers to swim a time, so we should be training them to swim at pace rather than to heart rates. We should train swimmers in the way that we want them to race (Atkinson and Sweetenham 1999).

As the season moves toward the competition time of the year (summer), all anaerobic work should be done as race-specific training and will include split (a training repeat with one break) and broken swims (a training repeat with more than one break). Stroke rate and stroke count as well as swimming speed (time) should also be incorporated into this type of work.

An example of broken swimming follows. A swimmer has a personal best time of 2:32 for the 200 m breaststroke, with the race details being the following:

	Running time	Splits	Stroke count	Stroke rate
50 m	0:35	35	20	35
100 m	1:14	39	23	37
150 m	1:53	39	24	39
200 m	2:32	39	25	41

The swimmer is aiming at a time of 2:30. The following set has been devised for the swimmer.

1 × 200 m broken by 10 seconds at 50 m, 100 m, and 150 m, holding the following:

	Running time	Splits	Stroke count	Stroke rate
50 m	0:34.5	34.5	19	35
100 m	1:13.0	38.5	22	37
150 m	1:51.5	38.5	22	37
200 m	2:30.0	38.5	22	37
The 50 m repeat to start this set is from a dive.				

The age-group swimmer completes this type of set incorporating time and stroke count. As the swimmer progresses, stroke rate is also included, as shown in the previous examples.

Lactate Production

Lactate production is the first type of lactate training introduced in the season. This type of training can include split and broken swims. Swimmers can do this training with 50 m to 100 m swims. An example follows:

> 10 × 50 m on 2:30 to 3:00 holding second 50 m pace of 100 m or 200 m goal times. The swimmer's goal time is 1:00.00 with splits 29.0 and 31.0. The target for the set is 31 seconds or faster.

As the season progresses a shift occurs from this type of training to lactate-tolerance training.

Lactate Tolerance

Because lactate-tolerance training is more intense than production training, fewer repeats are needed. Two examples follow:

Three sets of 3 × 100 m at second 100 m split of 200 m goal pace on 3:00 with a 200 m swim-down on each set.

8 × 100 m on 4:00 to 6:00 or 6 × 100 m holding second 100 m split of 200 m goal pace on 5:00 or on 3:00 holding 400 m goal pace.

The best repeat distances to use when performing lactate-tolerance training are 50 m to 200 m repeats. Lactate level reaches its peak postswim, and lactate in the muscle builds up throughout to the final swim in the set. This is the tolerance effect.

Recommended Training-Set Length

100 m swimmer: 600 to 1200 m

200 m swimmer: 600 to 1600 m

400 m swimmer: 600 to 2000 m

Peak Lactate

The swimmer produces peak or extremely close to peak lactate on each swim when doing peak lactate training. Therefore, this kind of training requires longer rest than tolerance work does. An example of this is 4 × 100 m on 15:00, with active recovery between repeats. Recommended swim-down protocols may be used between repeats.

This type of work can be best performed over distances of 100 m to 400 m, using straight or broken swims. An example of a broken swim is 3 × 200 m as 4 × 50 m on 60 seconds. The swimmer should dive start the first 50 m and then push start the next three 50 m swims in the set. The swimmer holds times based on the target goal for the event.

Zone 5—Sprint

Zone 5 is the short maximum-speed training that is commonly referred to as high-velocity overloads (HVO). Maximum speed and maximum effort are different. A swimmer may be going at maximum effort in the anaerobic training zone, but not at his or her maximum speed.

Training repeats of 10 m to 25 m are best for training in this zone. The swimmer should perform 25 m repeats with sufficient rest. If the rest on the 25 m repeats is inadequate, the swimmer will be performing lactate-production training, in the anaerobic zone.

A sample set could be 12 × 25 m as a 15 m maximum-speed sprint, 10 m distance per stroke (DPS) on 1:30. A target time should be set for each swimmer based on the method of calculating speed training pace as shown in the next section.

It is important to understand the difference between effort and speed.

Calculating Speed Training Pace

Because speed development is important, training must include sufficient speed work. Repeat training times for speed training can be calculated as follows.

Speed training for 100 m swimmers should be based on the following:

100 m personal best minus 5 seconds

For example, 60 seconds – 5 seconds = 55 seconds

55 ÷ 4 for 25 m training times = 13.75 seconds

55 ÷ 5 for 20 m training times = 11.00 seconds

55 ÷ 100 × 15 for 15 m training times = 8.25 seconds

55 ÷ 100 × 12.5 for 12.5 m training times = 6.87 seconds

55 ÷ 100 × 10 for 10 m training times = 5.50 seconds

Speed training for 200 m swimmers should be based on the following:

200 m personal best minus 10 seconds

For example, 2:10 = 130 seconds – 10 seconds = 120 seconds

120 ÷ 8 for 25 m training times = 15 seconds

120 ÷ 10 for 20 m training times = 12 seconds

Another method is useful for calculating targets for speed training. Suppose a 100 m backstroke swimmer has a personal best of 61 seconds. Speed work for this swimmer could be developed as follows.

Set 1

40 m target 24 seconds
40 m target 24 seconds
20 m target 12 seconds
Repeat time on 1:30 holding pace based on a target goal time of 60 seconds

Set 2

30 m target 18 seconds
40 m target 24 seconds
30 m target 18 seconds
Repeat time on 1:30 holding pace based on a target goal time of 60 seconds

Sets 3 to 8 are constructed in a similar way so that the swimmer receives eight minutes of work at this intensity. There are many different ways to break down 60 seconds of work. For example, it may be done as 20 m, 30 m, 30 m, 20 m, and so on. The idea is for the athlete to do the longest distance possible while maintaining pace and technique efficiency.

After each set the swimmer could do a 100 m, 200 m, 300 m, or 400 m swim-down. The distance should be long enough that the swimmer can swim the required speed on the next set. Heart rate on the swim-downs should be 50 beats per minute below maximum.

Aerobic Base and Endurance Swimming

Age-group swimmers may have recovery skills and adaptation abilities far different from those of mature, fully developed senior swimmers, masters, or triathletes.

Males will be different from the less muscled females, and specific events will require different levels of aerobic base training. Each athlete will be slightly different from any other in some way. The successful coach must evaluate the requirements of each individual and provide the correct coaching mix to achieve maximum aerobic and endurance fitness for each athlete.

This aerobic and endurance training and preparation begins before maturation on a simple and general application and will stay with the swimmer through post-maturation involvement in swimming. This training will often have great influence on the ability of females to improve in the 200 m and 100 m freestyle combination, the 200 m IM, and form-stroke events, as well as the traditional 400 m IM, 400 m, 800 m, and 1500 m freestyle events after maturation.

Although this effect is also true for males, it is not as significant. Compared with an age-group athlete, a senior athlete will require less exposure to any given stimulus for the same amount of improvement if an adequate aerobic background has been achieved through maturation. This consideration will therefore affect the length of macrocycles that the swimmer requires, shown in detail in chapter 12.

Aerobic training is defined as "doing the greatest amount of work in the shortest possible time, with the least amount of rest, without the heart rate exceeding 40 beats below maximum." This workload should also allow full (in this context *full* is not the same as *complete)* recovery for the next training session (usually 8 to 12 hours later). Endurance training is the same as aerobic training except that it involves a little more demand, 30 to 40 beats below maximum heart rate. The beginning of this chapter describes this as aerobic (A3) development. A recovery workout is longer in volume but with less intensity.

The preceding means that the parameters the coach works with in designing workouts are either to control the intensity at a higher level while holding other variables (rest interval, volume of work, and so on) steady or to maintain the intensity while decreasing the rest. The coach should implement only one of the parameters at any one time, although one design can be done once the other has been achieved.

Doing this in a team environment is far more beneficial and interesting, while accepting and understanding the significance of the athlete's ability to do this during the prematuration and maturation phases of development. The coach must not ignore or neglect an integrated training approach that balances the amount of other types of training, specifically quality speed training, which is required in the program on a regular basis, along with aerobic endurance training.

A gradual buildup of aerobic work is required. The progression should avoid sudden increases and increase only one training demand at a time. A beneficial approach is to increase kilometers (volume) one week and quality (intensity) the next. For senior swimmers an adaptation week can be scheduled as required. An example follows (the reference to pull is band-only pull).

Week 1

Six training sessions, 4000 m per session, 24 kilometers for the week.
Hold 38 seconds per 50 m pace on pull and swim, regardless of repeat distance.
Hold 50 seconds per 50 m kicking speed.
Pull or swim on a 50-second cycle.
Kick on a 60-second cycle.

Week 2

Like week 1, six training sessions, 4000 m per session, 24 kilometers for the week.
This week hold 37 seconds per 50 m pace on pull or swim and hold 48 seconds per 50 m kick.

Week 3

Increase to seven training sessions, 4000 m per session, 28 kilometers for the week.
Hold all variables the same as week 2.

Week 4

Seven training sessions, 4000 m per session, 28 kilometers for the week.
Hold 36 seconds per 50 m pace on pull or swim and hold 46 seconds per 50 m kick.

Week 5

For the senior swimmer this may be the holding or adaptation week if required.
Eight training sessions, 4000 m per session, 32 kilometers for the week.
Hold 36 seconds per 50 m pace on pull or swim and hold 46 seconds per 50 m kick.

Week 6

Like week 5, eight training sessions, 4000 m per session, 32 kilometers for the week.
Hold 36 seconds per 50 m pace on pull or swim and hold 46 seconds per 50 m kick. The
cycle times change. Swim and pull on 45 seconds and kick on 55 seconds.

Week 7

Hold all variables steady as in week 6, but increase the number of training sessions to
nine. Nine training sessions, 4000 m per session, 36 kilometers for the week.

Week 8

Hold all variables steady as in week 7, but increase the volume of each training session to
4500 m. Nine training sessions, 4500 m per session, 40.5 kilometers for the week.

Another sample progression follows:

Week 1

Eleven training sessions, 4000 m per session, 44 kilometers for the week.
Pull and swim on 50-second cycle holding 38 seconds per 50 m.
Kick on 60-second cycle holding 50 seconds per 50 m.

Week 2

Eleven training sessions, 4500 m per session, 49.5 kilometers for the week.
Hold all training variables while the volume increases.

Week 3

Eleven training sessions, 4500 m per session, 49.5 kilometers for the week.
Pull and swim on 50-second cycle holding 37 seconds per 50 m.
Kick on 60-second cycle holding 48 seconds per 50 m.

Week 4

Eleven training sessions, 5000 m per session, 55 kilometers for the week.
Hold all training variables while the volume increases.

Week 5

Eleven training sessions, 5000 m per session, 55 kilometers for the week.
Pull and swim on 50-second cycle holding 36 seconds per 50 m.
Kick on 60-second cycle holding 46 seconds per 50 m.
For the senior swimmer this is the holding or adaptation week if required.

Week 6

Eleven training sessions, 5500 m per session, 60.5 kilometers for the week.
Pull and swim on 50-second cycle holding 36 seconds per 50 m.
Kick on 60-second cycle holding 46 seconds per 50 m.

Week 7

All remains the same except that the repeat cycle changes.
Eleven training sessions, 5500 m per session, 60.5 kilometers for the week.
Pull and swim on 45-second cycle holding 36 seconds per 50 m.
Kick on 55-second cycle holding 46 seconds per 50 m.

Week 8

All remains the same except that the time to hold per 50 m repeat changes.
Eleven training sessions, 5500 m per session, 60.5 kilometers for the week.
Pull and swim on 45-second cycle holding 35 seconds per 50 m.
Kick on 55-second cycle holding 44 seconds per 50 m.

Week 9

Hold all training variables while the volume increases.
Eleven training sessions, 6000 m per session, 66 kilometers for the week.

These examples show how to manipulate the volume and intensity in planning the training program.

One of the keys to optimal adaptation involves even- or negative-split swimming on every repeat distance of 100 m or more. Another way of increasing intensity is to hold the repeat swim time and cycle time from a previous week's freestyle work but program a percentage of the training volume to be done on form stroke. Not every training session focuses on aerobic-endurance work as the primary objective, but at least three out of five sessions will, particularly in the first eight weeks of the swimming season. As the season progresses, anaerobic sessions or training sets can replace aerobic sessions.

After swimmers have achieved maximum volumes of training, intensity should increase. Training volume can then decrease as intensity increases after week 9 or when swimmers have developed optimal aerobic values. This simple goal minimizes the potential exposure to too much work at any given stimulus. An effective program will develop swimmers' aerobic-endurance base adequately and systematically while being both goal oriented and team motivating.

All coaches and swimmers should have an understanding of the training zones and how to individualize training to get the best result from the work they do. Coaches and swimmers must monitor all training to ensure that the swimmers are training at the required level and are therefore avoiding overtraining. This first chapter helps swimmers and coaches understand training zones, which in turn will help them use the test sets in chapter 2 to their maximum. The test sets allow coaches and swimmers to review how the training program is developing and make required adjustments to the amount of work each swimmer does in each of the training zones.

Benchmark Test Sets

The ultimate test for swimmers is the competitive result they achieve in races. The swimmer and coach need to evaluate the athlete's swimming through the training cycle and swimming season to ensure the best possible competitive result.

Test sets can be used to test almost any area of competitive swimming. In this chapter we have selected 12 tests and testing progressions, and we show how the swimmer and coach can use them to evaluate a certain type of training, make adjustments to stroke mechanics, or set training times for the future based on the test results. All test sets should have an objective.

Test sets should be consistently placed in the same position in the macrocycle, mesocycle, or microcycle so that a comparison can be made with the test results obtained in the previous cycle. Not all test sets may be necessary. The swimmer and coach must evaluate each test to see how well it worked and if they want to use it in the future. We will show an example of how to build the tests into training cycles.

The following are the 12 tests and test progressions shown in this chapter:

7×200 m step test

Double-distance 400 m test

Maximum heart-rate test

8×50 m efficiency test

Cold-swim test

High-performance endurance test-set progression

Individual medley pace test progression

Kick test set (800 m, 400 m, 200 m, 100 m, 50 m, 25 m)

Pull tests

Speed tests

IM and form-stroke count efficiency test

Individual checking speed (ICS) tests (100 m, 200 m, 300 m, and 400 m)

When completing these test sets, swimmers need to take responsibility for recording their stroke count, heart rate, and the total time for the swim repeats. They should write

The purpose of testing is to assess and fine-tune training and stroke mechanics with the goal of improving competition performance.

© David Sanders

the information on a poolside recording board using a china graph pencil, and then transfer the information into their training logs. The coach can take stroke rates, monitor technique, and record split times when required.

Swimmers can perform the tests in both long-course and short-course training facilities, but results will be comparable only on tests performed in pools of the same length. For example, the 7 × 200 m step test performed in January in a 50 m pool should not be compared with the same test performed in February in a 25 m pool. If both tests were performed in a 25 m, 50 m, or 25-yard pool, the results could be compared from test to test.

7 × 200 Meter Step Test

The 7 × 200 m step test should be conducted in one way for age-group and youth swimmers and in another for seniors, masters, and triathletes.

The test set on butterfly and breaststroke should comprise 5 × 200 m repeats. For freestyle and backstroke the test set will be 7 × 200 m. Note that the first 2 × 200 m repeats of the 7 × 200 m senior test set do not relate to the next 5 × 200 m repeats. These first 2 × 200 m swims are used as a comparison from test set to test set. The swimmer and coach compare the first two 200 m swims from the test set the swimmer has just completed to the first 2 × 200 m from the previous 7 × 200 m test set. These 2 × 200 m swims should be used in the same way that the individual checking speed test is used. The swimmer and coach record the same series of information—time, stroke count, heart rate, and splits. Please refer to the individual checking speed test in this chapter (page 50).

Swimmers should have their test-set results and graphs laminated, so that they can use them poolside during their training sessions. Swimmers can then perform a snapshot of the full test-set results at any given time for comparisons. The swimmer repeats the third, fourth, and fifth 200 m swims from the senior 7 × 200 m step test and compares all measures to the test-set results shown on the laminated sheet. This assessment will give the coach and swimmer an indication of the state of recovery at that moment in comparison with what the swimmer did in the step test. This 3 ×

200 m snapshot should be done in the warm-up of training sessions that are to have main sets from training zones 3 and 4.

Warm-Up

Swimmers should use the same warm-up whenever the test is conducted.

1000 m (20 minutes choice)
2 × 100 m ICS on 4:00
2 × 100 m at require pace for first 200 m swim of the 7 × 200 m step test

7 × 200 Meter Age-Group and Youth Test Set

Age-group and youth athletes should use this set, which is also an excellent test for swimmers to learn pace control. Senior, masters, and triathletes can also use this test. Age-group and youth swimmers can also occasionally complete the senior 7 × 200 m step test so that they learn the process expected from senior athletes. Youth swimmers should alternate between the two ways of doing the set.

7 × 200 m main stroke on 5:00
- All swims to be even split.
- Descend by four seconds on each swim.
- Record stroke count, splits, heart rate (HR), stroke rate, turning times, and breathing patterns.
- This set is for age-group and youth swimmers.
- The set is pace oriented, not heart-rate oriented.

Targets for each repeat of the 7 × 200 m are the following:

Swim	Targets for females	Targets for males
1	PB plus 20 seconds	PB plus 24 seconds
2	PB plus 16 seconds	PB plus 20 seconds
3	PB plus 12 seconds	PB plus 16 seconds
4	PB plus 8 seconds	PB plus 12 seconds
5	PB plus 4 seconds	PB plus 8 seconds
6	PB pace	PB pace
7	Goal PB pace	Goal PB pace

The sixth 200 m is split at 100 m. The freestyle repeat is on 1:40, and the form-stroke repeat is on 2:00. The target time is the current personal best for 200 m.

The seventh 200 m is broken at each 50 m. The freestyle repeat is on a 50-second interval, and the form-stroke repeat is on a 60-second interval. The target time is the goal 200 m time.

The main difference between this set and the senior 7 × 200 m step test is that this test is based on pace, whereas the senior test is based on heart rate (Atkinson and Sweetenham 1999).

7 × 200 Meter Senior Test Set

This set is recommended for seniors, masters, and triathletes.

- All swims to be even split and performed as straight swims. Therefore, swims 6 and 7 are not split or broken.

- Record the stroke count, splits, heart rate, stroke rate, turning times, and breathing patterns.
- This set for seniors, masters, and triathletes is heart-rate oriented. Youth swimmers can alternate between the senior 7 × 200 m step test and the age-group and youth 7 × 200 m step test.
- Postswim lactates can be taken, but they are not essential. Swimming coaches and parents should not take blood lactates from swimmers. Only a qualified person such as an exercise physiologist working with elite swimmers should do this. Lactate measures can be graphed, but they are not essential to the success of the test.

Targets for the test are the following:

Swim	*Pace and heart rate*
1	Pace at 60 beats below maximum heart rate
2	Pace at 50 beats below maximum heart rate
3	Pace at 40 beats below maximum heart rate
4	Pace at 30 beats below maximum heart rate
5	Pace at 20 beats below maximum heart rate
6	Pace at 10 beats below maximum heart rate
7	Pace at maximum heart rate

All swimmers should be able to swim efficiently at low intensity levels such as 60 and 50 beats below maximum effort.

Butterfly swimmers should have the capacity to swim full-stroke butterfly at a controlled low intensity. Some butterfly swimmers may well swim the first 100 m of each 200 m swim on controlled freestyle and swim the second 100 m on butterfly until they are capable of completing the whole test on butterfly (Atkinson and Sweetenham 1999). Age group swimmers need to train on butterfly, completing sets of up to 2400 meters on full stroke butterfly at least two to three times each week before they are expected to perform the whole test on butterfly.

Recording Information

Alternating tests between the age-group and youth test set and senior test set provides valuable comparisons, training-speed information, efficiency (broken 200s) information, even-paced swimming, and immediate heart-rate recordings. Table 2.1 shows the information that can be recorded during the swim.

The 7 × 200 m step test can be performed and graphed as all straight swims as in the senior test or as an efficiency pace test as in the age-group and youth test with the last 2 × 200 m swims broken. If the swimmer does the last 2 × 200 m broken, these would not be graphed. The following information should be graphed:

- Lactate (mmol/l) versus velocity (average for 100 m in seconds) as shown in figure 2.1
- Heart rate (bpm) versus velocity (average for 100 m in seconds) as shown in figure 2.2
- Stroke rate (strokes per minute) versus velocity (average for 100 m in seconds) as shown in figure 2.3
- Stroke count (strokes per 50 m) versus velocity (average for 100 m in seconds) as shown in figure 2.4

TABLE 2.1 SAMPLE TEST-SET RESULTS FOR SENIOR 7 × 200 METERS

Swim	Time	1st 100 m	2nd 100 m	Avg 100 m	HR	Lac	SR	SC	RPE
1	2:40.50	80.3	80.2	80.25	151	1.8	33.5	23.0	7
2	2:39.00	79.0	80.0	79.50	161	2.0	34.5	24.0	9
3	2:34.50	76.6	77.9	77.25	172	2.4	35.6	24.5	11
4	2:29.40	74.1	75.3	74.70	180	3.1	37.5	25.0	14
5	2:24.50	71.7	72.8	72.25	187	5.0	39.3	27.0	17
6	2:22.10	70.9	71.2	71.05	190	6.9	39.8	27.5	19
7	2:18.00	68.5	69.5	69.00	201	12.1	42.5	28.5	20

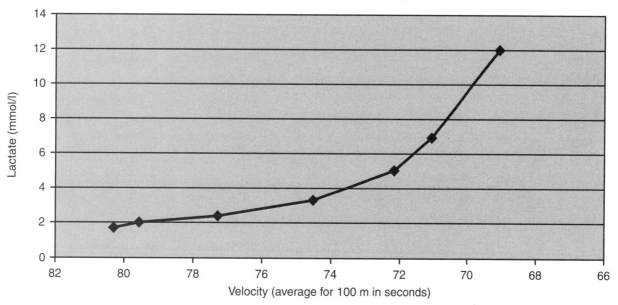

FIGURE 2.1   *7 × 200 m lactate versus velocity graph.*

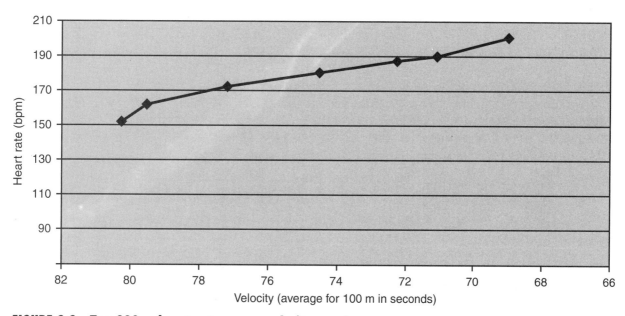

FIGURE 2.2   *7 × 200 m heart rate versus velocity graph.*

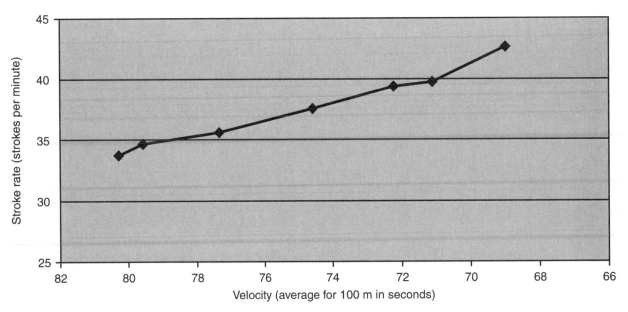

FIGURE 2.3 *7 × 200 m stroke rate versus velocity graph.*

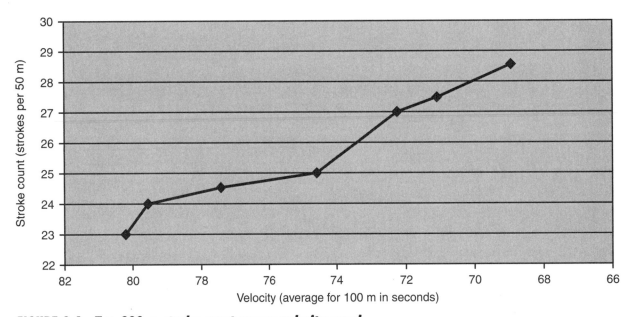

FIGURE 2.4 *7 × 200 m stroke count versus velocity graph.*

- Rating of perceived exertion (RPE) versus velocity (average for 100 m in seconds) as shown in figure 2.5

The graph showing heart rate versus velocity should be laminated and used by the swimmer poolside for all training sets. Only accurate information should be recorded. The swimmer should be sure to leave at the correct time when commencing swims on the test set.

As the season progresses a graph of the test-set results on a single chart will indicate differences in the curves. A recording sheet that can be used is shown in figure 2.6 on page 24. Swimmers and coaches can use the heart rate versus velocity curve on a daily basis to set paces for training sets.

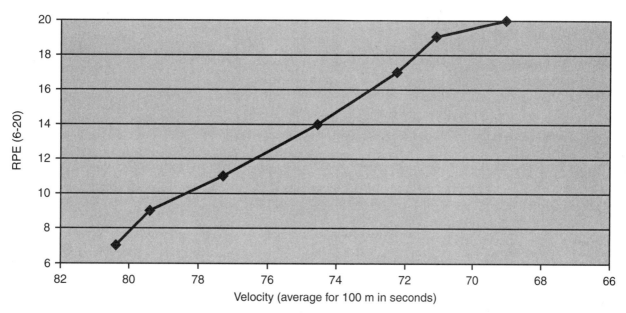

FIGURE 2.5   *7 × 200 m rate of perceived exertion versus velocity graph.*

A swimmer who has an old 7 × 200 m step test (heart rate versus velocity curve) should use the 3 × 200 m check during the warm-up of the training session. For example, a swimmer returning to training after a break would swim 3 × 200 m at the third, fourth, and fifth 200 m paces from the 7 × 200 m senior step test.

These results from the 3 × 200 m should then be drawn with a china graph pencil on the laminated poolside heart rate versus velocity graph from the previous 7 × 200 m step test. The results from the 3 × 200 m snapshot test are then drawn on the laminated poolside graph, and new training paces are established for the swimmer according to the current level of fitness.

Swim-Down

Swimmers do the swim-down in the same way they do the warm-up, repeating until all values are in balance and equal to the ICS in the warm-up.

    1000 m (20 minutes choice)
    2 × 100 m ICS on 4:00

7 × 200 Meter Step Test for IM Swimmers

In the individual medley event the percentage contribution of each stroke will vary. Use of the strengths and weaknesses charts can establish this percentage, as shown in figures 2.14 and 2.15 on pages 39 and 40.

The target percentages for swimmer X for the 400 m IM are the following, as shown in figure 2.14:

    100 butterfly split, 24.77% = 1:05.80

    100 backstroke split, 25.61% = 1:08.04

    100 breaststroke split, 26.83% = 1:11.28

    100 freestyle split, 22.77% = 1:00.48

7 × 200 METER STEP TEST RECORDING SHEET

Name_____ Date_____

		Target	Time recorded	100 m split	Stroke count	Stroke rate	Heart rate	Other
1	PB + 24 M PB + 20 F or 60 BBM							
2	PB + 20 M PB + 16 F or 50 BBM							
3	PB + 16 M PB + 12 F or 40 BBM							
4	PB + 12 M PB + 8 F or 30 BBM							
5	PB + 8 M PB + 4 F or 20 BBM							
6	PB Pace, broken at the 100 m or 10 BBM							
7	Goal pace, broken at each 50 m or maximum HR							

FIGURE 2.6 *7 × 200 m step test recording sheet.*
(Atkinson and Sweetenham 1999)

The target time for the 400 IM is 4:25.60. The set for the IM swimmer is 7 × 200 m repeats as 100 m backstroke and 100 m breaststroke. These are even-paced swims on a five-minute cycle, descending as follows.

First, the swimmer's 400 IM goal time is determined using the strengths and weaknesses chart in figure 2.15. Working in reverse order from the sixth repeat, which is at target 400 m IM splits, add two seconds to each 100 m, which is four seconds for each 200 m swim. The seventh 200 m swim is maximal effort. Based on the preceding information and rounding up the target splits to the next second, the set is as shown in table 2.2. The same information should be recorded on this set as on the 7 × 200 m senior and age-group and youth step test.

TABLE 2.2 7 × 200 METER STEP TEST FOR IM SWIMMERS

Swim	100 m backstroke split	100 m breaststroke split	Target time
1	1:19.00	1:23.00	2:41.00
2	1:17.00	1:20.00	2:37.00
3	1:15.00	1:18.00	2:33.00
4	1:13.00	1:16.00	2:29.00
5	1:11.00	1:14.00	2:25.00
6	Goal split 1:09.00	Goal split 1:12.00	2:21.00
7	Maximum effort	Maximum effort	

Double-Distance 400-Meter Test

Senior 200 m swimmers do a 400 m time trial in a reasonably fresh state, usually on Monday afternoon. Individual medley specialists do this test over a period of time on all four strokes. All age-group and youth swimmers do this test over 400 m.

A training speed for high-performance endurance speed can be evaluated by deducting the swimmer's 200 m personal best time from the 400 m double-distance time trial and evaluating the speed from this value (differential).

Sample Double-Distance 400-Meter Test

A swimmer with a 200 m personal best time of 2:12.00 swims the double-distance 400 m time trial and records a time of 4:50.00. To work out the training paces, one would go through the following process:

> 200 m PB of 2:12.00 = 132 seconds ÷ 4 = 33.0 seconds per 50 m
> 400 m double-distance test of 4:50 = 290 seconds ÷ 8 = 36.2 seconds per 50 m
> 36.2 – 33.0 seconds = 3.2 seconds
> 3.2 seconds ÷ 2 = 1.6 seconds

The estimated training speed is 36.2 seconds minus 1.6 seconds or 34.6 seconds, which is rounded to the nearest but higher second, that is, 35.0 seconds.

This training speed of 35 seconds is used for 100 m and longer training repeats up to a maximum of 200 m. A speed of 34.6 seconds is used for the 50 m repeats in the middle to later part of the 2000 m to 3000 m workout. A sample set using this information is the following:

> 16 × 100 m on 1:45 holding training pace of 1:10.0
> 8 × 50 m on 50 holding training pace of 34.6

Double-Distance Test Progression

The initial double-distance test can be used in a testing progression:

Week 1 Double-distance time trial 1 × 400 m and record time.

Week 2 2 × 400 m with 30 seconds of rest after each swim, trying to hold or swim a faster average than week 1.

Week 3   3 × 400 m with 30 seconds of rest after each swim, trying to hold a faster average than week 2.

Week 4   4 × 400 m with 30 seconds of rest after each swim, trying to hold or swim a faster average than week 3.

The swimmer can repeat this progression after a three-week, four-week, or even five-week progression with the goal of going faster in the second run-through of the whole progression. Week 1 the second time through still has the 1 × 400 m swim, and the coach and swimmer then reevaluate the estimated training speed (high-performance endurance). Following the first week the aim is to improve the average times for the 2 × 400 m, 3 × 400 m, and the 4 × 400 m tests. Distance swimmers and females in particular may do a fifth week and perform the 5 × 400 m test set.

This 400 m double-distance time trial is normally completed one week or two weeks before the 7 × 200 m step test. The recording sheet for the double-distance 400 m test is shown in figure 2.7.

Maximum Heart-Rate Test

All swimmers should know their maximum heart rate so that they can monitor their training accurately. The maximum heart-rate test will establish that value. A swimmer may have a different maximum heart rate for different strokes. This test should therefore be conducted on the swimmer's main form stroke as well as freestyle (Atkinson and Sweetenham 1999). Maximum heart rates are sometimes recorded on training sets. Swimmers and coaches should monitor heart rates on all training sets.

Warm-Up

Before each maximum heart-rate test, swimmers should do the same warm-up, perhaps using this example:

200 m choice swim on 3:30
200 m freestyle, build from easy to moderate pace (approximately 30 beats below maximum heart rate) on 3:00
200 m IM on 3:30
4 × 50 m choice as 25 kick, 25 swim on 1:00
100 m main stroke, build to fast on 1:45
5 × 50 m as 15 m explode, 35 m distance per stroke (DPS) on 1:00

Test Set

The set is conducted on the same stroke throughout (no drill permitted). A slightly different test is used for 50 m and 100 m swimmers as opposed to 200 m and farther swimmers (Atkinson and Sweetenham 1999). Figures 2.8 and 2.9 show recording sheets for both test sets.

200-Meter and Farther Swimmers

2 × 100 m build to maximum effort.
Rest interval (RI)15 seconds per 100 m, and swimmers take their HR.
3 × 100 m race pace, RI 10 seconds. Target PB plus four seconds or faster for each 100 m. Swimmers take HR following each swim.
3 × 50 m race pace, RI 10 seconds (if required). The number of 50 m swims can be extended if required.
400 m recovery, then swim-down.

DOUBLE-DISTANCE 400-METER TEST RECORDING SHEET

Name_____

Date:	1 × 400 m	Splits and total time
1st 400 m		
Date:	**2 × 400 m**	**Splits and total time**
1st 400 m swim		
2nd 400 m swim		
Average 400 m time		
Date:	**3 × 400 m**	**Splits and total time**
1st 400 m swim		
2nd 400 m swim		
3rd 400 m swim		
Average 400 m time		
Date:	**4 × 400 m**	**Splits and total time**
1st 400 m swim		
2nd 400 m swim		
3rd 400 m swim		
4th 400 m swim		
Average 400 m time		
Date:	**5 × 400 m**	**Splits and total time**
1st 400 m swim		
2nd 400 m swim		
3rd 400 m swim		
4th 400 m swim		
5th 400 m swim		
Average 400 m time		

FIGURE 2.7 Double-distance 400 m test recording sheet.

50-Meter and 100-Meter Swimmers

1 × 100 m build to maximum effort.

1 × 100 m race pace, RI 10 seconds. Target PB plus seconds or faster.

Rest 15 seconds per 100 m, and swimmers take their HR.

4 × 50 m race pace, RI 10 seconds (swim four if required).

Extra 50 m swims to be added as required. The number of 50 m repeats can be extended if required.

400 m recovery, then swim-down.

MAXIMUM HEART-RATE TEST RECORDING SHEET

200 m and Farther Swimmers

Name_____ Date_____

Distance	Notes	Time recorded	Heart rate
100 m	Build to maximum		
100 m	Build to maximum		
1st 100 m	Target PB plus 4 seconds		
2nd 100 m	Target PB plus 4 seconds		
3rd 100 m	Target PB plus 4 seconds		
1st 50 m	If required		
2nd 50 m	If required		
3rd 50 m	If required		

FIGURE 2.8 *Maximum heart-rate test recording sheet for 200 m and farther swimmers.*

MAXIMUM HEART-RATE TEST RECORDING SHEET

50 m and 100 m Swimmers

Name_____ Date_____

Distance	Notes	Time recorded	Heart rate
100 m	Build to maximum		
1st 100 m	Target PB plus 4 seconds		
1st 50 m	At race pace		
2nd 50 m	At race pace		
3rd 50 m	At race pace		
4th 50 m	At race pace		

FIGURE 2.9   Maximum heart-rate test recording sheet for 50 m and 100 m swimmers.

When performing this test the heart rate will increase rapidly at the start. Some swimmers will require over three minutes of work to attain their maximum heart rate. Following each repeat the heart rate will drop quickly in well-trained athletes. Therefore, broken and split swims should be avoided when testing for maximum heart rate.

Swimmers may not achieve maximum heart rate on swims of shorter distances at maximum speed. Maximum speed is different from maximum effort. Age, sex, and genetic profiles of the athletes influence maximum heart rate. Girls may have heart rates 5 to 10 beats lower than boys do. Another factor influencing maximum heart rate is the health status of the swimmer and the training conducted in the days before the test. We do not recommend prescribing a set heart-rate level at which to work. One swimmer working at 170 beats per minute may be working at a significantly different level than another swimmer working at the same heart rate.

The maximum heart-rate test should be conducted regularly, about every month or two. Swimmers should record all heart rates attained in training sets so that they can keep a check on their maximum heart rate and know if they have attained a new level (Atkinson and Sweetenham 1999).

Determining if Maximum Heart Rate Has Been Achieved

When the heart rate drops following the repeat swims, the set can end. A sample test result for a 200 m and farther swimmer follows.

100 m build to maximum	178 bpm
100 m build to maximum	184 bpm
100 m target PB plus 4 seconds	188 bpm
100 m target PB plus 4 seconds	192 bpm
100 m target PB plus 4 seconds	195 bpm
50 m target half of 100 m swims	196 bpm
50 m target half of 100 m swims	192 bpm

At the completion of the 100 m swims the heart rate is still rising, so the 50 m swims are added to the test. Following the first 50 m repeat the heart rate is still rising, so the set continues. Following the second 50 m repeat the heart rate drops, so the set ends.

If the heart rate had risen after the second 50 m repeat, the third 50 m swim would be added. If the heart rate following the second 50 m swim was the same as it was in the previous swim, an additional 50 m swim could be added. Following the third 50 m repeat a decision would be made about whether to extend or conclude the set.

8 × 50 Meter Efficiency Test

This set has been designed to test the swimmer's efficiency and then help the swimmer and coach design training sets with the results.

The 8 × 50 m swims are completed on a 2:30 cycle, and the swims descend through the set. The swimmer and coach record the time, stroke count, and stroke rates. Each swim should become faster by approximately two seconds, with a target on the final 50 m swim of PB plus one second or faster. The final swim of the 8 × 50 m repeats is maximum effort. Tables 2.3 and 2.4 show a sample test, and results from this test are shown in figures 2.10 and 2.11.

Following the set the swimmer should plot the velocity (in time per 50 m) against stroke count for each 50 m repeat on a graph, as shown in figure 2.10. A second graph can be produced showing velocity (in time per 50 m) against stroke rate (strokes per minute) as shown in figure 2.11. Figure 2.12 shows a recording sheet that can be used for this set. All the swims in the 8 × 50 m descending set will be from a push start.

Following this test set the swimmer and coach can set training speeds from which to work. Table 2.3 shows a large increase in the number of strokes taken between swims 7 and 8. A large increase in the stroke rate used on swims 7 and 8 also occurred, as shown in table 2.4. Using that information, the following training set could be structured for

TABLE 2.3 SAMPLE TEST SET RESULTS 8 × 50 METER, TIME VERSUS STROKE COUNT

Swim	Time	Stroke count
1	44.01	10
2	42.28	10
3	39.83	11
4	38.81	12
5	35.58	14
6	34.31	15
7	32.86	17
8	32.07	20

TABLE 2.4 SAMPLE TEST SET RESULTS 8 × 50 METER, TIME VERSUS STROKE RATE

Swim	Time	Stroke rate
1	44.01	20.5
2	42.28	21.7
3	39.83	21.7
4	38.81	23.7
5	35.58	30.3
6	34.31	33.6
7	32.86	42.4
8	32.07	47.1

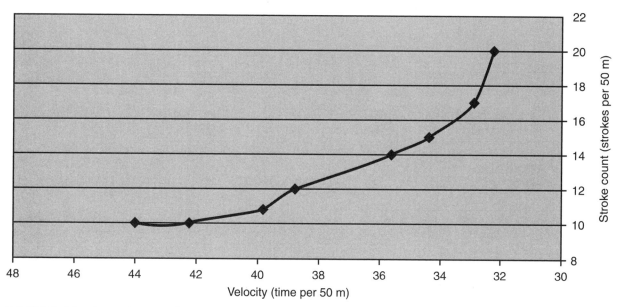

FIGURE 2.10 8 × 50 m stroke count versus velocity graph.

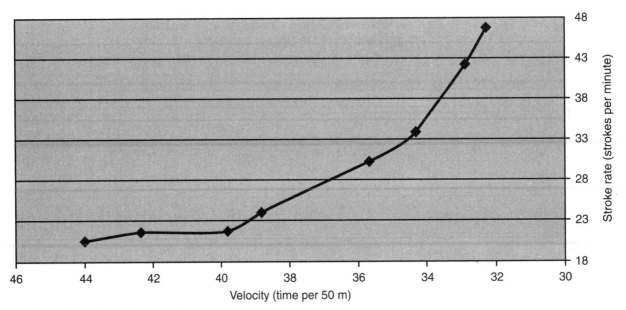

FIGURE 2.11 *8 × 50 m stroke rate versus velocity graph.*

the swimmer: 10 × 50 m on 1:30, holding 32.0 to 32.5 seconds for each 50 m repeat of the set. The swimmer is also given a stroke count to hold, which could be set at 17 to 18 strokes per 50 m swim while maintaining a stroke rate of 42.

The set can be manipulated in many ways. If the swimmer completed the set with no problems, the swimmer and coach would have these options the next time the swimmer performs that set:

- Repeat on a faster leaving time, that is, 1:15 instead of 1:30.
- The swimmer could maintain a lower stroke count of 16 to 17 and still repeat on 1:30.
- The swimmer could maintain all values and swim with a slower stroke rate.

This test set can be used over an eight-week period leading into a competition. This approach keeps the swimmer working on efficiency and control with speed.

- Eight weeks out from the meet on the Monday morning session, swim 8 × 50 m descending to race pace (stroke count, stroke rate, and time).
- Seven weeks out from the meet on the Monday morning session, swim 7 × 50 m descending to race pace (stroke count, stroke rate, and time).
- Six weeks out from the meet on the Monday morning session, swim 6 × 50 m descending to race pace (stroke count, stroke rate, and time).
- Five weeks out from the meet on the Monday morning session, swim 5 × 50 m descending to race pace (stroke count, stroke rate, and time).
- Four weeks out from the meet on the Monday morning session, swim 4 × 50 m descending to race pace (stroke count, stroke rate, and time).
- Three weeks out from the meet on the Monday morning session, swim 3 × 50 m descending to race pace (stroke count, stroke rate, and time).
- Two weeks out from the meet on the Monday morning session, swim 3 × 50 m descending to race pace (stroke count, stroke rate, and time).
- One week out from the meet on the Monday morning session, swim 3 × 50 m descending to race pace (stroke count, stroke rate, and time).

8 × 50 METER EFFICIENCY TEST RECORDING SHEET

Name_____ Date_____

Swim	Target	Target time	Time recorded	Stroke count	Stroke rate	Heart rate
1	PB + 15					
2	PB + 13					
3	PB + 11					
4	PB + 9					
5	PB + 7					
6	PB + 5					
7	PB + 3					
8	PB + 1					
9	If required					

FIGURE 2.12 8 × 50 m efficiency test recording sheet.
(Atkinson and Sweetenham 1999)

All test speeds and efficiencies can be trained, that is, 24 × 50 m, with odds at one speed from the test and evens at another speed from the test.

Cold-Swim Test

The cold-swim test can confirm the current racing speed value of the athlete. It should be conducted 10 to 14 days following the 7 × 200 m step test.

A cold swim is a swim performed by the athlete at maximum effort, in a mock-trial situation, without swimming a warm-up, in the training pool. To prevent injuries from occurring, the swimmer should perform a comprehensive dryland warm-up before the cold swim. To eliminate the risk of aggravating an injury, the coach should ensure that the swimmer performing the test is injury free. The swimmer wears training gear, not a racing swimsuit. This test teaches athletes to perform under difficult conditions to a set level determined by the coach. This test should only be performed with swimmers who are fully committed to the training program; hence the coach knows their entire training and competition history.

During a swimming season the coach should schedule 10 to 12 occasions to conduct cold swims. The tests should be unannounced and done both in morning and afternoon sessions. Swimmers do half the swims when the coach determines that the athletes feel good, and the other half in tough situations when they are fatigued or undergoing heavy training. The coach and swimmer would record splits, total time, and heart rate for the cold swim. The cold swim time would be compared to the swimmer's personal best time, and a percentage either over or under his or her best time would be worked out—for example, if the swimmer's PB time is 60 seconds and he recorded 61 seconds on the cold swim, the percentage is plus 1.66 percent.

When cold swims are built into the program, all swimmers can do mock trials at 6 percent, 4 percent, and 2 percent of their personal best times with perfect racing protocols—great starts, perfect turns, perfect finishes, and so on.

For example, a swimmer with a personal best time of 60 seconds for the 100 m freestyle completes a trial aiming at the targets of 6 percent, 4 percent, and 2 percent of his or her personal best time, which works out like this:

$$60 \div 100 = 0.6 \times 106 = 63.60, \text{ which is } 6\%$$
$$60 \div 100 = 0.6 \times 104 = 62.40, \text{ which is } 4\%$$
$$60 \div 100 = 0.6 \times 102 = 61.20, \text{ which is } 2\%$$

This progresses to doing a single cold swim at 4 percent of personal best time. This in turn progresses to doing a single cold swim at 3 percent of personal best time. Doing all cold swims at 3 percent of personal best time is the goal, but swimmers build up to that using the previous progression.

The coach can change the emphasis by making the percentages applicable to the goal time. The same swimmer with a personal best time of 60 seconds for the 100 m freestyle then has the percentages based on the goal time of 59 seconds, which produces these targets:

$$59 \div 100 = 0.59 \times 106 = 62.54, \text{ which is } 6\%$$
$$59 \div 100 = 0.59 \times 104 = 61.34, \text{ which is } 4\%$$
$$59 \div 100 = 0.59 \times 102 = 60.18, \text{ which is } 2\%$$

This could again progress to doing a single cold swim at 4 percent of goal time, which in turn progresses to doing a single cold swim at 3 percent of goal time. Doing all cold swims at 3 percent of goal time is the target.

Following the swim at 3 percent of personal best time or 3 percent of goal time, the swimmer can perform a broken swim at 2 percent. When completing a broken swim the swimmer should always be at racing profile with perfect starts, turns, finishes, and so on.

This percentage progression can be applied to racing situations. In a midseason meet when swimmers are under work conditions, they can practice the following: heats at 3 percent of personal best time, semifinals at 2 percent of personal best time, and final at 1 percent of personal best time.

If athletes are competing at a midseason meet when rested, they aim for heats to be at 3 percent of goal time, semifinals at 2 percent of goal time, and final at 1 percent of goal time. Swimmers must be trained to achieve heats at 2 percent of goal time, semifinals at 1 percent of goal time, and the final at their goal time.

High-Performance Endurance Test-Set Progression

This high-performance endurance test-set progression is an example of how high-performance endurance training can be progressed over a period of weeks.

The swimmer needs to achieve a set of 40 × 100 m freestyle before progressing to the second set in the progression. Figure 2.13 shows the recording sheet for the first set; it can be amended for use with the other sets as well.

Set 1: 40 × 100 m test

Achieve 40 × 100 m freestyle on a cycle (1:20) before progressing to set 2. If the swimmer makes cycle at any intensity, he or she can progress to the next set. The aim is to swim this set at a heart-rate level of 30 BBM.

Set 2: 30 × 100 m test

All swims on 1:30.
The swimmer should do this set in the heart-rate range of 30 to 20 BBM, aiming to swim faster times than in set 1. On consecutive cycles, speed and heart rate from this set can be compared with performance on this set in previous cycles.

Set 3: 24 × 100 m test

18 × 100 m on 1:45, heart rate at 20 BBM to 10 BBM.
6 × 100 m on 2:00, heart rate at 20 BBM to 10 BBM.
Record times, stroke counts, and breathing patterns.
Record the average of the total set.
Record the average of the first 18 × 100 m.
Record the average of the last 6 × 100 m.
Do not include fastest and slowest time when working out averages.
Compare heart rate to speed.

Set 4: 18 × 100 m test

All 18 × 100 on 2:00.
The swimmer should hold the fastest average from set 3 during either the 18 × 100 m section or the 6 × 100 m section. Record heart rates and stroke counts from set 1. Compare speed to heart rates.

Set 5: 2000 m or 3000 m test

This set is either a timed 2000 m or timed 3000 m test.

The swimmer repeats the progression of sets 1 to 4 on a biweekly basis after several progressions early season. This progression can be used with 50 m, 100 m, 150 m, and 200 m repeat distances or combinations of those repeat distances. But 50 m repeats

40 × 100 METER FS HIGH-PERFORMANCE ENDURANCE TEST RECORDING SHEET

Name_____   Date_____

Swim	Time	Heart rate	Stroke count	Swim	Time	Heart rate	Stroke count
1				21			
2				22			
3				23			
4				24			
5				25			
6				26			
7				27			
8				28			
9				29			
10				30			
11				31			
12				32			
13				33			
14				34			
15				35			
16				36			
17				37			
18				38			
19				39			
20				40			
	Average time	HR drift					

FIGURE 2.13   *40 × 100 m freestyle high-performance endurance test recording sheet.*

should be done at the back end of the set after fatigue has occurred. Progress 200 m repeat distances down through the week and season.

Workouts containing these sets should use a common set warm-up, and sets 1, 2, 3, and 4 should be followed by a submaximal moderate but controlled and descending overdistance swim of approximately 1500 m to 2000 m. A drill progression should lead into these sets. All repeats must be even-split swims (Sweetenham 1998a, 1999a).

The coach should record splits, stroke rates, and breathing patterns, and swimmers should record times and stroke rates and if possible breathing patterns.

Swimmers should complete the 3000 m and 2000 m timed swims at an even pace that is as fast as they can maintain throughout the swim. Around 30 minutes of work completed at an even, fast pace will be close to the anaerobic threshold. Swimmers need a high level of motivation if they are to perform these tests at the required level (Atkinson and Sweetenham 1999; Maglischo 1993).

Sample 3000-Meter Time Trial

This example shows how to use the collected data to set training repeat times.

Time for the 3000 m = 36 minutes = 2,160 seconds
Average 100 m time = 1:12.00

Correction factors to adjust average times to anaerobic-threshold training repeat times are as follows:

200 m repeat swims minus 2 seconds

100 m repeat swims minus 1.5 seconds

50 m repeat swims minus 1 second

Prescribing Training Repeat Times

Prescribed anaerobic-threshold training times with 10- to 20-second rest intervals:

400 m = average 100 m time of 1:12 × 4 = 4:48.00   400 m = 4:48.00
200 m = average 100 m time of 1:12 × 2 = 2:24.00 – 2 seconds   200 m = 2:22.00
100 m = average 100 m time of 1:12 = 1:12.00 – 1.5 seconds   100 m = 1:10.50
50 m = average 100 m time of 1:12 ÷ 2 = 0:36.00 – 1 second   50 m = 35.00

(Atkinson and Sweetenham 1999; Maglischo 1993)

Sample 2000-Meter Time Trial

This example shows how to use the collected data to set training repeat times.

Time for the 2000 m swim time = 26 minutes = 1,560 seconds
Average 100 m time = 1:18.00

Correction factors to adjust the average times to anaerobic-threshold training repeat times are as follows:

200 m repeat swims minus 2 seconds

100 m repeat swims minus 1.5 seconds

50 m repeat swims minus 1 second

Prescribing Training Repeat Times

Prescribed anaerobic-threshold training times with 10- to 20-second rest intervals.

400 m = average 100 m time of 1:18 × 4 = 5:12.00   400 m = 5:12.00
200 m = average 100 m time of 1:18 × 2 = 2:36.00 – 2 seconds   200 m = 2:34.00
100 m = average 100 m time of 1:18 = 1:18.00 – 1.5 seconds   100 m = 1:16.50
50 m = average 100 m time of 1:12 ÷ 2 = 39.00 – 1 second   50 m = 38.00

(Atkinson and Sweetenham 1999; Maglischo 1993)

Individual Medley Pace Test Progression

The IM swimmer should complete the IM strengths and weaknesses chart as shown in figures 2.14 and 2.15 before progressing to doing this test set. The following example is based on swimmer X as shown in the sample strengths and weaknesses chart in figure 2.14. The strengths and weaknesses chart will allow the swimmer to establish target percentages of each stroke for the individual medley.

This test progression can be used with the IM swimmer over a period of weeks during which the swimmer completes one section of the test each week. The IM swimmer can use sections of this test instead of or as well as the 7 × 200 m step test. The swimmer can also do the test over a week by performing a section of the test for four days in succession (Atkinson and Sweetenham 1999).

Butterfly 10 × 100 Meter and 1 × 200 Meter Test

4 × 100 m BF at PB plus 12 seconds, target = 1:13.00, on 2:00
3 × 100 m BF at PB plus 8 seconds, target = 1:09.00, on 2:20
2 × 100 m BF at PB plus 4 seconds, target = 1:05.00, on 2:40
1 × 100 m BF as fast as possible, target = under 1:04.00, on 3:00
1 × 200 m backstroke at goal split pace for the 400 m IM, 1:08.00 × 2, target = 2:16.00

The swimmer descends through the set of 100 m swims on an increasing rest cycle. The recording sheet for the 10 × 100 m and 1 × 200 m test is shown in figure 2.16.

Backstroke and Breaststroke 6 × 200 Meter Test

Based on goal 400 m IM backstroke split time of 1:08.00

First 200 m BK target 2:32.00 on 5:00
Second 200 m BK target 2:28.00 on 5:00
Third 200 m BK target 2:24.00 on 5:00
Fourth 200 m BK target 2:20.00 on 5:00
Fifth 200 m BK target 2:16.00 on 5:00

Target on the fifth 200 m is goal backstroke split pace of 2:16.00 (1:08.00 × 2).
Target on the sixth 200 m for breaststroke is 400 m IM goal pace of 2:22.00 (1:11.00 × 2).
Reduce each 200 m by 4 seconds.

Breaststroke and Freestyle 6 × 200 Meter Test

Based on goal 400 m IM breaststroke split time of 1:11.00

First 200 m BR target 2:38.00 on 5:00
Second 200 m BR target 2:34.00 on 5:00
Third 200 m BR target 2:30.00 on 5:00
Fourth 200 m BR target 2:26.00 on 5:00
Fifth 200 m BR target 2:22.00 on 5:00

Target on the fifth 200 m is goal breaststroke split pace of 2:22 (1:11.00 × 2).
Target on the sixth 200 m FS is 400 m IM goal pace of 2:00.00 (1:00.00 × 2).
Reduce each 200 m by 4 seconds.

Freestyle and IM 6 × 200 Meter Test

Based on goal 400 m IM freestyle split time of 1:00.00

First 200 m FS target 2:16.00 on 5:00
Second 200 m FS target 2:12.00 on 5:00
Third 200 m FS target 2:08.00 on 5:00

COMPLETED INDIVIDUAL MEDLEY STRENGTHS AND WEAKNESSES CHART

Swimmer: Swimmer 'X'
Short course or long course: Short course
Date when completing the chart: December 2002

	Butterfly	Backstroke	Breaststroke	Freestyle	
100 m and 200 m best times for all strokes and differential (diff)	100 m = 1:01 200 m = 2:16 Diff = 15	100 m = 1:03 200 m = 2:13 Diff = 10	100 m = 1:06 200 m = 2:24 Diff = 18	100 m = 56 200 m = 1:59 Diff = 13	
Splits from 400 m IM personal best time and difference between 100 m PB and splits	1:03 2 seconds difference between splits for 400 m IM and 100 m PB time	1:13 10 seconds difference between splits for 400 m IM and 100 m PB time	1:15 9 seconds difference between splits for 400 m IM and 100 m PB time	1:00 4 seconds difference between splits for 400 m IM and 100 m PB time	4:31.00 = current 400 m IM personal best time
Actual 400 m IM splits as a percentage	23.24%	26.93%	27.67%	22.14%	
PB (100 m + 6%) × 2 = goal time for 200 m	PB 100 m + 6% = 1:04.60 × 2 = **200 m BF goal = 2:09.20**	PB 100 m + 6% = 1:06.70 × 2 = **200 m BK goal = 2:13.40**	PB 100 m + 6% = 1:09.90 × 2 = **200 m BR goal = 2:19.80**	PB 100 m + 6% = 59.10 × 2 = **200 m FS goal = 1:58.20**	
PB 100 m + 8% = target 400 m IM splits	1:05.80	1:08.04	1:11.28	1:00.48	**4:25.60 = 400 m IM goal time**
Target 400 m IM splits as a percentage	24.77%	25.61%	26.83%	22.77%	
400 m target time for each stroke = 200 m goal time × 2 + differential between 100 m and 200 m best times	**400 m BF goal = 4:33.40** 2:09.20 × 2 = 4:18.40 + 15 = 4:33.40	**400 m BK goal = 4:36.80** 2:13.40 × 2 = 4:26.80 + 10 = 4:36.80	**400 m BR goal = 4:57.60** 2:19.80 × 2 = 4:39.60 + 18 = 4:57.60	**400 m FS goal = 4:09.40** 1:58.20 × 2 = 3:56.40 + 13 = 4:09.40	
200 m IM target splits 100 m PB + 4% ÷ 2	**31.72** 1:01 + 4%= 1:03.44 ÷ 2 = 31.72	**32.76** 1:03 + 4% = 1:05.52 ÷ 2 = 32.76	**34.32** 1:06 + 4% = 1:08.64 ÷ 2 = 34.32	**29.12** 56 + 4% = 58.24 ÷ 2 = 29.12	**2:07.92 = 200 m IM goal time**
200 m targets based on target 400 m IM splits	**200 m BF/BK goal = 2:13.84**	**200 m BK/BR goal = 2:19.32**	**200 m BR/FS goal = 2:11.76**		

FIGURE 2.14 Completed individual medley strengths and weaknesses chart.
(Atkinson and Sweetenham 1999)

INDIVIDUAL MEDLEY STRENGTHS AND WEAKNESSES CHART

Swimmer_____

Short course or long course_____

Date when completing the chart_____

	Butterfly	**Backstroke**	**Breaststroke**	**Freestyle**	
100 m and 200 m best times for all strokes and differential	100 m = 200 m = Diff =	100 m = 200 m = Diff =	100 m = 200 m = Diff =	100 m = 200 m = Diff =	
Splits from 400 m IM personal best time and difference between 100 m PB and splits	Split = Diff =	Split = Diff =	Split = Diff =	Split = Diff =	Current 400 m IM personal best time =
Actual 400 m IM splits as a percentage					
PB (100 m + 6%) × 2 = goal time for 200 m	PB 100 m + 6% = × 2 = **200 m BF goal =**	PB 100 m + 6% = × 2 = **200 m BK goal =**	PB 100 m + 6% = × 2 = **200 m BR goal =**	PB 100 m + 6% = × 2 = **200 m FS goal =**	
PB 100 m + 8% = target 400 m IM splits	PB 100 m + 8% =	PB 100 m + 8% =	PB 100 m + 8% =	PB 100 m + 8% =	**400 m IM goal time =**
Target 400 m IM splits as a percentage					
400 m target time for each stroke = 200 m goal time × 2 + differential between 100 m and 200 m best times	**400 m BF goal =**	**400 m BK goal =**	**400 m BR goal =**	**400 m FS goal =**	
200 m IM target splits 100 m PB + 4% ÷ 2					**200 m IM goal time =**
200 m targets based on target 400 m IM splits	**200m BF/BK goal =**	**200 m BK/BR goal =**	**200 m BR/FS goal =**		

FIGURE 2.15 Blank individual medley strengths and weaknesses chart.
(Atkinson and Sweetenham 1999)

10 × 100 METER AND 1 × 200 METER INDIVIDUAL MEDLEY PACE TEST RECORDING SHEET

Name_____   Date_____

Set	Swim	Splits	Stroke rate and stroke count	Target	Time	Heart rate
4 × 100 m	1					
	2					
	3					
	4					
3 × 100 m	1					
	2					
	3					
2 × 100 m	1					
	2					
1 × 100 m	1					
1 × 200 m	1					

FIGURE 2.16   *10 × 100 m and 1 × 200 m individual medley pace test recording sheet.*

Fourth 200 m FS target 2:04.00 on 5:00

Fifth 200 m FS target 2:00.00 on 5:00

Target on the fifth 200 m is goal freestyle split pace of 2:00.00 (1:00.00 × 2).

The sixth 200 m IM is a straight 200 m IM, but the target is half of 400 m IM pace of 2:13.00.

Each section of this test progression is 1200 m. The constant in this progression is the goal time, not the heart rate.

Test heart rates and stroke counts at goal pace. Do not test times at set heart rates. Goal-orientated tests are by far the best way for the individual medley swimmer to train sets. The recording sheet for each 6 × 200 m section of this test is shown in figure 2.17.

6 × 200 METER INDIVIDUAL MEDLEY PACE TEST RECORDING SHEET

Name_____   Date_____

Swim	Stroke	Target	Time recorded	100 m split	Stroke rate and stroke count	Heart rate
1						
2						
3						
4						
5						
6						

FIGURE 2.17 *6 × 200 m individual medley pace test recording sheet.*

Kick Test Sets

Swimmers should also be tested on their ability to perform kick training. This kick test set has been designed to provide a goal-oriented approach to testing kicking ability. The results can also be compared with the training sets that the swimmers perform on kick.

1 × 800 m kick target time 12 minutes or faster
200 m swim-down
1 × 400 m kick target time 6 minutes or faster
200 m swim-down
1 × 200 m kick target time 3 minutes or faster
200 m swim-down
1 × 100 m kick target time within 20 seconds of personal best time for 100 m
200 m swim-down
1 × 50 m kick
150 m swim-down
1 × 25 m kick
75 m swim-down

Test Protocol

This test can be conducted long course or short course. Swimmers should use one stroke for the entire test. Breaststroke swimmers should build up to doing the whole of this test on breaststroke, and they may do the 800 m swim on freestyle. The warm-up for this test should include some breaststroke because the only true way to warm up for breaststroke kick is to swim breaststroke kick at low intensity and build up to get ready for the test. Swimmers may alternate 50 m freestyle and 50 m breaststroke on the 800 m kick if they are breaststroke swimmers. In time they may build up to performing the whole 800 m on breaststroke kick, but they should do this in consultation with the coach. Swimmers must keep their hands on the kickboard until the touch at each turn and use the kickboard for all strokes.

Any swimmer completing the kick tests under the target times shown in a long-course pool for the 800 m kick, 400 m kick, and 200 m kick sections of the test can be awarded special kicking certificates. A coach may wish to establish 12-minute, 6-minute, and 3-minute kicking clubs in the program (Atkinson and Sweetenham 1999). A recording sheet used for this test is shown in figure 2.18.

Another method for establishing target times is to swim the 800 m kick as fast as possible and then cut the time recorded in half to set the target time for the 400 m kick. This procedure is repeated for establishing target times through the remainder of the set, as in this example:

800 m kick, time recorded 17:30.00
400 m kick target becomes 8:45.00 or faster
400 m kick, time recorded 8:30.00
200 m kick target becomes 4:15.00 or faster
200 m kick, time recorded 4:05.00
100 m kick target becomes 2:02.50 or faster
100 m kick, time recorded 1:56.00
50 m kick target becomes 58 seconds or faster
50 m kick, time recorded 52 seconds
25 m kick target becomes 26 seconds or faster
25 m kick, time recorded 24 seconds

KICK TEST SET RECORDING SHEET

Name_____   Date_____

	Test 1	Test 2	Test 3
800 m kick 12-minute club			
400 m kick 6-minute club			
200 m kick 3-minute club			
100 m kick Within 20 seconds of PB 100 m swim time			
50 m kick Target half of time recorded on the 100 m kick or faster			
25 m kick Target half of time recorded on the 50 m kick or faster			

FIGURE 2.18   Kick test set recording sheet.

Pull Tests

Most coaches test their swimmers on full stroke and on kick, but it is equally important to test swimmers' ability on pull sets. This set tests the swimmer while using a combination of pull with a band or a band with pull buoys. The pull buoy will provide some flotation for the legs while swimmers perform that section of the test. Removing the pull buoy will make the test more challenging.

> 100 m timed breaststroke pull, with a pull buoy and band, ensuring that the time and stroke count are recorded.
> 100 m timed backstroke pull, with band only, ensuring that the time and stroke count are recorded.
> 50 m backstroke end of stroke drill, with a band. Elbows are fixed at the swimmers' sides. They count the number of sculling actions for the 50 m swim. Record the number of sculling actions and the time. This pull test will develop the end of stroke phase of the stroke.

The information from this test should be recorded on the sample sheet in figure 2.19.

PULL TEST RECORDING SHEET

Name_____ Date_____

	Time recorded	Stroke count	Heart rate
100 m BR pull			
100 m BK pull			
50 m BK end of stroke scull			

FIGURE 2.19   Pull test recording sheet.

Speed Tests

Swimming speed is important, but also important is being able to perform an effective transition from the dive start to swimming at full speed, to perform the turning action with speed, and to maintain speed at the back of a race while fatigued. The speed tests are broken down into four areas—starts, turns, finishes, and swimming speed—to test the swimmer's speed in all areas of a competitive race.

Starts

6 × 20 m. From a command start the swimmer is timed to the head passing 15 m. The swimmer continues to sprint to the 20 m mark in the pool.

Turns

6 × 25 m. The swimmer commences each swim at least 12.5 m from the wall. The swimmer is timed from when the head passes a point 7.5 m from the turn and returns to the 7.5 m mark after the turn. The athlete continues to sprint back to the 12.5 m point. The coach should also time hand entry on the final stroke before the turn to the point when the feet hit the wall. The swimmer should aim at a target of 0.6 seconds for this action for freestyle and backstroke. On butterfly and breaststroke the coach should time from when the hands touch the wall to when the feet hit the wall. Chapter 10 outlines targets and more details about turns.

Finishes

6 × 20 m. The swimmer sprints in to a finish from 20 m out from the wall. Each finish is timed from the flags to the wall. When the head passes under the flags (5 m out) the timing starts, and it ends as the swimmer finishes on the wall.

Swimming Speed

6 × 25 m. From a push the swimmer is timed over 6 × 25 m swims.

Do not count the fastest and slowest repeat from each section. Add together the four times from each section that remain and then divide by four to give the swimmer an average time to improve on through the season (Atkinson and Sweetenham 1999).

The purpose of this swimming-speed test set is to work on improving all elements of a race while maintaining efficiency with speed. An example of the swimming-speed section of the test is the following:

First 25 m	14.00
Second 25 m	14.50
Third 25 m	13.70
Fourth 25 m	14.20
Fifth 25 m	13.90
Sixth 25 m	14.60

The third and sixth swim are not counted because they are the fastest and slowest repeats. The remaining four swims are added together and divided by four.

$$14.00 + 14.50 + 14.20 + 13.90 = 56.60 \div 4 = 14.15$$

The information from this test can be recorded on the recording sheet shown in figure 2.20.

IM and Form Stroke Count Efficiency Test for Age-Group Swimmers 13 Years and Younger

This test is designed to ensure that the swimmer is swimming as efficiently as possible on all four strokes. The test involves a progression of a 100 m IM to a 200 m IM and then to a 400 m IM. This test is designed for junior age-group swimmers aged 13 years and younger (Atkinson and Sweetenham 1999).

SPEED TEST RECORDING SHEET

Name_____   Date_____

Effort number	Starts	Turns	Finishes	Swimming speed
1				
2				
3				
4				
5				
6				
Fastest				
Slowest				
Average of the remaining 4 swims				

FIGURE 2.20   Speed test recording sheet.

100-Meter Individual Medley

For age-group swimmers have a target of the following stroke counts—8 butterfly, 12 backstroke, 8 breaststroke, and 12 freestyle. The underwater stroke is counted in the total of 8 for the breaststroke. This is for the test performed in a 25 m pool.

Another aim is to improve any inefficient strokes. As a rule the butterfly and breast-stroke stroke counts match each other, as do the backstroke and freestyle stroke counts. Swimmers must perform the technique of the strokes on each section of the test without using an exaggerated glide.

A swimmer who performed with the following stroke counts—6 butterfly, 14 backstroke, 9 breaststroke, and 12 freestyle—would have to work on improving the breaststroke to match the butterfly and improving the backstroke to match the freestyle (Atkinson and Sweetenham 1999).

200-Meter Individual Medley

A swimmer who attains 100 m IM stroke counts of 8 butterfly, 12 backstroke, 8 breast-stroke, and 12 freestyle doubles those stroke counts to establish 200 m IM target stroke counts of 16 butterfly, 24 backstroke, 16 breaststroke, and 24 freestyle.

The swimmer who performs this test in a 50 m pool records the stroke counts and then establishes targets for the 400 m IM (Atkinson and Sweetenham 1999).

400-Meter Individual Medley

The swimmer who attains stroke-count targets for the 200 m IM transfers those targets to the 400 m IM. The following procedure is used to progress the swimmer to attaining the target stroke counts in a 400 m IM.

In a 25 m pool the first 400 m swim as outlined is added to start the progression. In a 50 m pool the swimmer starts with the second 400 m swim.

400 m IM performed as 4 × 100 m IMs with no rest, aiming at these stroke counts on each 100 m IM—8 butterfly, 12 backstroke, 8 breaststroke, and 12 freestyle.

400 m IM performed as 2 × 200 m IMs with no rest, aiming at these stroke counts on each 200 m IM—16 butterfly, 24 backstroke, 16 breaststroke, and 24 freestyle.

400 m IM as a straight 400 m IM, aiming at these stroke counts—32 butterfly, 48 backstroke, 32 breaststroke, and 48 freestyle—on each 100 m of each stroke (Atkinson and Sweetenham 1999).

Form Test

When the swimmer has competed the IM testing process, the values attained can be applied to swimming a test on a form stroke over 100 m, 200 m, and 400 m in a similar way to the IM progression (Atkinson and Sweetenham 1999).

The sample swimmer shown in the IM section of this test would need to hold the following stroke counts on the form-test progression:

Butterfly
100 m 32 strokes (8 strokes per 25 m lap or 16 strokes per 50 m lap)
200 m 64 strokes (8 strokes per 25 m lap or 16 strokes per 50 m lap)
400 m 128 strokes (8 strokes per 25 m lap or 16 strokes per 50 m lap)

Backstroke
100 m 48 strokes (12 strokes per 25 m lap or 24 strokes per 50 m lap)
200 m 96 strokes (12 strokes per 25 m lap or 24 strokes per 50 m lap)
400 m 192 strokes (12 strokes per 25 m lap or 24 strokes per 50 m lap)

Breaststroke
100 m 32 strokes (8 strokes per 25 m lap or 16 strokes per 50 m lap)
200 m 64 strokes (8 strokes per 25 m lap or 16 strokes per 50 m lap)
400 m 128 strokes (8 strokes per 25 m lap or 16 strokes per 50 m lap)

Freestyle
100 m 48 strokes (12 strokes per 25 m lap or 24 strokes per 50 m lap)
200 m 96 strokes (12 strokes per 25 m lap or 24 strokes per 50 m lap)
400 m 192 strokes (12 strokes per 25 m lap or 24 strokes per 50 m lap)

Figure 2.21 shows a recording sheet for both the IM and form-stroke sections of this test.

IM STROKE COUNT EFFICIENCY AND FORM STROKE COUNT EFFICIENCY TEST RECORDING SHEET

Name_____ Date_____

IM

Date of test	Length of swim	Swim time	Stroke counts	Heart rate
	100 m IM		BF BK BR FS	
	200 m IM		BF BK BR FS	
	400 m IM		BF BK BR FS	

Form stroke_____

Date of test	Length of swim	Swim time	Stroke counts	Heart rate
	100 m			
	200 m			
	400 m			

FIGURE 2.21 *IM stroke count efficiency and form stroke count efficiency tests recording sheet.*

Individual Checking Speed Tests

The individual checking speed (ICS) test is a swim of submaximal intensity that can be used to establish a relationship between areas of swimming performance such as swimming speed, heart rate, and stroke count (Atkinson and Sweetenham 1999). The information from this test can be recorded on the sheet shown in figure 2.22. We suggest that checking speed values be established for 100 m, 200 m, 300 m, and 400 m repeats.

The test or sections of the test should be done at the beginning of the training session before the swimmer becomes fatigued by any training set. The swim can also be used in a swim-down to test whether the swimmer is sufficiently recovered. If the swimmer has not recovered enough, the swim-down can continue. If the swimmer has recovered sufficiently, the swim-down can end. The values at the end of the swim-down would be compared with the values established on the initial test.

The checking speed values will probably change throughout the season as the swimmer progresses and improves his or her personal best time. We suggest that the ICS times be changed once per macrocycle and that swimmers work to the same time throughout each cycle.

The ICS is based on the swimmer's 100 m personal best time plus 15 seconds for butterfly, backstroke, and freestyle. For breaststroke the ICS is personal best time plus 20 seconds. When the test is conducted for the first time, the swimmer must be sure to swim to the required pace. Swimming at the right pace may take a few attempts when the test is first conducted.

As an example, a swimmer with a 100 m freestyle personal best time of 59.10 would have a target time for the ICS of 1:14.10 with a heart rate of 135.

This test has been used successfully to check the recovery status of swimmers on the Monday morning session following a weekend competition. The swimmer just offered as an example swam the ICS test following a weekend competition and had a heart rate of 165 after recording a time of 1:14.50. This result gave the coach a solid indication of the recovery status of the athlete. Any distance of the ICS can be used in isolation in many training situations.

This test swim gives the coach and swimmer the information about speed, efficiency, and technical and tactical aspects of performance.

Speed

Swimming speed remains constant between distances: 100 m at 1:30, 200 m at 3:00, 300 m at 4:30, and 400 m at 6:00. As swimmers hit the splits through the swim they must maintain even pace (Atkinson and Sweetenham 1999). Sprinters, breaststroke swimmers, and butterfly swimmers should perform the test up to the distance of 300 m. They should not go beyond 300 m if their technique does not hold. For some sprinters the maximum distance of the test may be 200 m.

Efficiency

The stroke count recorded at the ICS swimming speed gives the swimmer and coach a measure of efficiency. This stroke count is then repeated as the swimmer progresses through the test. Expanding on the previous example, targets would be the following:

INDIVIDUAL CHECKING SPEED TEST RECORDING SHEET

Name_____ Date_____

Date and stroke	Target time	Distance	Time recorded	Splits	Stroke counts	Heart rate
		100 m				
		200 m				
		300 m				
		400 m				

FIGURE 2.22   Individual checking speed test recording sheet.
(Atkinson and Sweetenham 1999)

100 m 1:30 pace, with 20 strokes per 50 m, equaling 40 strokes per 100 m

200 m 1:30 pace equals a time of 3:00, with 20 strokes per 50 m, equaling 80 strokes per 200 m

300 m 1:30 pace equals a time of 4:30, with 20 strokes per 50 m, equaling 120 strokes per 300 m

400 m 1:30 pace equals a time of 6:00, with 20 strokes per 50 m, equaling 160 strokes per 400 m

The stroke rate is also important, because the swimmer should swim the repeats with an even stroke rate as well as an even stroke count (Atkinson and Sweetenham 1999).

Fitness

The heart rate should be taken at the conclusion of each repeat distance. The heart rates at the end of all the distances should be taken and recorded.

The heart-rate increase through the test progression should be noted. A heart-rate increase of 8 beats or fewer through the swim would be excellent. A large increase in heart rate of 30 to 40 beats per minute when swimming at the same pace over longer distances could result from two causes. First, the swimmer may not be aerobically fit and may require additional aerobic conditioning. Second, if previous test results are known and the swimmer did not have a large increase, he or she may be fatigued or about to come down with some type of illness (Atkinson and Sweetenham 1999).

Technical and Tactical

Starts, turns, and finishes can be timed as outlined in the speed test set to give a better overall picture of efficiency and help improve this aspect of swimming performance (Atkinson and Sweetenham 1999).

Psychological

Swimmers can gain substantial psychological benefits by doing this test. Improvement in aerobic fitness, stroke count, or pacing skills will boost confidence (Atkinson and Sweetenham 1999).

Planning the Use of Test Sets

The placement of test sets into the annual plan and the macrocycle is important. Coaches must not overtest at the expense of training. As an example, the following testing pattern may occur in a 15-week macrocycle.

Week 1

Mesocycle 1, endurance week, 60 kilometers

- Double-distance 1 × 400 m Monday afternoon session
- High-performance endurance test-set progression 40 × 100 m

Week 2

Mesocycle 1, endurance week, 65 kilometers

- Double-distance 2 × 400 m Monday afternoon session
- High-performance endurance test-set progression 24 × 100 m
- Maximum heart-rate test

Week 3

Mesocycle 1, endurance week, 70 kilometers

- Double-distance 3 × 400 m Monday afternoon session
- High-performance endurance test-set progression 18 × 100 m

Week 4

Mesocycle 1, endurance week, 70 kilometers

- Double-distance 4 × 400 m Monday afternoon session
- High-performance endurance test-set progression 30 × 100 m

Week 5

Mesocycle 2, quality week, 65 kilometers

- 7 × 200 m step test on Monday
- Distance swimmers may do the double-distance 5 × 400 m Monday afternoon session
- Distance swimmers may do the final step in the high-performance endurance test-set progression 2000 m or 3000 m timed

Week 6

Mesocycle 2, quality week, 65 kilometers

- Cold swim 10 to 14 days after the first 7 × 200 m step test

Week 7

Mesocycle 2, quality week, 65 kilometers

- Maximum heart-rate test

Week 8

Mesocycle 2, quality week, 60 kilometers

- 8 × 50 m efficiency test

Week 9

Mesocycle 3, specifics week, 60 kilometers

- 7 × 200 m step test on Monday
- 7 × 50 m efficiency test

Week 10

Mesocycle 3, specifics week, 55 kilometers

- 6 × 50 m efficiency test
- Maximum heart-rate test

Week 11

Mesocycle 3, specifics week, 50 kilometers

- 5 × 50 m efficiency test
- Speed tests

Week 12

Mesocycle 3, specifics week, 50 kilometers

- 4 × 50 m efficiency test
- Speed tests

Week 13

Mesocycle 4, specifics or taper week, 45 kilometers

- 7×200 m step test on Monday
- 3×50 m efficiency test
- Speed tests

Week 14

Mesocycle 4, specifics or taper week, 40 kilometers

- Cold swim 10 to 14 days after the first 7×200 m step test. This fits into the policy as outlined in chapter 12 that the swimmer should perform a full-blooded hit out at maximum effort 10 days out from the competition. This swim is shorter than race distance and on a different stroke.
- 3×50 m efficiency test
- Speed tests

Week 15

Mesocycle 4, taper week, 35 kilometers

- 3×50 m efficiency test

Not all the test sets in this chapter need to be used in every 15-week macrocycle. The swimmer and coach should determine which tests they will use during the cycle. This may change from cycle to cycle while the swimmer maintains the core tests that the swimmer and coach feel work for them.

The IM pace set is a test that can be broken down into four sections. The IM swimmer could perform sections of this test when the remainder of the squad performs the 7×200 m step test.

Individual checking speed tests and the IM and form-stroke efficiency test will be used as required through the macrocycle. For example, one or two swims from the checking speed test can be incorporated in warm-ups and swim-downs in training sessions. The same approach can be used for the kick and pull tests, which can be done either as a straight set or broken up and performed in the training session.

Swimmers should always check their heart rates on all training sets to learn their training intensity or recovery status or to know if they have recorded a new maximum heart rate.

During the second 15-week macrocycle, the same progression of testing can take place to allow comparisons to be made with the first macrocycle. For example, suppose that in week 13 in the first 15-week macrocycle a swimmer recorded a time of 2:35.00 for the seventh 200 m swim in the 7×200 m step test. If on the same test in the second macrocycle the swimmer recorded 2:31.00, both the swimmer and the coach would have a good indication of the form in comparison to that in the previous macrocycle.

This chapter provides the coach and swimmer an understanding of the swimming tests that can be done and the information that can be gained from the results. Essential to the usefulness of tests is the accuracy of all recorded information. Swimmers and coaches can now choose which tests will work best in their program.

Drilling for Performance

Most coaches who have enjoyed success with senior international-class swimmers agree that, within reasonable limits, an older athlete will respond significantly faster to a training stimulus than will an age-group athlete or an athlete who has a limited training background. This effect also applies to technique and training-efficiency skills—body position, distance per stroke, distance per kick, flexibility, hand acceleration, and so on.

Swimming is a technique-driven sport. An athlete who possesses adequate core body strength and range of movement (flexibility) can at a young age learn quality stroke mechanics and receive reinforcement with low-intensity skill-based training. We do not believe and have never witnessed efficiency at high speed or high effort if it is not practiced and evident at low speed.

Stroke-Efficiency Progressions

Stroke efficiency is the most challenging area of skill enhancement for the coach and swimmer. When the athlete is first obtaining and then maintaining optimum range of movement and core body strength, he or she must go through a series of stroke-efficiency progressions to high speed and maximum effort. The swimmer must develop efficiency at race-pace values and strive to imitate the stroke rates and stroke lengths of successful athletes at the international level. Therefore, the stroke enhancement or drill progression must link the basics to the goal of attaining the biomechanics of successful international swimmers.

To achieve this, we believe that all swimming pools must be accurately marked every 5 m, and preferably every 1 m. For instance, if it takes a senior male 100 m freestyle swimmer (approximately 22 to 24 years old) between 24 and 26 strokes per 50 m in 22 seconds, then surely it is wise to have an age-group male measuring his efficiency by using stroke counts as the constant and measuring time and distance as the variable. So too should the swimmer use distances other than 50 m as the constant. Three variables exist: stroke count, distance, and time. We believe that coaches should do training sets that constantly change emphasis using one of these three as a constant and the other two values as variables.

Stroke rates, although somewhat of an innovation, have been used and recorded for many years. Coaches can introduce them to senior athletes, youth swimmers, masters, and triathletes, but they should be used cautiously (if at all with junior and age-group swimmers for most events and distances).

Because most drills are performed over 50 m or less with intensive repeats, heart rates cannot play as important a role with monitoring effort or fatigue. Therefore, goal-pace simulation is required. In our opinion, race pace is future race pace and therefore must be goal oriented with regard to future performance of speed, stroke count (length), and distance. A knowledge of pacing, stroke counts, and stroke efficiency used by successful senior swimmers is a prerequisite for all practicing coaches if they are to deliver sound advice to their athletes. Most coaches seem to use distance as the only constant.

Specific strength, or power per body weight, and buoyancy are also relevant in this progression of skill acquisition. A coach should be aware of the buoyancy of the athlete.

Resistance pull for the prematuration swimmer is extremely important in developing power per body weight in the water, and flexibility, recovery, and adaptation skills of the athlete are of maximum value. This becomes important at age 13 to 15 years after the athlete has developed core body strength to an optimum level. How many coaches know accurately the core body strength, range of movement, buoyancy, and specific power per body weight of each athlete they coach? How many have in practice specialized remedial antidotes for each area and each individual?

As a swimmer, can you swim a series of repeats like 20 × 50 m freestyle on 60 seconds holding 36 seconds for each 50 m repeat without using the pace clock (turning the pace clock off)? Can you do this accurately and hold stroke count and even stroke rate for the whole set? If you cannot do this, it is an area of your swimming that you need to work on.

The answer to the preceding question is to have a well-supervised, well-disciplined stroke-drill progression program for your swimming. This progression gives constant feedback to the athlete and coach where perfection is the only passing grade.

Each swimmer should have an individual stroke-drill progression for each stroke that he or she can use to improve any area of weakness in stroke technique. Athletes will win because of their strengths and lose because of their weaknesses.

100 percent correct is 100 percent correct; 99 percent correct is 100 percent wrong. The 1 percent margin can mean the difference between gold and silver.

At the senior level every aspect of skill development must be constantly revised with minimum time and effort. Any compromise in this area of development at the age-group level will become magnified many times over at the senior level.

Triathletes must conserve as much energy as possible during the swim. Improving technique and minimizing resistance will allow them to do this. Masters and triathletes should strive to attain the best possible technique.

The stroke-drill progressions contained in chapters 4 through 10 will help swimmers of all ages improve their stroke technique, starts, turns, and finishes for every event.

Progression Example

Stroke drills have absolutely nothing to do with easy swimming. They are about doing fewer strokes with maximum effort and concentration. Eventually, under demanding pressure, stroke drills lead to speed and perfection. As an example, a butterfly progression drill is shown to explain the link between basic stroke drills and specific race-pace performance drills and speed drills. The drill progression shown here is progression 4 in chapter 4 on butterfly. The explanation for Biondi butterfly drill is shown in butterfly drill progression 1.

1	50 m kick. 25 m front underwater kick, 25 m choice position kick (side or back). Streamlined arms, torpedo position.
2	50 m drill. Biondi drill, breathe only every six kicks. Breathe early, drop chin, and kick into and out of the stroke. Concentrate on accelerating hand speed through to the back of the stroke.
3	50 m drill. Biondi drill plus one full stroke.
4	50 m drill. Biondi drill plus two full strokes.
5	50 m swim. Slow-motion butterfly breathing every three. Concentrate on the kick into and out of the stroke. Count strokes.
6	50 m drill. Males use two right-arm pulls, two left-arm pulls, and four full strokes. Females use three right-arm pulls, three left-arm pulls, and three full strokes. The swimmer should breathe to the front every two strokes. The aim is to make the 50 m going through the preceding cycles twice. Start alternate 50 m repeats with the right arm and then the left arm. This step of the progression can be done breathing every three.
7	50 m drill. Minimum-maximum drill. Males aim at 16 strokes; females aim at 18 strokes.

The minimum-maximum drill is swimming at maximum effort with the minimum number of strokes. The two added together produce an efficiency figure. An example follows:

50 m BF in 30 seconds in 20 strokes = efficiency rating of 50

50 m BF in 32 seconds in 22 strokes = efficiency rating of 54

For this progression the amount of underwater swimming is adjusted for the skill and maturation level of the athlete. The coach should carefully monitor underwater kicking and swimming. The swimmer builds up this type of work over the season, being sure not to push too far too soon.

When the swimmer has completed this progression, it is important to record the stroke counts and times. The goal for the swimmer is to improve the efficiency rating.

Linking the Drill Progression to Improve the Whole Stroke

Step 1 of the progression teaches streamlining and stable body position, with the athlete feeling water pressure both above and below the body. Having to travel through the water, the athlete will learn to take the line of least resistance. By combining this with taking no breath for the 25 m, the swimmer will learn accelerated fast kick, streamlined body position, and stable body position.

© Sport the Library

Swimmers will attain efficiency at high speed only by first learning and perfecting stroke mechanics at low speed and then progressing to higher speeds.

This first step of the progression moves eventually to an arms-folded position that is significantly more difficult and provides additional stimulus to develop this skill further. Kicking on the back develops upper-body stabilization and an accelerated kick with minimum upper-body undulation.

Step 2 in the shown progression enhances body position (water pressure above and below body), timing of the breath, hand acceleration through to the back of the stroke, and head position. The head position has the face looking at the bottom of the pool, the chin only slightly tucked and on the surface, and the forehead forward on the breathing section just before the arm recovery. The swimmer does this while maintaining kicking speed and body position as developed in the first 50 m.

Steps 3 and 4 further develop the skills learned in steps 1 and 2 while adding more arm strokes and again maintaining kicking speed and body position. This also develops the weakest and least propulsive sections of the stroke, those being the initial and final parts. It is extremely difficult to commence a pull pattern incorrectly and still perform the stroke correctly. The swimmer must learn to start and finish the stroke properly.

Step 5 is completed by swimming as slowly as possible with absolutely perfect technique and timing with the least possible number of strokes. The swimmer must master the timing of the kicks, breathing, and arm stroke at slow speeds without the pressure of speed or effort.

Step 6 in the progression is completed by putting first priority on the number of strokes and less emphasis on the timing of the breathing, kicks, and arm stroke, as a contrast to the emphasis at step 5. For a 50 m swim the goal is 16 strokes for males and 18 strokes for females. These stroke counts are based on the stroke counts of international-level swimmers.

Step 7, the final step of the progression, requires the swimmer to combine all the skills of the previous steps, put them together under pressure for time and stroke count over 50 m, and maintain perfect technique and eventually race pace.

The swimmer must maintain the skill as the speed increases. He or she must not maintain speed integrity by a compromise in technique of either stroke length or stroke rate.

This progression can also include underwater sculling with the arms as a further development after the swimmer learns and perfects the streamlining and arms-folded progressions.

Specific Drill Progressions

This type of progression and similar ones are shown for all four strokes in chapters 4 through 7. Turning and starting progressions are also shown and can be developed. All progressions must start with the basics and link to full stroke, using any combination of distance, stroke count, stroke rate, and speed under pressure of race pace.

This approach can be incorporated into many test sets as outlined and shown in chapter 2. Is performance threatened by a breakdown in fitness or efficiency? (Or by lack of technique?) A drill done in isolation is of minimum benefit when compared with a progression that the swimmer completes perfectly and frequently. Done correctly, progressions will guarantee permanent precision performance.

With all the sections of the drill progressions shown in chapters 4 through 7, the coach can determine the distance that swimmers will perform on each drill, which will be based on the age and ability of the athlete performing the drill.

4

Butterfly

When working with swimmers on butterfly the coach must consider some key issues, such as the requirement that the stroke be balanced by a strong kick that has a significant propulsive contribution. Butterfly is the second least efficient of the competitive strokes. The complex nature of the stroke increases the potential for flaws in the swimmer's technique. Work should be conducted on the butterfly kick to ensure that the swimmer is efficient and fast when performing the kick underwater off the start and turns. This concern pertains to backstroke and freestyle as well. The drill progressions in this chapter break down the stroke into sections, which build back to full stroke. It is our belief that swimmers need to train on full stroke butterfly. For age-group swimmers to progress to completing the 7×200 m step test in chapter 2, they must build up to at least two or three sets per week of 2000 to 2400 m on full stroke butterfly, with repeats of 100 m, 200 m, or 300 m.

Butterfly Stroke Technique

Entry of the hands into the water is in line with the shoulders, and the legs are positioned ready to start the first downward kick as shown in figure 4.1a. The first downward kick of the legs occurs as the hands and arms are positioning for the catch.

As the hands and arms move into the high-elbow position, the legs have moved upward ready for the next downward propulsive kick, as shown in figure 4.1b.

As the hands and arms reach the position under the body, the hands are close together under the body ready to start the push-through of the stroke, shown in figure 4.1c. The legs are beginning their second downward kick. The face is leaving the water to take a breath. As the legs are moving downward the hands and arms can move through the push phase of the stroke and the face will have risen out of the water for the breath.

The hands and arms accelerate through the final extension of the push phase of the stroke. When the hands and arms leave the water for the recovery phase, the legs recover upward ready to start the downward kicking action. The face returns to the water slightly ahead of the entry of the hands to enable the smooth flow of the stroke as the hands go forward of the shoulders.

a   **b**   **c**

FIGURE 4.1   Underwater butterfly stroke technique.

Butterfly Drill Progressions

Drill progressions are crucial to the development of the stroke technique of the swimmer performing the progression. They are developed with the aim of improving specific areas of stroke technique. Before performing the drill progression the coach and swimmer should understand what the progressions are designed to do. Each progression should conclude with a full stroke so that the swimmer can transfer improvements from the drill back into full-stroke swimming.

PROGRESSION 1: BREATHING, TIMING, AND KICKING

1 Undulation action with the arms by the side, as shown in figures a and b.

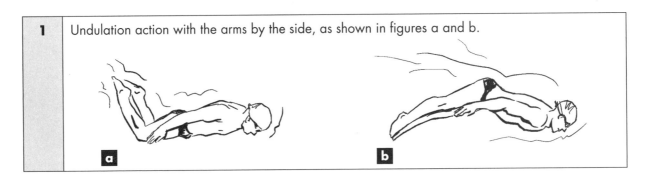

a   **b**

2	Butterfly Biondi drill. The swimmer starts this drill with a streamlined push off the wall underwater. As the swimmer begins to surface, he or she performs a pull underwater with the hands, then flicks back behind as if going into a recovery. The hands and lower arms of the junior swimmer leave the water, whereas the hands and arms of the older swimmers stop by the side of the thighs without leaving the water. The swimmer lifts the head to take a breath as the hands are pushing through. The swimmer has the head up taking a breath at the same time he or she is flicking back. After a powerful flick the swimmer does not recover the arms over the water but brings them back underneath the body. After completing the flick, the swimmer pushes the head back down into the water. At this point the hips should rise. The arms now recover underwater with the swimmer returning to a streamlined position. The swimmer undulates in the streamlined position (six downward beats of the legs). As the arms come up to the surface, the swimmer prepares to start the cycle again. Figures a through d below show this drill. 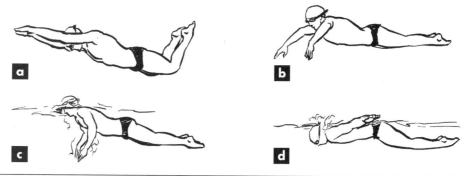
3	The swimmer this time performs the Biondi drill alternative with a full stroke; this is called Biondi drill plus one.
4	The swimmer now progresses to Biondi drill plus two.
5	The final progression is to full-stroke butterfly.

(Sweetenham 1998g)

The Biondi drill for juniors is sometimes referred to as half-stroke or push butterfly. When teaching the Biondi drill it is best to find a swimmer who can demonstrate the drill to the swimmers learning it. The following progression can then be used.

1. A swimmer who can perform the required action demonstrates the drill.
2. The group stands out of the water and does the push-through of the hands and arms without the recovery.
3. The group stands in the water and does the push-through (flick), and as they push through with the hands and arms they push their heads down.
4. Like step 3 except as they push through with hands and arms and push their heads forward, they jump forward off the bottom of the pool and perform the push-through with hands and arms.
5. Like step 4 except when they have done the jump off the bottom and the push-through, they complete the underwater recovery with the hands coming forward to the streamlined position in front (with six dolphin kicks).
6. Like step 5 except when the swimmers extend their arms forward, they perform a Biondi drill.
7. Swimmers start at the wall with a push-off and then perform a Biondi drill.

When learning this progression swimmers can wear fins from step 4 onward.

PROGRESSION 2: FISTS AND PADDLES

The aim of the progression is to improve the swimmer's feel for the water and stroke efficiency.	
1	50 m butterfly stroke count.
2	50 m butterfly with fists timed and stroke count. The swimmer performs this drill with the hands in a clenched fist.
3	50 m butterfly distance per stroke and stroke count.
4	50 m butterfly with hand paddles, distance per stroke, and stroke count.
5	50 m butterfly maximum effort with hand paddles, counting strokes, and trying to hold stroke count from step 4.
6	50 m butterfly maximum effort, counting strokes, and aiming to hold stroke count from step 3. No hand paddles.
7	50 m butterfly slow-motion minimum strokes.
8	50 m butterfly minimum-maximum drill. See chapter 3 for an explanation of minimum-maximum drill.

PROGRESSION 3: POWER KICK AND TIMING DRILL

1	Streamlined kick 15 m underwater to develop power for starting and turning. See figures a and b.
2	Right arm only, breathing to the side with the nonpulling arm extended, working on the timing of the kicks and a straight-arm recovery.
3	Left arm only, breathing to the side with the nonpulling arm extended, working the timing of the kicks and a straight-arm recovery. See the figure below.
4	Like step 2 except breathing to the front with the nonpulling arm by the side, working on the timing of the kicks and breathing.
5	Like step 3 except breathing to the front with the nonpulling arm by the side, working on the timing of the kicks and breathing.

6	Females: three right arm pulls, three left arm pulls, three full strokes through twice for 50 m. The aim is for the swimmer to do three-three-three through twice for 50 m, which is 18 strokes for the first 50 m of the 200 m butterfly. The nonpulling arm is by the side. Males: two right arm pulls, two left arm pulls, four full strokes through twice for 50 m. The aim is for the swimmer to do two-two-four through twice for 50 m, which is 16 strokes for the first 50 m of the 200 m butterfly. The nonpulling arm is by the side.
7	Full-stroke butterfly in slow motion.
8	Full-stroke butterfly.
	On steps 7 and 8 of progression 3 the swimmer emphasizes a strong two-beat kicking action.

(Sweetenham 1998g)

In butterfly, all successful swimmers at the international level have an extremely powerful butterfly kick. Swimmers can use the following practices to develop their kicking action.

Kick Development

1. 25 m maximum effort kick timed.
   25 m maximum effort swim timed.
   The two times are added together. The swimmer's target is to beat his or her long-course best time for 50 m if the swims are performed long course. If the swim is performed short course, the target is to beat the short-course time.

2. The swimmer should know his or her best 100 m time and how many strokes it took to do it. The swimmer then kicks the same number of kicks in the same time and measures how far he or she went. The target is 75 m or farther.

PROGRESSION 4: BREATHING AND TIMING (WITH OR WITHOUT FINS)

1	50 m kick. 25 m front underwater kick, 25 m choice position kick (side kicking, as shown in the figure below, or back kicking). Streamlined arms, torpedo position. 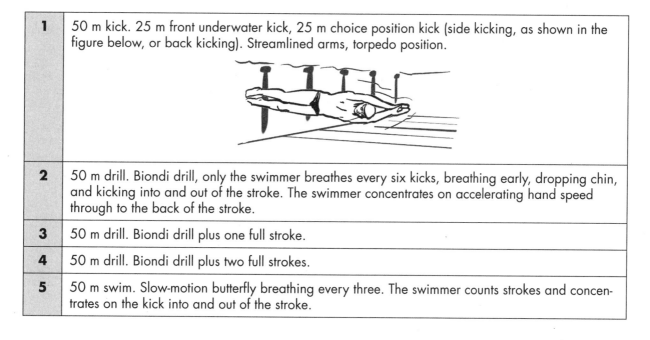
2	50 m drill. Biondi drill, only the swimmer breathes every six kicks, breathing early, dropping chin, and kicking into and out of the stroke. The swimmer concentrates on accelerating hand speed through to the back of the stroke.
3	50 m drill. Biondi drill plus one full stroke.
4	50 m drill. Biondi drill plus two full strokes.
5	50 m swim. Slow-motion butterfly breathing every three. The swimmer counts strokes and concentrates on the kick into and out of the stroke.

6	50 m drill. Males: two right arm pulls, two left arm pulls, four full strokes. Females: three right arm pulls, three left arm pulls, three full strokes. The swimmer should be breathing to the front every two strokes. The aim is to make the 50 m going through the cycles twice. Start alternate 50 m repeats with the right arm and then the left arm. This step of the progression can be done breathing every three.
7	50 m drill. Minimum-maximum. Males aim at 16 strokes, and females aim at 18. This drill is performed as outlined in chapter 3.
8	50 m kick. 25 m front underwater kick, 25 m kick. Streamlined arms, torpedo position.

Swimmers should do the first and last 50 m maximum effort. If the swimmer is using fins, the time should be faster than the swimmer's best swimming time for 50 m butterfly. The swimmer or coach can pick any other two 50 m repeats of the progression to swim at maximum effort. The set can also be done performing the kick with the arms folded.

With arms folded the swimmer must hold each elbow with the opposite hand. This encourages and supports a clean entry at shoulder-width and develops strong kicking patterns. The Biondi drill progression develops rhythm and timing of the stroke, breathing, and the kick.

This drill progression can be done in many different ways—short course, long course, with fins, or without fins.

(Sweetenham 1998g)

PROGRESSION 5: FEEL-THE-STROKE DRILL

This drill requires a pair of goggles that have been blacked out. The objective of the drill is to increase the sense of awareness that the swimmer has for the stroke. The swimmer is now unable to see the surrounding lane lines, the end of the pool, the pace clock, or anything else. The progression is conducted as follows.

1	The first step is for the swimmer to do 50 m in a certain but appropriate number of strokes.
2	The swimmer progresses to combine a number of strokes and a target time for 50 m.
3	The final step of the progression is to maintain either time or stroke count for 50 m and improve the other, or maintain a predetermined stroke rate while controlling the breathing pattern.

Care must be taken to protect the swimmer at the finish end of the 50 m repeat without compromising the drill.

Constant feedback must be sought from the swimmer to know exactly how he or she is feeling in timing, stroke, and technique. The coach and swimmer may decide to concentrate on a different aspect of the stroke in each 50 m of the drill. The swimmer should be encouraged to offer feedback to the coach after each 50 m repeat. This progression may be practiced on stroke drills as well as on full stroke.

(Sweetenham 1997a)

JUNIOR SQUAD BUTTERFLY DRILL PROGRESSION

This drill progression is designed to introduce the arms into the kicking action to develop the butterfly stroke.

1	25 m butterfly back torpedo dolphin kick. Hand-over-hand streamlining as shown in figures a and b. 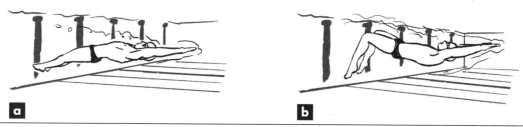
2	25 m butterfly front torpedo dolphin kick. Hand-over-hand streamlining.
3	25 m butterfly kick arms folded in front. In this drill the swimmer must kick much harder. The position is shown in the figure below. 
4	25 m butterfly torpedo dolphin kick. The swimmer starts the 25 m with two full strokes and then finishes the 25 m with two full strokes. After the first two strokes the swimmer performs dolphin torpedo kick until he or she needs to perform the two strokes to finish the 25 m.
5	25 m butterfly front torpedo dolphin kick with a sculling action at the front of the stroke. This brings the feel for the front of the stroke into the action. This drill is shown in figures a and b. 
6	25 m butterfly torpedo dolphin kick. The swimmer starts the 25 m with three full strokes and then finishes the 25 m with three full strokes. After the first three strokes the swimmer performs dolphin torpedo kick until he or she needs to perform the three strokes to finish the 25 m.
7	25 m butterfly front torpedo dolphin kick with a sculling action at the front of the stroke, as outlined in step 5.
8	25 m butterfly torpedo dolphin kick. The swimmer starts the 25 m with four full strokes and then finishes the 25 m with four full strokes. After the first four strokes the swimmer performs dolphin torpedo kick until he or she needs to perform the four strokes to finish the 25 m.

9	25 m butterfly kick on the back, arms folded, as shown in the figure below. In this drill the swimmer must kick much harder. 
10	25 m full-stroke butterfly stroke counting.

In this drill progression the swimmer aims to progress to swimming the 25 m butterfly in 8 to 12 strokes with perfect technique.

(Sweetenham 1998k)

Butterfly Technique Stroke Analysis

As a coach you must have the ability to analyze the technique of a swimmer. The stroke-analysis sheet will enable you to write comments for the technique of your swimmer on butterfly. The sheet can be very effective when viewing videotape of your swimmer. As you view the video you can write comments on the sheet and give a copy to the swimmer to refer to when viewing himself or herself swimming. See pages 69-70 for an example of a butterfly technique stroke analysis sheet that you can use with your swimmer.

Because the butterfly stroke is complex, swimmers need to work hard to avoid flaws in their technique. In addition, working on the kick helps increase speed, efficiency, and propulsive force.

BUTTERFLY TECHNIQUE STROKE ANALYSIS SHEET

Name _____

Date _____

Venue _____

Body position	Comments
Head position	
Shoulders	
Rotation	
Legs	
Amount of undulation	
General comments	

Legs	Comments
2-beat kick?	
1-beat kick?	
Amount of bend at the knees	
Ankles	
Butterfly kicks underwater on push-offs	
General comments	

(continued)

(continued)

Arms	Comments
Position of arms/hands on entry	
Position of arms/hands on catch	
Pull pattern	
Elbow position on pull	
Hand position on pull	
Push phase and acceleration	
Recovery, straight or bent arm	
General comments	

Timing and breathing	Comments
Timing of first kick	
Timing of second kick	
Timing of the lift of the face to breathe	
Timing of the head returning to the water after the breath	
General comments	

Butterfly Checklist

❑ The swimmer should work on controlled-frequency breathing patterns when asked, such as breathing every three, four, or five.

❑ Holding the stroke length is of vital importance in butterfly. The swimmer should try to hold stroke length at the end of sets in training, while aiming to maintain or even increase the stroke rate (distance per stroke).

❑ The coach should insist that the swimmer touch the wall with two hands in training on both turns and finishes.

❑ The swimmer should not grip the poolside guttering when turning. If possible arrange for the touch pads to be placed into the pool for training so that swimmers can practice flat wall turns as often as possible.

❑ The swimmer should have the ability to turn both ways (left and right).

❑ The butterfly swimmer should perform butterfly kick sets so that they are specific. Kick is important, and the butterfly swimmer must have good conditioning in the legs. The swimmer should be timed performing butterfly kick. For example, the coach should know that the swimmer covered 12 m in 12 kicks in a certain length of time.

❑ The coach should plan to include butterfly training on all types of sets, both sprint and endurance sets, so that swimmers use the specific muscle fibers required in butterfly. Freestyle is similar to butterfly, but not the same.

❑ Ankle flexibility and extension are important for the butterfly swimmer in performing effective kicks.

❑ Short rest sets can be used for endurance butterfly sessions.

❑ Some endurance butterfly sets can be done using a combination of full stroke with two, two, four or three, three, three butterfly drills being incorporated into the set.

❑ On all push-offs in training the swimmer should maximize streamlining, including push starts and turns. The swimmer should practice the number of butterfly kicks he or she wishes to use in a race. The swimmer should practice butterfly kicking on the front and on the side. Butterfly kicks should be practiced for speed in preference to distance. The differences in time should be compared between kicking on the front and on the side.

❑ Following all push-offs and turns with streamlined kick, the swimmer should do at least two strokes before taking the first breath. The swimmer should also note that the better the streamline off the turns and from the start, the less distance remains to swim.

❑ The swimmer should strive in training for a smooth flowing stroke, working on distance per stroke and minimizing resistance. The minimum-maximum drill, outlined in chapter 3, is great for developing this.

❑ A race model should be developed taking into consideration stroke counts, stroke rates, splits, starting times, turning times, and finishing times.

❑ The swimmer should know exactly the individual checking speed values at distances of 100 m, 200 m, 300 m, and 400 m.

(continued)

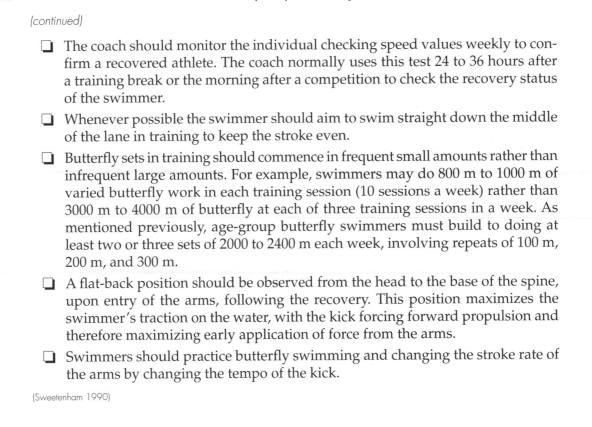

(continued)

❏ The coach should monitor the individual checking speed values weekly to confirm a recovered athlete. The coach normally uses this test 24 to 36 hours after a training break or the morning after a competition to check the recovery status of the swimmer.

❏ Whenever possible the swimmer should aim to swim straight down the middle of the lane in training to keep the stroke even.

❏ Butterfly sets in training should commence in frequent small amounts rather than infrequent large amounts. For example, swimmers may do 800 m to 1000 m of varied butterfly work in each training session (10 sessions a week) rather than 3000 m to 4000 m of butterfly at each of three training sessions in a week. As mentioned previously, age-group butterfly swimmers must build to doing at least two or three sets of 2000 to 2400 m each week, involving repeats of 100 m, 200 m, and 300 m.

❏ A flat-back position should be observed from the head to the base of the spine, upon entry of the arms, following the recovery. This position maximizes the swimmer's traction on the water, with the kick forcing forward propulsion and therefore maximizing early application of force from the arms.

❏ Swimmers should practice butterfly swimming and changing the stroke rate of the arms by changing the tempo of the kick.

(Sweetenham 1990)

This chapter provides valuable information for enhancing stroke technique on butterfly. Minimizing resistance is important for all events, particularly for butterfly. By using the drill progressions in this chapter, swimmers can improve their stroke technique. The butterflyer should swim the butterfly in all training zones, including training zone 1. This approach is important for building a training base from which to progress the butterfly training throughout the season. Both swimmer and coach should use the checklist regularly to remind them of things that the swimmer should be practicing for butterfly.

5

Backstroke

In backstroke, trunk rotation is crucial to allowing the swimmer to have a deep catch at the start of the pull, with the palm facing downward. The straight-arm recovery and early application of force in the deep catch makes backstroke a great stroke to teach to help with the development of the other strokes. Many swimmers started their swimming careers as backstroke swimmers before eventually specializing in other strokes. Another advantage with backstroke is that breathing on need can take place. This, along with no movement of the head, means that breathing has no effect on stroke mechanics. With no interruption to body position because head position does not vary, swimmers can attain early application of force in the catch. Swimmers can develop aerobically on backstroke, and it is a great stroke to offset all the work done on freestyle. The drill progressions shown in this chapter can enhance the principles outlined in this introduction.

Backstroke Stroke Technique

As the swimmer's hand enters the water, the opposite hip rotates upward, ready for the recovery of the arm on that side. The hand entry is shown in figure 5.1a.

Following the entry, the hand catches the water with the palm facing downward, keeping a firm fixed-elbow position. The sweeps of the arms should be minimized as recommended for freestyle. The catch should be deep enough to position the arm to set the elbow (lock) on the water. The line of pull is direct, with a minimum of sweeping. The rotations of the hips, trunk, and shoulders drive the body past the anchored arm.

After finishing the upward phase of the stroke, the hand and arm are ready for the push phase. The body is in a flatter position ready for the rotation through the hips to the opposite side, as shown in figure 5.1b.

As the swimmer completes the push phase, the hips rotate and the opposite hand enters the water. The right hand enters the water, and the palm then rotates downward to get the catch on the water, as shown in figure 5.1c. The same sequence is repeated on the other side of the body. During this full sequence the legs make six propulsive upward kicks. As the legs kick upward they will straighten. The hand exits the water with the thumb or forefinger knuckle first.

FIGURE 5.1   Underwater backstroke stroke technique.

Backstroke Drill Progressions

Drill progressions are crucial to the development of the stroke technique of the swimmer performing the progression. The progressions have the aim of improving specific areas of stroke technique. Before performing the drill progressions, the coach and swimmer should understand what the progressions are designed to do. Each progression should conclude with full stroke so that the swimmer can transfer improvements from the drill back into full-stroke swimming.

PROGRESSION 1: SCULL CATCH

1	Side lateral kick on the side. One arm is extended in the palm-down position. The opposite arm is by the side of the swimmer. Every 12 kicks the swimmer pulls with the extended arm and recovers with the arm from the side, assuming the side lateral kicking position. During this action the swimmer rotates to the opposite side. The scull catch position is shown in figures a and b. 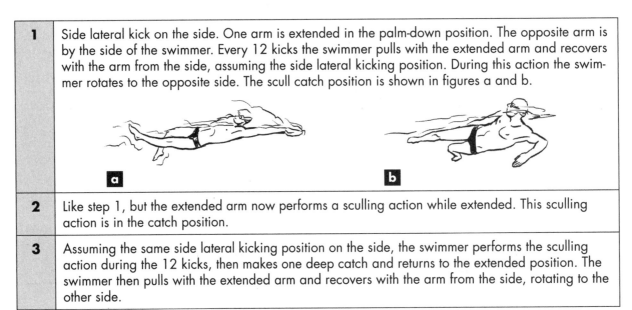
2	Like step 1, but the extended arm now performs a sculling action while extended. This sculling action is in the catch position.
3	Assuming the same side lateral kicking position on the side, the swimmer performs the sculling action during the 12 kicks, then makes one deep catch and returns to the extended position. The swimmer then pulls with the extended arm and recovers with the arm from the side, rotating to the other side.

4	Like step 3, but the swimmer performs two deep catches, then recovers and rotates. The deep catch position is shown in figures a and b. 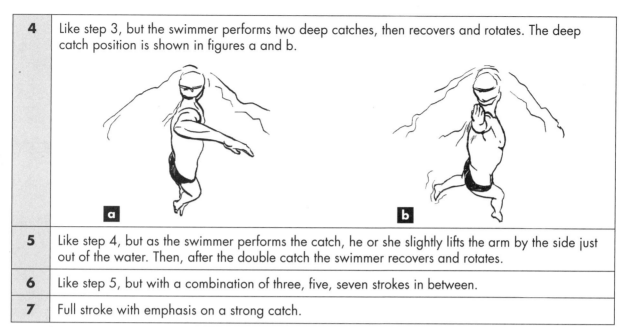
5	Like step 4, but as the swimmer performs the catch, he or she slightly lifts the arm by the side just out of the water. Then, after the double catch the swimmer recovers and rotates.
6	Like step 5, but with a combination of three, five, seven strokes in between.
7	Full stroke with emphasis on a strong catch.

(Sweetenham 1998e)

PROGRESSION 2: HIP, SHOULDER, AND TRUNK ROTATION

1	Kicking on the side position with the head still. After 12 kicks the swimmer rotates to the other side, keeping the head still and making sure that the rotation is fast and continuous. Both arms are by the side.
2	Kicking in the same position as in step 1. The swimmer recovers the arm on the side that is highest in the water for a half recovery and then lowers back into the water by the side of the body, maintaining the kicking position. When lowered, the swimmer rotates to the other side and the drill continues, as shown in figures a and b. 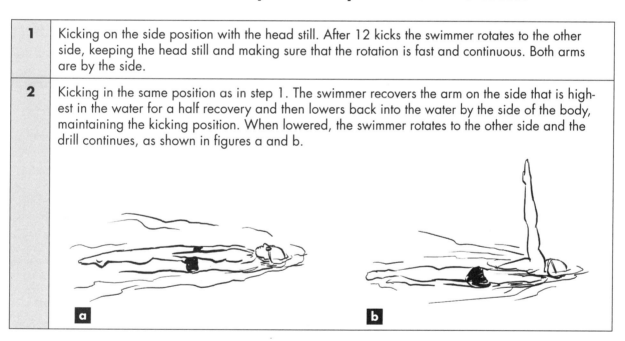

3	Kicking as in step 2, except this time the swimmer performs a full recovery and then a pull, with the other arm maintaining a position by the side. As the arm recovers, the other shoulder pops out of the water, ready for the other arm to recover once the pull has finished. (Catch up at the hips, as shown in figures a through c.)
	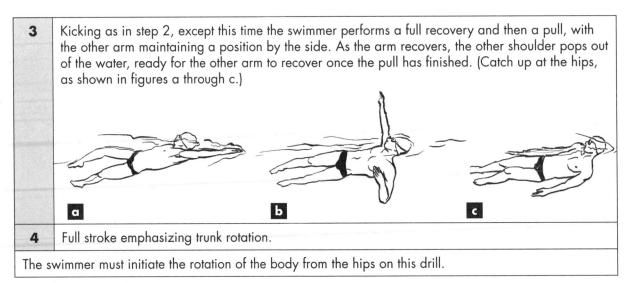
4	Full stroke emphasizing trunk rotation.

The swimmer must initiate the rotation of the body from the hips on this drill.

(Sweetenham 1998e, 1999c)

PROGRESSION 3: ROTATION SCULL FEEL

1	Side lateral kicking position with one arm extended and the other arm by the side. Rotation after 12 kicks.
2	Side lateral kicking position with extended arm sculling. Recovery and rotation after 12 kicks.
3	Like step 2 with three strokes between.
4	Like step 2 with five strokes between.
5	Like step 2 with seven strokes between.
6	Full stroke with emphasized catch and rotation.

As the number of arm strokes increases, the number of kicks between can decrease.

(Sweetenham 1998e)

PROGRESSION 4: FISTS AND PADDLES

The aim of this progression is to improve efficiency and feel for the water.	
1	50 m backstroke stroke counting.
2	50 m backstroke fists timed and stroke count. Perform this drill with the hands in a clenched fist.
3	50 m backstroke distance per stroke and stroke count.
4	50 m backstroke with hand paddles, distance per stroke, and stroke count.
5	50 m backstroke maximum effort with hand paddles, counting strokes, and trying to hold stroke count from step 4.
6	50 m backstroke maximum effort, counting strokes, and aiming to hold stroke count from step 3. No hand paddles.
7	50 m backstroke slow-motion minimum strokes.
8	50 m backstroke minimum-maximum drill. See chapter 3 for an explanation of this drill.

PROGRESSION 5: LATERAL SIDE KICK ROTATION

	The purpose of this drill progression is to increase the number of arm strokes, reduce the kick between, and increase rotation of the body from the hips.
1	Side lateral kicking position with one arm extended and the other arm by the side. Rotation after 12 kicks (12-1-12).
2	10 kicks, 5 pulls, and 10 kicks (10-5-10).
3	8 kicks, 7 pulls, and 8 kicks (8-7-8).
4	6 kicks, 9 pulls, and 6 kicks (6-9-6).
5	4 kicks, 11 pulls, and 4 kicks (4-11-4).
6	Full-stroke backstroke.

(Sweetenham 1998e)

PROGRESSION 6: ARM SCULL DRILL

1	Side lateral kicking position with one arm extended and the other arm by the side. Both the extended arm and the arm at the side are sculling.
2	Extended arm has pressed down to the catch position and continues to scull. The opposite arm has recovered to a third of the way on the recovery.
3	The hand progresses from the catch position to the midway point and sculls in that position. The opposite arm has now completed at least half of the recovery.
4	Full stroke to finish the progression.
	The swimmer repeats the progression on the opposite arm.

(Sweetenham 1998e)

PROGRESSION 7: BENT-ARM SCULLING DRILLS

	The sculling drills and recovery take place underwater.
1	Double bent-arm sculling as shown in figures a and b. 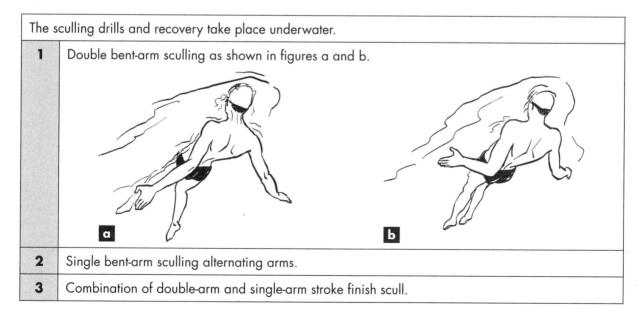
2	Single bent-arm sculling alternating arms.
3	Combination of double-arm and single-arm stroke finish scull.

4	Double-arm (bent-arm) midstroke push.
5	Single-arm alternate midstroke push.
6	Combination of double-arm and single-arm midstroke push.
7	Alternate single-arm midstroke push. The swimmer starts with a push through to the finish of the stroke aiming at maximum trunk rotation.
8	Full-stroke backstroke.
	After the hand or hands have pushed through to the end of the stroke, the recovery takes place underwater with the thumb leading back.

(Sweetenham 1998e)

PROGRESSION 8: CROSSOVER KICK WITH ROTATION

1	The swimmer performs the kick with the arms bent and the hands behind the head as shown in the figure. The hands are in the hand-on-hand position, with the palms pressing onto the back of the swimmer. 50 m kick on the left side (right arm up and left arm down).
2	Like step 1 with the swimmer on his or her right.
3	The swimmer performs six to eight kicks on one side and then rotates through the hips to the opposite side, maintaining the correct head position during the rotation.
4	Like step 3 with the swimmer releasing into a deep catch with the lower arm and extending upward with the upper arm, every six to eight kicks. This is shown in the figure below. At the catch position the swimmer performs three to five sculling presses on the water before doing three arm strokes and then resuming the crossover kick position on the opposite side.

| 5 | Like step 3 with five strokes in between. |
| 6 | Full-stroke backstroke. |

Steps 4 and 5 can be performed without the sculling action after the release into the deep catch position.

(Sweetenham 1998e)

PROGRESSION 9: OVERREACHING CORRECTION

1	Double-arm backstroke pull with a pull buoy (no kick).
2	Double-arm backstroke with backstroke kick.
3	Right arm only with the nonpulling arm by the side. Concentration on correct entry position is important.
4	Like step 3 but with the left arm.
5	Full-stroke backstroke.

PROGRESSION 10: END-OF-STROKE DRILL

1	The swimmer performs the kick in the flat body position, rotating from the hip and in doing so pushing through with the hand and driving the hip around. Following this, the swimmer returns to the flat-body kicking position, using the right arm only for an end-of-stroke push. The swimmer starts each push action at midbody position on this drill.
2	Like step 1 but with the left arm.
3	Left arm and right arm alternate sides for the end-of-stroke push.

(Sweetenham 1998e)

PROGRESSION 11: FEEL-THE-STROKE DRILL

This drill requires a pair of goggles that have been blacked out. The objective of the drill is to increase the sense of awareness that the swimmer has for the stroke. The swimmer is now unable to see the surrounding lane lines, the end of the pool, the pace clock, or anything else. The progression is conducted as follows.

1	The first step is for the swimmer to do 50 m in a certain but appropriate number of strokes.
2	The swimmer progresses to combine a number of strokes and a target time for 50 m.
3	The final step of the progression is to maintain either time or stroke count for 50 m and improve the other, or maintain a predetermined stroke rate while controlling the breathing pattern.

Care must be taken to protect the swimmer at the finish end of the 50 m repeat without compromising the drill.

Constant feedback must be sought from the swimmer to know exactly how he or she is feeling in timing, stroke, and technique. The coach and swimmer may decide to concentrate on a different aspect of the stroke in each 50 m of the drill. The swimmer should be encouraged to offer feedback to the coach after each 50 m. This progression may be practiced on stroke drills as well as on full stroke.

(Sweetenham 1997a)

JUNIOR SQUAD BACKSTROKE DRILL PROGRESSION

	For backstroke, the following drill progression can be used with junior squads.
1	25 m backstroke crossover kick position, holding the body in a side lateral kicking position. The swimmer should work to maintain body position with the hips high and head still. One elbow is high, and one elbow is lower and in the water. This drill is explained at step 1 of progression 8.
2	25 m backstroke crossover kick position with rotation from one side to the other. The coach specifies the number of kicks before each rotation.
3	25 m backstroke pressure-point scull. The swimmer is in a side lateral kicking position. The arm that is extended is in the water in the catch position, and the other arm is by the side. The swimmer is working for a deep catch position and a high elbow on the extended arm while performing this sculling action.
4	25 m backstroke double-arm end-of-stroke drill with a deep push at the end of the scull.
5	25 m backstroke right arm and left arm end-of-stroke scull and rotation. The swimmer assumes a side lateral kicking position on the side, with both arms by the side. The lower arm in the water performs an end-of-stroke push and scull. While pushing through, the swimmer rotates to the other side. The swimmer then performs the same action on the other side.
6	25 m backstroke exchange recovery arm drill. The swimmer is in a side lateral kicking position with one arm extended in the entry position and the other arm by the side. As the drill name suggests, the swimmer then exchanges the arms without performing a propulsive pulling action. The swimmer lifts both arms out of the water, the arm by the side in a normal recovery action and the arm that is extended in a backward action. The arms cross and assume their exchange positions. The swimmer has now rotated onto the opposite side. This drill promotes a high recovery lead by the hips. The drill is shown in figures a through c.
7	25 m full-stroke backstroke aiming to swim with perfect technique and aiming at 12 to 18 strokes.
8	25 m choice of steps 1 to 7. This step will require the most attention by the swimmer.

(Sweetenham 1998k)

Backstroke Technique Stroke Analysis

As a coach you must have the ability to analyze the technique of a swimmer. The stroke-analysis sheet will enable you to write comments for the technique of your swimmer on backstroke. The sheet can be very effective when viewing videotape of your swimmer. As you view the video you can write comments on the sheet and give a copy to the swimmer to refer to when viewing himself or herself swimming. See pages 83-84 for an example of a backstroke technique stroke analysis sheet that you can use with your swimmer.

Backstroke Checklist

❏ The swimmer should start the first stroke on alternate arms in backstroke sets to develop turning skills on both arms.

❏ Swimmers should know how many butterfly kicks to do off the start and turns. They should have kicks from the start and the turns timed frequently at workouts in warm-ups, main sets, and swim-downs.

❏ Backstrokers should swim up to one-half of weekly volume on backstroke. This can include swim, drill, kick, and pull.

❏ Ensure that the backstroke flags are up for every session and are the correct distance from the wall (5 m).

❏ The backstroke swimmer needs to do more backstroke kick and kicking drills than the freestyle swimmer does. The backstroke swimmer should use a continuous six-beat kick, being sure that the knees stay underwater. A common fault is a pedaling action in the knees; this can be corrected by kicking with short fins or sneakers (when kicking in sneakers the toes should be cut out of the shoe).

❏ The coach should plan to use kick sets to improve aerobic endurance.

❏ The swimmer should kick some sprint sets.

❏ Correct kicking mechanics are important; the swimmer should perform some kick sets on the back and some on each side.

❏ In a short-course race a backstroker could do 60 percent of the race underwater using dolphin kicks. The backstroker should use butterfly kicks in all types of backstroke training. The underwater butterfly kick should be a shorter, faster kick at double the normal rating. The purpose of the butterfly kicks is speed, not distance. The swimmer starts with slower, deeper kicks, which transfer to shallower, faster kicks as the streamlined position is held through the underwater phase. Each swimmer should experiment with different plans and have them timed. Butterfly kicks are practiced for speed in preference to distance.

❏ Backstrokers must have the ability to maintain their stroke rate throughout the race. Higher stroke rates are desirable for the 50 m and 100 m events.

❏ Backstrokers commence the turn as a continuation of the rolling movement from back to front.

(continued)

(continued)

❏ The coach should insist on a six-beat continuous kicking action in training on all sprint sets.

❏ The swimmer should strive for a smooth flowing stroke, maximum distance per stroke, and minimum resistance during training. Minimum-maximum drills should be used for this purpose as outlined in backstroke drill progression 4.

❏ A specific race model (race profiling) should be developed, taking into consideration stroke count, stroke rate, splits, starting time, turning time, and finishing time.

❏ The swimmer should know precise individual checking speed values at distances of 100 m, 200 m, 300 m, and 400 m.

❏ The coach should monitor individual checking speed values weekly to confirm a recovered athlete. The coach normally uses this test 24 to 36 hours after a training break or the morning after a competition to check the recovery status of the athlete.

❏ The better the swimmer streamlines, the less distance he or she must swim.

❏ Whenever possible the swimmer should swim straight down the middle of the lane in training (Sweetenham 1990).

© Michael Zito/SportsChrome

This chapter provides valuable information for enhancing backstroke technique. Minimizing resistance is important for all events. By using the drill progressions in this chapter swimmers can improve their stroke technique. Backstroke is an important stroke for all swimmers, and they can use it to enhance recovery during training sessions. Both the swimmer and the coach should use the checklist regularly to remind them of things that the swimmer should be practicing for backstroke.

The ease of breathing during the backstroke (as compared to other strokes) enables the young swimmer to focus on developing the stroke technique itself.

BACKSTROKE TECHNIQUE STROKE ANALYSIS SHEET

Name _____

Date _____

Venue _____

Body position	Comments
Head position	
Shoulder rotation	
Hip rotation	
Legs	
Lateral movement of the body	
General comments	

Legs	Comments
6-beat kick?	
4-beat kick?	
2-beat kick?	
Amount of bend at the knees—do they break the surface?	
Ankles/toes	
Butterfly kicks underwater on push-offs	
General comments	

(continued)

(continued)

Arms	Comments
Position of arms/hands on entry, left	
Position of arms/hands on entry, right	
Position of arms/hands on catch, left	
Position of arms/hands on catch, right	
Pull pattern, left	
Pull pattern, right	
Elbow position on pull, left	
Elbow position on pull, right	
Hand position on pull, left	
Hand position on pull, right	
Push phase and acceleration of hand, left and right	
Recovery, straight or bent arm, left	
Recovery, straight or bent arm, right	
General comments	

Timing and breathing	Comments
Breathing pattern	
Any catch up in the stroke	
General comments	

6

Breaststroke

Breaststroke is the least efficient of all the competitive swimming strokes, and it requires excellent ankle and lower-leg rotation. The stroke requires a great amount of skill training and coaching supervision during workouts. The kick is essential to the efficiency of the stroke. The swimmer's flexibility, core strength, and individual size play a part in determining his or her stroke technique. The swimmer will probably perform this stroke less on full stroke than he or she will the other strokes and do more work on drills, kick, and pull in training. The breaststroke drill progressions outlined in this chapter can develop the technique of the swimmer.

Breaststroke Stroke Technique

As the arms are extending, the legs are in a position ready to start their propulsive phase. The face enters between the arms to achieve a streamlined position and get maximum propulsion from the legs.

Following this streamlined extension and propulsion from the leg kick, the hands and arms start their outsweep (see figure 6.1a). During this outsweep the legs stay in a streamlined position to maximize propulsion from the arms.

As the arms and hands reach the widest point, the elbows remain fixed while the hands and forearms commence the insweep. The head is now moving upward to fit the breathing into the stroke cycle. The legs have not yet broken their streamlined position.

The hands are now halfway through their insweep, and the face is clear of the water to take a breath, as shown in figure 6.1b. The thumbs are upward during this insweep.

As the insweep takes place the legs begin to bend, as shown in figure 6.1c, in order to kick backward as the hands and arms recover forward into the streamlined position. During this kick and streamlined extension, the face goes back into the water.

FIGURE 6.1 *Underwater breaststroke stroke technique.*

Breaststroke Drill Progressions

Quality of execution is important when completing drills, but it is essential when practicing breaststroke. As with the other strokes, drill progressions are crucial to the development of stroke technique. The progressions have the aim of improving specific areas of stroke technique. Before performing the drill progression the coach and swimmer should understand what the progressions are designed to do. Each progression should conclude with full stroke so that the swimmer can transfer improvements from the drill back into full-stroke swimming.

PROGRESSION 1: FISTS AND PADDLES

	The aim of the progression is to improve efficiency and feel for the water.
1	50 m breaststroke stroke counting.
2	50 m breaststroke with fists timed and stroke count. The swimmer performs this drill with the hands in a clenched fist.
3	50 m breaststroke distance per stroke and stroke count.
4	50 m breaststroke with hand paddles, distance per stroke, and stroke count.
5	50 m breaststroke maximum effort with hand paddles, counting strokes, and trying to hold stroke count from step 4.
6	50 m breaststroke maximum effort, counting strokes, and aiming to hold stroke count from step 3. No hand paddles.
7	50 m breaststroke slow-motion minimum strokes.
8	50 m breaststroke minimum-maximum drill. See chapter 3 for an explanation of minimum-maximum drill.

PROGRESSION 2: KICK DRILL AND TIMING DEVELOPMENT

1	The swimmer kicks with the arms back, drawing the heels to the fingertips as shown figures a and b.
2	The swimmer kicks with the arms extended in the streamlining position, as shown in the figure below, concentrating on the timing of the kick and the breathing. The swimmer should be sure not to push down with the extended arms while taking a breath.
3	Three kicks and one pull, streamlined during the powerful kicks. The swimmer performs three breaststroke kicks while maintaining a streamlined position with the arms. Following the third kick the swimmer performs one pull.
4	Two kicks and one pull, streamlined during the powerful kicks. This is performed as step 3 but with two kicks.
5	Lay-out drill concentrating on timing of the kick. After completing the kick the swimmer lies out in the streamlined position before starting the next powerful arm stroke.
6	Minimum-maximum drill. See chapter 3 for an explanation of minimum-maximum drill.

(Sweetenham 1998f)

PROGRESSION 3: PULL AND TIMING DRILL

1	Pull with fins (no kicking action) distance per stroke.
2	Pull with fins and a slight flowing undulating kick from the legs to each arm stroke.
3	Three pulls, with two butterfly kicks and one breaststroke kick.
4	Two pulls, with one butterfly kick and one breaststroke kick.

5	Lay-out drill concentrating on timing of the kick. After completing the kick the swimmer lies out in the streamlined position before starting the next powerful arm stroke.
6	Minimum-maximum drill (see chapter 3).

PROGRESSION 4: BREASTSTROKE SPEED DRILL

1	25 m kick with hand-on-hand streamlined torpedo position (see figure in step 2 of progression 2).
2	25 m pull, arms only, legs still not using a pull buoy.
3	25 m speed drill with head up, smaller pull than normal breaststroke, with butterfly kicks. This is shown in figures a and b.
4	25 m fast breaststroke full stroke.
5	25 m as follows: push off the wall, three streamlined kicks, three pulls, three speed drills, and three full strokes at maximum effort (3-3-3-3).
6	Like step 5 with two on each section, then full-stroke swim for the rest of the 25 m repeat (2-2-2 then as many full strokes as required to reach the end of the 25 m repeat).
7	Minimum-maximum drill (see chapter 3).

PROGRESSION 5: BREASTSTROKE KICK AND PULL

1	Kick hand-on-hand streamlined torpedo position.
2	Four kicks with the arms in a folded position underwater, then one pull and breathe. The swimmer repeats this for the duration of the repeat distance. The arms-folded position is shown in the figure below.
3	Three kicks with arms folded underwater, then one pull and breathe and so on for the remainder of the repeat distance.
4	Two kicks with arms folded underwater, then two pulls and so on for the remainder of the repeat distance.

5	One kick with arms folded underwater, then three pulls and so on for the remainder of the repeat distance.
6	Minimum-maximum drill (see chapter 3).

(Sweetenham 1998f)

PROGRESSION 6: BREASTSTROKE

1	Kick with a kickboard. The kickboard should be extended in front with the timing of the breathing in the correct position to simulate the full-stroke breathing pattern.
2	Kick without the kickboard, arms extended in the streamlined position, with the breathing conducted as in step 1.
3	Pull with hand paddles, pull buoy, and fins.
4	Pull with hand paddles and band only.
5	Minimum-maximum drill (see chapter 3).

PROGRESSION 7: DISTANCE PER STROKE BREASTSTROKE (LANE ROPES)

1	The swimmer swims across the pool, undulating under each lane rope across the pool width as shown in figures a through c. 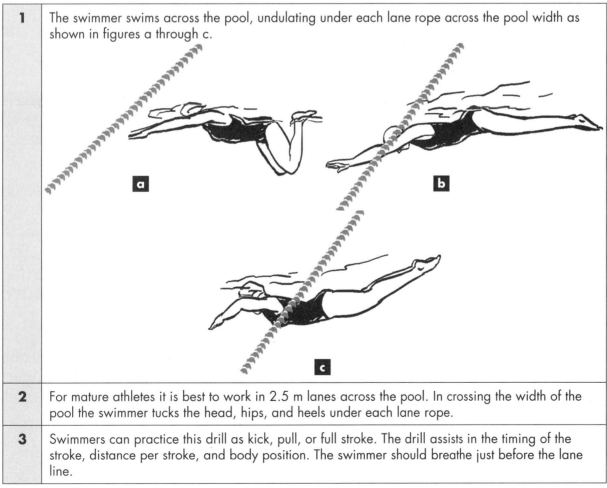
2	For mature athletes it is best to work in 2.5 m lanes across the pool. In crossing the width of the pool the swimmer tucks the head, hips, and heels under each lane rope.
3	Swimmers can practice this drill as kick, pull, or full stroke. The drill assists in the timing of the stroke, distance per stroke, and body position. The swimmer should breathe just before the lane line.

(Sweetenham 1998f)

PROGRESSION 8: KICK AND SCULL-PULL

1	50 m as 25 m streamlined torpedo kick, 25 m kick with 25 percent arm pull or front scull (as described in chapter 9).
2	50 m as 25 m streamlined torpedo kick, 25 m kick with 50 percent arm pull or wide midpoint breaststroke scull (as described in chapter 9).
3	50 m as 25 m streamlined torpedo kick, 25 m kick with 75 percent arm pull.
4	50 m as 25 m streamlined torpedo kick, 25 m swim concentrating on reducing resistance and timing, that is, maximizing distance from the kicks while maintaining a streamlined position.
5	50 m as breaststroke pull minimum-maximum as outlined in chapter 3.
6	50 m as breaststroke swim minimum-maximum. Compare efficiency ratings of the pull with the swim minimum-maximum drill.
7	50 m as 25 m breaststroke with dolphin kick, 25 m four underwater kicks, then one pull.
8	50 m as 25 m breaststroke with dolphin kick, 25 m three underwater kicks, then one pull.
9	50 m as 25 m breaststroke with dolphin kick, 25 m two underwater kicks, then one pull.
10	50 m as 25 m breaststroke with dolphin kick, 25 m normal stroke working timing.
11	50 m as breaststroke kick minimum-maximum.
12	50 m as breaststroke swim minimum-maximum. Compare efficiency ratings of the pull with the swim minimum-maximum drill.
13	50 m as breaststroke minimum-maximum drill as 25 m torpedo kick and 25 m pull. Compare efficiency ratings.
14	50 m as breaststroke swim minimum-maximum aiming to beat efficiency rating from step 6.
	Practice this progression only after the swimmer can perform flat wrist, wrist up, wrist down, front horizontal, and vertical sculling, as shown in chapter 9.

(Sweetenham 1998c, 1998f)

SAMPLE BREASTSTROKE PROGRESSION 8

50 m breaststroke pull minimum-maximum. Time recorded 43 seconds in 32 arm pulls equals an efficiency rating of 75.
50 m breaststroke swim minimum-maximum. Time recorded 35 seconds in 25 strokes equals an efficiency rating of 60.
50 m breaststroke kick minimum-maximum. Time recorded 49 seconds in 26 leg kicks equals an efficiency rating of 75.
50 m breaststroke swim minimum-maximum. Time recorded 35 seconds in 25 strokes equals an efficiency rating of 60.

50 m breaststroke pull-kick minimum-maximum combination.
- 25 m breaststroke pull in 16 arm strokes and 21.5 seconds, total equals 37.5.
- 25 m breaststroke kick in 13 leg kicks and 24.5 seconds, total equals 37.5.
- Overall efficiency rating equals 75.

50 m breaststroke swim minimum-maximum. Time recorded 35 seconds in 25 strokes equals an efficiency rating of 60.

Following this progression and using the example, the efficiency rating of the pull and kick are the same.

PROGRESSION 9: STRONG KICK DEVELOPMENT

This drill can be used to correct the fault of bringing the knees too far underneath the body.

| 1 | Vertical kicking facing the wall. The arms are held in a streamlined position out of the water. This drill is shown in figures a and b. |

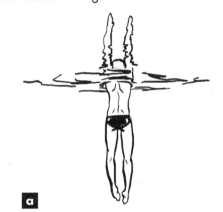 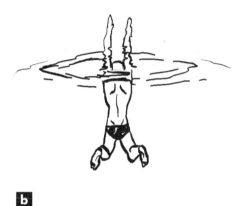

2	Legs only on the front, arms trailing behind, bringing the heels up to the fingers and hands. The head is out of the water, as shown in the figure in step 1 of progression 2 (page 87).
3	Like step 2, allowing breathing every two kicks.
4	Legs only on the back, concentrating on dropping the heels and not lifting the knees out of the water, as shown in figures a and b. The swimmer can use a kickboard over the thighs to ensure that they do not move. If not using a kickboard, the swimmer performs the drill with the hands in a streamlined position.

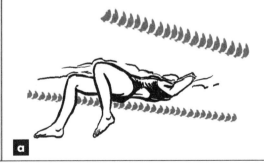 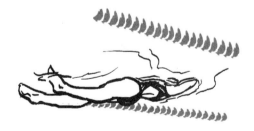

PROGRESSION 10: TENNIS BALLS AND SINKERS FOR PULL DEVELOPMENT

1	The swimmer swims breaststroke holding a tennis ball between the thumb and forefinger (junior swimmers can use squash balls).
2	A sinker is attached to a rubber band. The swimmer puts a hand through the rubber band and swims with the sinker on the palm side of the hand. If the sinker stays midpalm as the athlete swims, the pressure on the water has been maintained in the correct position.
3	Holding a tennis ball between the chin and chest ensures that the swimmer maintains good head position and does not drop the chin as the face goes into the water.

(Sweetenham 1998j)

PROGRESSION 11: FEEL-THE-STROKE DRILL

	This drill requires a pair of goggles that have been blacked out. The objective of the drill is to increase the sense of awareness that the swimmer has for the stroke. The swimmer is now unable to see the surrounding lane lines, the end of the pool, the pace clock, or anything else. The progression is conducted as follows.
1	The first step is to have the swimmer do 50 m in a certain but appropriate number of strokes.
2	The swimmer progresses to combine a number of strokes and a target time for 50 m.
3	The final step of the progression is to maintain either time or stroke count for 50 m and improve the other, or maintain a predetermined stroke rate while controlling the breathing pattern.
	Care must be taken to protect the swimmer at the finish end of the 50 m repeat without compromising the drill.
	Constant feedback must be sought from the swimmer to know exactly how he or she is feeling in timing, stroke, and technique. The coach and swimmer may decide to concentrate on a different aspect of the stroke in each 50 m of the drill. The swimmer should be encouraged to offer feedback to the coach after each 50 m. This progression may be practiced on stroke drills as well as on full stroke.

(Sweetenham 1997a)

JUNIOR SQUAD BREASTSTROKE DRILL PROGRESSION

	The following breaststroke drill progression is appropriate for the junior squad swimmer.
1	25 m breaststroke kick with a kickboard, breathing every two kicks. The swimmer fits breathing into the kicking action so that when kicking back, the face is returning into the water.
2	25 m breaststroke kick torpedo position. The swimmer must be sure not to push down with the arms when in this position.
3	25 m breaststroke with hand paddles, fins, and pull buoy. The swimmer should use a continuous arm action with the little finger up in the outsweep and the thumb leading the insweep.
4	25 m breaststroke with hand paddles, band, and pull buoy. The swimmer should use a continuous arm action with the little finger up in the outsweep and the thumb leading the insweep. On this step the swimmer must work harder than he or she did on step 3.

5	25 m breaststroke four kicks to one pull, using a streamlined position following the forward extension of the arms and during the four kicks.
6	25 m breaststroke three kicks to one pull, using a streamlined position following the forward extension of the arms and during the three kicks.
7	25 m breaststroke two kicks to one pull, using a streamlined position following the forward extension of the arms and during the two kicks.
8	25 m breaststroke lay-out drill concentrating on the timing of the kick. After completing the kick the swimmer lies out in the streamlined position before starting the next powerful arm stroke.
9	25 m breaststroke full stroke concentrating on distance per stroke.
10	25 m choice of steps 1 to 9. This step will require the most attention by the swimmer.
	In this drill progression the swimmer aims to progress to swimming the 25 m breaststroke in 8 to 12 strokes with perfect technique.

(Sweetenham 1998k)

Breaststroke Technique Stroke Analysis

As a coach you must have the ability to analyze the technique of a swimmer. The stroke-analysis sheet will enable you to write comments for the technique of your swimmer on breaststroke. The sheet can be very effective when viewing videotape of your swimmer. As you view the video you can write comments on the sheet and give a copy to the swimmer to refer to when viewing himself or herself swimming. See pages 94-96 for an example of a breaststroke technique stroke analysis sheet that you can use with your swimmer.

BREASTSTROKE TECHNIQUE STROKE ANALYSIS SHEET

Name_____

Date _____

Venue_____

Body position	Comments
Head position when in the water	
Shoulders level or not?	
Hip position on extension	
Hip position at highest point out of the water	
Hips undulate too much?	
Hips too high?	
Streamlining at the end of the propulsive kick phase	
General comments	

Legs	Comments
Knees come too far under the body on the recovery	
Prior to being fully recovered the ankles turn out	
Acceleration during the propulsive kick phase?	
Position of ankles on recovery	
Position of knees on recovery	

Legs	Comments
Whip kicking action or not?	
Knees too wide on the propulsive kick phase?	
General comments	

Arms	Comments
Thumbs down and little fingers up for commencement of the outsweep of the pull?	
Too much elbow movement at the start of the outsweep?	
Firm or loose wrists?	
Elbows deep or high at the end of the outsweep?	
No wrist rotation?	
Uneven pull, one hand moving through the pull faster than the other?	
Not a streamlined recovery?	
General comments	

Timing and breathing	Comments
The pull commences before the leg kick finishes or not?	
Breathing is late or early?	

(continued)

(continued)

Timing and breathing	Comments
Head movements during breathing	
Recovery of feet is too slow	
Even stroke or not?	
General comments	

A swimmer's flexibility, core strength, and individual size determine the stroke technique for the breaststroke, the least efficient of the competitive strokes.

© Sport the Library

Breaststroke Checklist

❏ Breaststrokers require great flexibility of the hips, knees, and ankles. Swimmers can improve flexibility by doing regular stretching exercises, as shown in chapter 15. This practice will prevent injuries.

❏ The swimmer should practice flat-wall two-handed turns as often as possible (the swimmer does not curl the hands around the lip of the pool). The swimmer should practice turning to the left and right.

❏ Breaststrokers should warm up the legs by swimming and kicking slowly at first, then building into a normal pace on training sets.

❏ The amount of breaststroke swum in each session should increase throughout the season. If the swimmer experiences knee pain, he or she should switch strokes, change to a breaststroke pull set, or perform breaststroke with a butterfly kick.

❏ Pulling drills are important for the breaststroke swimmer. The palms must be pitched at the correct angle, that is, with thumbs down with the little fingers up on the outsweep.

❏ The breaststroke swimmer should aim at a starting time of four to four and a half seconds underwater from the racing start until the head breaks the surface. Maintaining speed on the start is the crucial factor that both the swimmer and the coach should consider.

❏ Pace work should be done with the required stroke rate and stroke count. Combination of time, stroke rate, and stroke count should be used on breaststroke training sets.

❏ Stroke drills for are essential for correct timing in breaststroke.

❏ The swimmer should finish every kick with accelerating foot speed and be sure that the legs finish straight with the toes pointed to maximize streamlining. The swimmer should not turn the feet out for the propulsive effect until the legs and feet are recovered fully.

❏ During breaststroke endurance sets the swimmer tends to relax the arms; in other strokes the legs relax. Therefore, upper-body stress may be slightly less in some swim sets, so training sessions should include pulling sets.

❏ Breaststroke pull with a dolphin kick is a drill. A breaststroker having a weak pull will compensate by letting the kick do most of the work. This is another reason to build breaststroke pull sets into training sessions. This pull should be done with a pull buoy, band, and paddles.

❏ Swimmers at training should strive for a smooth flowing stroke, maximum distance per stroke, and minimum resistance. Minimum-maximum drills are helpful in achieving this, as shown in breaststroke drill progression 1.

❏ A race model (race profiling) should be developed using stroke count, stroke rate, splits, starting time, turning time, and finishing time.

❏ The arm-stroke insweep should move the body upward and forward, not upward and backward.

❏ To accommodate the underwater pull and kick phase, the angle of the body during the entry into the water following a dive start is usually steeper and deeper than it is in the other strokes.

(continued)

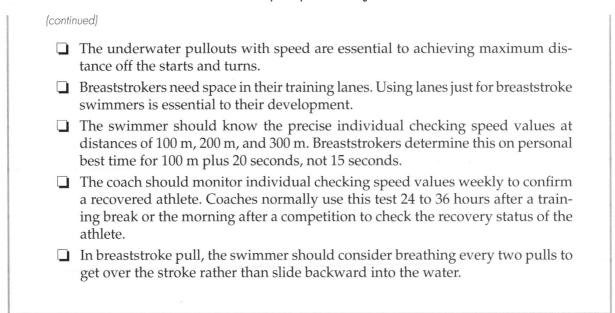

(continued)

❏ The underwater pullouts with speed are essential to achieving maximum distance off the starts and turns.

❏ Breaststrokers need space in their training lanes. Using lanes just for breaststroke swimmers is essential to their development.

❏ The swimmer should know the precise individual checking speed values at distances of 100 m, 200 m, and 300 m. Breaststrokers determine this on personal best time for 100 m plus 20 seconds, not 15 seconds.

❏ The coach should monitor individual checking speed values weekly to confirm a recovered athlete. Coaches normally use this test 24 to 36 hours after a training break or the morning after a competition to check the recovery status of the athlete.

❏ In breaststroke pull, the swimmer should consider breathing every two pulls to get over the stroke rather than slide backward into the water.

This chapter provides valuable information for enhancing stroke technique on breaststroke. As with butterfly, minimizing resistance is important for breaststroke. By using the drill progressions in this chapter the swimmer can improve stroke technique. Both the swimmer and the coach should use the checklist regularly to remind them of things that the swimmer should be practicing for breaststroke.

Freestyle

When swimmers begin squad training they should have the basics well in place. Because freestyle is traditionally the stroke most used for aerobic development, swimmers develop the greatest number of faults in that stroke. As a rule, swimmers should have a balanced stroke that has sufficient trunk rotation to allow them to attain maximum distance per stroke and an early catch leading into a high stable elbow position underwater. This action will result in maximum application of force when the stroke is fully rotated, with minimum resistance. All swimmers will benefit from using the drill progressions outlined in this chapter.

Freestyle Stroke Technique

The entry by the hand is made in line with the shoulders and with the palm pitched at approximately 45 degrees. As the hand enters, it extends forward as the other arm pushes through to the back of the stroke, as shown in figure 7.1a.

The swimmer then applies pressure to the water while making the catch. After the catch is made, the hand travels in an outward and downward direction while the elbow remains firm and assumes a high elbow position, as shown in figure 7.1b.

Following this initial pull phase in the outward and downward direction, the angle at the elbow is about 45 to 65 degrees. Inward and upward movement occurs before the push through to the back of the stroke.

Figure 7.1c shows the hand pushing through to the back of the stroke. The hand accelerates though this phase of the underwater stroke. The arm leaves the water with the elbow leading in a traditional high elbow recovery stroke. If the swimmer swims with a straight arm, the arm will be straight at the start of the recovery.

Following the recovery the hand enters the water and the sequence starts again. During this full stroke cycle, the legs will have made six downward kicks. Variations are a two-beat or four-beat kick.

FIGURE 7.1   *Underwater freestyle stroke technique.*

Freestyle Drill Progressions

Drill progressions are crucial to the development of stroke technique. The progressions have the aim of improving specific areas of stroke technique. Before performing the drill progression the coach and swimmer should understand what the progressions are designed to do. Each progression should conclude with full stroke so that the swimmer can transfer improvements from the drill back into full-stroke swimming.

PROGRESSION 1: SCULL CATCH

1	Side lateral kick on the side, breathing every 12 kicks. One arm is extended in the palm-down position, and the other arm is by the swimmer's side. Every 12 kicks the swimmer pulls with the extended arm and recovers with the arm from the side. During this action the swimmer rotates to the other side.
2	Like step 1 but the extended arm performs a sculling action while extended. The swimmer keeps the wrist high while sculling, as shown in figures a and b.
3	Assuming the same side lateral kicking position on the side, the swimmer performs the sculling action during the 12 kicks, performs one catch, and then returns to the extended position. The swimmer pulls with the extended arm and recovers with the arm from the side, rotating to the other side.
4	Like step 3 but the swimmer performs two catches and then recovers and rotates.
5	Like step 4 but when the swimmer performs the catches he or she lifts the arm by the side just out of the water. Then after the double catch the swimmer recovers and rotates.
6	Like step 5 but with a combination of three, five, and seven strokes in between (3-5-7).
7	Full stroke with an emphasis on a strong catch.

(Sweetenham 1998d)

PROGRESSION 2: HIP, SHOULDER, AND TRUNK ROTATION

1	The figure below shows kicking on the side with the hands in the pocket position. The swimmer performs a left-side kick followed by a right-side kick. 
2	Like step 1 with one rotation from the left side to the right side. Arms stay in the hands-in-pockets position. The rotation takes place at a position determined by the coach.
3	Kicking on the side position with the head still. The hands are in the pockets position with the thumbs downward. After 12 kicks the swimmer rotates to the other side, keeping the head still. The rotation should be fast and continuous. The swimmer can breathe at will in the initial stage of learning this drill, although the coach may want to set breathing patterns for the swimmer. The swimmer should be in the head-set position before the rotation and then be sure not to go straight into having a breath following the rotation. The coach could set breathing patterns in this way: • The swimmer assumes the kicking position with hands in the pockets and performs 6 to 12 kicks. • Following the 6 to 12 kicks the swimmer takes a breath. • Following the 6 to 12 kicks the swimmer rotates to the opposite side, being sure to keep the head in the set position, and performs another 6 to 12 kicks before taking the next breath.
4	Kicking in the same position as step 3, the swimmer recovers the arm on the side that is highest in the water for a half recovery and then lowers the arm back into the water to the hands-in-pockets position, maintaining the kicking as shown in the figure below. After lowering the arm the swimmer rotates to the other side and the drill continues. As shown in step 3 the coach may ask the swimmer to perform the drill to a set breathing and kicking pattern. 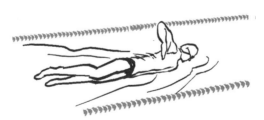

5	Kicking as in step 4, the swimmer this time performs a full recovery and then a pull, with the other arm maintaining the position by the side (hip catch-up). As the arm recovering extends into the water, the body should rotate—hip, shoulder, and then chin. When the swimmer pulls, the body has rotated. As the pull finishes by the side of the body, the other arm starts its recovery (this is a catch-up action at the hips).
6	Like step 5 but with half to three-quarter catch-up by the side.
7	Full stroke in slow motion with maximum rotation.

The swimmer can do this progression with hand paddles. The rotation from one side to the other must be fast with no pause when the body is facing downward. In the early stages of learning the drill, the swimmer may wear fins. As the swimmer becomes more proficient at this progression, the coach sets advanced breathing patterns for the athlete to follow.

(Sweetenham 1998d, 1999c)

PROGRESSION 3: HIGH ELBOW RECOVERY AND ROTATION

1	Side lateral kicking with extended-arm sculling. Recovery and rotation after 12 kicks.
2	The orientation drill is shown in figures a and b. The swimmer starts in the side lateral kicking position as in step 1. The swimmer performs one lift with the arm by the side while kicking in that position. The lift is with the elbow leading and is approximately one-third of a normal recovery. The hand and arm then descend to the side of the body into the water. During this lift and descent the body maintains its side lateral kicking position. After the 12 kicks the swimmer performs a recovery and pull with rotation to the opposite side to perform the cycle again.
3	Like step 2 but with the swimmer performing two lifts and then a stroke and rotation. After performing two controlled lifts the swimmer does the recovery and pull rotation.
4	Like step 3 but with three full strokes between the lifts.

5	Shark-fin drill as shown in figures a through c. The swimmer performs a very slow lift recovery with the other arm extended. The recovering arm is a high elbow recovery. As the hand approaches the armpit, there is acceleration in the extension of that arm. As that arm moves forward, the extended arm pulls back. The swimmer then performs the same drill on the other side.
	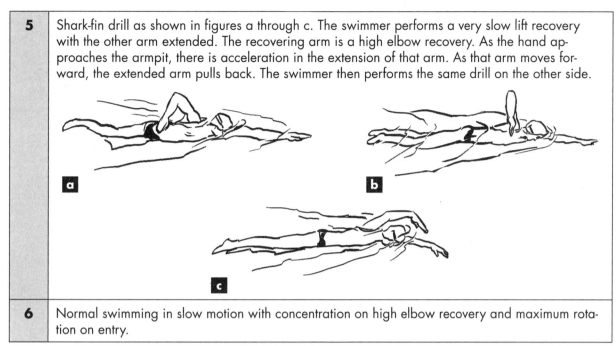
6	Normal swimming in slow motion with concentration on high elbow recovery and maximum rotation on entry.

(Sweetenham 1998d)

PROGRESSION 4: ROTATION SCULL FEEL

1	Side lateral kicking position with one arm extended and the other arm by the side. Rotation after 12 kicks.
2	Side lateral kicking position with extended-arm sculling. Recovery and rotation after 12 kicks.
3	Like step 2 but with three strokes between.
4	Like step 2 but with five strokes between.
5	Like step 2 but with seven strokes between.
6	Full stroke with emphasis on catch and rotation.
As the number of arm strokes increases, the number of kicks between can decrease.	

(Sweetenham 1998d)

PROGRESSION 5: WEAK-ARM, STRONG-ARM HAND PADDLE ROTATION DRILL

1	Single-arm swimming with the nonpulling arm extended as shown in the figure below (weak-arm pulling). This drill can also be done with the nonpulling arm by the side.

2	Like step 1 but on the strong arm.
3	Like step 1 but with hand paddles.
4	Like step 2 but with hand paddles.
5	Minimum-maximum drill. The swimmer holds best time possible with minimum stroke count and starts laps with the weak arm. See chapter 3 for an explanation of minimum-maximum drill.
6	Like step 5 but with racing stroke rate.
	Start the repeats on steps 5 and 6 with the weak arm.

(Sweetenham 1998d)

PROGRESSION 6: FISTS AND HAND PADDLES

	The aim of the progression is to improve efficiency and feel for the water.
1	50 m freestyle stroke counting.
2	50 m freestyle fists timed and stroke count. The swimmer performs this drill with the hands in a clenched fist.
3	50 m freestyle distance per stroke and stroke count.
4	50 m freestyle with hand paddles, distance per stroke, and stroke count.
5	50 m freestyle maximum effort with hand paddles, counting strokes, and trying to hold stroke count from step 4.
6	50 m freestyle maximum effort, counting strokes, and aiming to hold count from step 3. No hand paddles.
7	50 m freestyle slow-motion minimum strokes.
8	50 m freestyle minimum-maximum drill as outlined in chapter 3.
	When the swimmer has completed this progression, it is important to record the stroke counts and times.

PROGRESSION 7: FRONT LATERAL KICK WITH HIP ROTATION

1	With the right arm extended and sculling, the swimmer is on the front with the left arm by the side. The swimmer pushes the hip up first to start the rotation, followed by the shoulders. The rotation continues until the body is in a high lateral position. The hip then leads the body back down to a flat position with the right arm still extended.
2	Like step 1 but with the left arm extended.
3	One arm catch-up with the right arm extended. The swimmer follows through the progression, leading with the hips, followed by the shoulders.
4	One arm catch-up as in step 3 but with the left arm.

5	Hip rotation with hands-in-pockets position catch-up. The swimmer must lead through each stroke as shown in step 1.

On this progression the swimmer must always lead with hip first. One-arm catch-up is single-arm freestyle with the nonpulling arm extended.

(Sweetenham 1998d)

PROGRESSION 8: TOUCH-THE-KICKBOARD DRILL

1	The swimmer performs freestyle pull holding a long kickboard between the thighs. After each push through to the back of the stroke, the swimmer touches the kickboard before recovering the arm, as shown in the figure below. 
2	Like step 1 but with leg kick, still holding the kickboard.
3	Full-stroke freestyle.

The drill corrects the crossover kick in freestyle. Another drill to correct this is a vertical kick with a sculling action by the side, against the wall.

PROGRESSION 9: FEEL-THE-STROKE DRILL

This drill requires a pair of goggles, which have been blacked out. The objective of the drill is to increase the sense of awareness that the swimmer has for the stroke. The swimmer is now unable to see the surrounding lane lines, the end of the pool, the pace clock, or anything else. The progression is conducted as follows.

1	The first step is to have the swimmer do 50 m in a certain but appropriate number of strokes.
2	The swimmer progresses to combine a number of strokes and a target time for 50 m.
3	The final step of the progression is to maintain either time or stroke count for 50 m and improve the other, or maintain a predetermined stroke rate while controlling the breathing pattern.

Care must be taken to protect the swimmer at the finish end of the 50 m repeat without compromising the drill.

Constant feedback must be sought from the swimmer to know exactly how he or she is feeling in timing, stroke, and technique. The coach and swimmer may decide to concentrate on a different aspect of the stroke in each 50 m of the drill. The swimmer should be encouraged to offer feedback to the coach after each 50. This progression may be practiced on stroke drills as well as on full stroke.

(Sweetenham 1997a)

JUNIOR SQUAD FREESTYLE DRILL PROGRESSION

	For freestyle, the following drill progression can be used with junior squads.
1	25 m freestyle drill as left-side lateral kicking position. Hands-in-pockets position. The swimmer should work to keep the body and the head still.
2	25 m freestyle drill as right-side lateral kicking position. Hands-in-pockets position. The swimmer should work to keep the body and the head still.
3	25 m freestyle drill with three full strokes to start the 25. Then as the arm enters and extends on the fourth stroke, the swimmer assumes the side lateral kicking position for the 25 m. On the approach to the finish, the swimmer performs four strokes to finish the 25 m.
4	25 m freestyle drill starting in the right-side lateral kicking position. After 12.5 m the swimmer performs one rotation to the left side. Hands-in-pockets position. As the swimmer rotates no pause should occur on the front. The rotation is continuous. As the swimmer completes the rotation, he or she must be sure that the head does not follow the body around and must maintain the head-set position.
5	25 m freestyle drill as five full strokes to start the 25 m. As the arm enters and extends on the sixth stroke, the swimmer assumes the side lateral kicking position for the 25 m. On the approach to the finish, the swimmer performs six strokes to finish the 25 m.
6	25 m freestyle drill starting in the hands-in-pockets position. After 12 kicks the swimmer rotates to the other side, keeping the head still. The rotation is fast and continuous. The swimmer breathes at will. The swimmer should maintain head-set position before the rotation and should not go straight into having a breath after the rotation.
7	25 m full-stroke freestyle aiming to swim with perfect technique and with 12 to 18 strokes.
8	25 m choice of steps 1 to 7. This step will require the most attention by the swimmer.
	For the junior squad swimmer, kick and swim combinations are important for the development of full-stroke freestyle.

(Sweetenham 1998k)

Freestyle Technique Stroke Analysis

As a coach you must have the ability to analyze the technique of a swimmer. The stroke-analysis sheet will enable you to write comments for the technique of your swimmer on freestyle. The sheet can be very effective when viewing videotape of your swimmer. As you view the video you can write comments on the sheet and give a copy to the swimmer to refer to when viewing himself or herself swimming. See pages 107-108 for an example of a freestyle technique stroke analysis sheet that you can use with your swimmer.

FREESTYLE TECHNIQUE STROKE ANALYSIS SHEET

Name_____

Date _____

Venue_____

Body position	Comments
Head position, level of water	
Head position during breathing	
Shoulder rotation	
Hip rotation	
Legs	
Lateral movement of the body	
General comments	

Legs	Comments
6-beat kick?	
4-beat kick?	
2-beat kick?	
Amount of bend at the knees—do they break the surface?	
Ankles/toes	
Butterfly kicks underwater on push-offs	
General comments	

(continued)

(continued)

Arms	Comments
Position of arms/hands on entry, left	
Position of arms/hands on entry, right	
Position of arms/hands on catch, left	
Position of arms/hands on catch, right	
Pull pattern, left	
Pull pattern, right	
Elbow position on pull, left	
Elbow position on pull, right	
Hand position on pull, left	
Hand position on pull, right	
Push phase and acceleration of hand, left and right	
Recovery, straight or bent arm, left	
Recovery, straight or bent arm, right	
General comments	

Timing and breathing	Comments
Breathing pattern	
Any catch up in the stroke	
General comments	

Sprint Checklist

❏ The senior sprint swimmer should consider following a reverse periodization macrocycle plan as outlined in chapter 12, pages 184-185.

❏ The swimmer should perform dryland training for 10 to 40 minutes before each swimming training session to a light sweat.

❏ The successful sprinter needs superior kicking ability, which he or she can develop by practicing fast kick sets.

❏ The swimmer should practice holding racing stroke rate with hand paddles and fins on 15 m to 100 m swims. The time, stroke rate, and stroke count should be recorded, and the swimmer should aim to match or beat all measures the next time he or she performs this type of training.

❏ The swimmer should regularly perform high-velocity overloads (HVOs) (400 m to 600 m daily). Refer to chapter 12 for more details on how many HVOs to incorporate.

❏ The sprint program should include tethered sprints with surgical tubing working against tension (speed-resistance work) as well as with tension (speed-assistance work) on a weekly basis. These sprints should take into account racing stroke rate and racing breathing patterns.

❏ The sprint swimmer can use turning drills as speed drills. Refer to chapter 10 for turning drills.

❏ The great sprinter needs to have strong abdominals and core stability (created by doing sit-ups and crunches each day). See chapter 15 for information about dryland conditioning. The younger developing sprinter can benefit by doing pull sets using long kickboards held between the thighs, rather than pull buoys, so that core strength is required to keep the kickboard in position.

❏ The sprinter should not breathe bilaterally or breathe too much in a 50 m sprint. The swimmer should know exactly how many breaths to take. Senior male sprinters may not need to breathe at all. The program of the sprint swimmer should include controlled-frequency breathing on all sprints of 50 m or less.

❏ If in doubt when tapering a sprint swimmer, the coach should give the athlete more rest. (If in doubt, leave it out.) Swimmers should wear racing costumes only for major competitions, not for training or for meets they have not tapered for.

❏ The sprint swimmer needs to attain top speed in the first two strokes when sprinting. On racing-start practice, the swimmer should get the stroke rate from the breakout stroke to develop this skill. The swimmer must focus all concentration on the breakout stroke because the ability to reach top speed can determine success or failure. Performing starts using one hand paddle on the hand that the swimmer pulls with first is a good drill for improving the breakout stroke.

❏ The coach should ensure that the sprint swimmer practices HVOs on kick, pull, swim, and drill. HVOs can be included in warm-up and swim-down routines. A good strategy is to alternate the placement from one training session to the next. Speed in warm-ups develops speed. Speed in (pre) swim-downs develops specific race endurance and some speed.

❏ Sprinters should spend more time on resistance training, at speed, than other swimmers do.

(continued)

(continued)

❏ Sprinters should maintain a consistent training volume of 40 to 55 kilometers per week while manipulating the total intensity of each training week.

❏ Relay sprints are a great way to develop fast swimming as well as improve relay changeovers.

❏ Swimming across the width of the pool is another good way to develop speed, and this drill can include turns and finishes.

❏ Developing a water circuit session for the sprinter is a good way to enhance speed and power. This circuit could be scheduled once a week in addition to regular training. Surgical tubing sprints (assisted), tethered swimming (resisted), vertical sprint kicking, power sprint pulling (with buckets, sponges), monofin sprints, timed starts, and timed turns can form the circuit. Circuits are usually regulated by controlling the time at each station or the number of repeats performed.

❏ Coaches should insist on six-beat kicking on all race-pace and sprint sets during training. Many sprinters overkick, however, and these athletes can benefit from a reduction in kicking.

❏ Sculling drills can help the sprinter develop feel for the water. Swimming with the eyes closed or in darkness can help the swimmer develop feel for the water. Teaching the wrong way before teaching the right way sometimes works very well.

❏ The better the swimmer streamlines, the less distance the swimmer has to swim. Swimmers should try to avoid rough water out of the turn by having great streamlining and distance off the wall, with speed. Butterfly kicks used off the wall are to maintain speed, not just distance.

Distance-Swimming Checklist

❏ All types of training will increase through the cycle, and the training programs should be methodically planned. The percentage of aerobic and anaerobic training may not change, but the absolute volume of work done will change. See chapter 12 for sample macrocycle plans.

❏ Coaches need to have a two-year plan as a minimum when coaching distance swimmers.

❏ Swimmers should work an overdistance swim at high intensity at least once every two to three weeks (above the anaerobic threshold level).

❏ Some speed work is important to distance swimmers. They must have an ability to produce speed at the back end of their races. This type of training should be conducted regularly throughout the year. An example is 20 to 30 × 50 m on 1:30 to 2:30, at maximum speed, conducted as a main set once a week.

❏ Swimmers should develop a volume base before working race-specific sets at high intensity. The speed, intensity, and volume of the set can increase after an aerobic phase. Males should work at 20 to 15 BBM heart rate and females at 15 to 10 BBM heart rate.

- ❏ A 5000 m timed swim under 60 minutes should be the target for all distance swimmers.
- ❏ Distance swimmers should judge pace in their heads, not by always using a pace clock. The coach should switch off the pace clock occasionally to help swimmers develop this skill.
- ❏ Resistance pull sets are important for age-group distance swimmers. Hand paddles need to be only slightly larger than the hand for developing age-group swimmers. As with all aids, the rule for the swimmer should be 50 percent with and 50 percent without.
- ❏ Age-group and distance swimmers can do resistance pull training up to 20 percent of the total training volume. Two sets of band-only resistance pull each week should be conducted.
- ❏ Use backstroke as a recovery stroke for freestyle.
- ❏ A physiotherapist should conduct muscular skeletal screening regularly (that is, each season). This screening will identify any potential injury risk and permit prescription of a preventative series of exercises if required.
- ❏ Light to moderate swimming enhances recovery more than complete rest does. Recovery days should be at the same or higher volume but performed at lower intensity.
- ❏ The distance swimmer needs to develop core body strength, but not necessarily from weight training.
- ❏ The distance swimmer requires sustained effort and speed sets, not descending sets. That is, the distance swimmer should do 6 × 400 m on 5:00 holding 4:30 on each swim, not 6 × 400 m descending one to three and four to six on 5:30. Descending sets may be a first phase before the introduction of sustained pace sets, and they can be used as a last phase into a race situation.
- ❏ The distance swimmer should develop the ability to sustain endurance-training loads. Being a distance swimmer requires a great deal of mental and physical stamina. The coaching stimulus must be positive.
- ❏ The recovery skill of the distance swimmer determines his or her training capacity for distance, as it does for all athletes.
- ❏ Use active recovery strategies such as contrasting showers, hydrotherapy, massage, spas, and controlled evaluated swim-downs.
- ❏ Like all swimmers, the 800 m and 1500 m swimmer should train for a longer event at the start of the season. The first 20 percent of the season is a preparation phase, the next 40 percent of the season is spent training for an event of greater distance than the 800 m and 1500 m, and the final 40 percent of the season is spent on specifics for the 800 m and 1500 m. We believe that using the 12-week cycle in preference to the 20- to 24-week cycle has harmed distance swimming.
- ❏ Short-rest interval training, such as 30 × 100 m freestyle on 1:15 holding 1:04, is unquestionably beneficial for the high-recovery female athlete but has extreme limitations for the senior male with less recovery skills. Age-group male athletes should be trained as the females are.
- ❏ For female distance swimmers, 32 seconds per 50 m repeat on freestyle is the key to success. Every day, the female distance swimmer should swim some 50 m repeats, at 32 seconds to feet on wall pace, in their training. They should aim at 31.8 to 32.2 seconds. For males, the target is 29.8 to 30.2 seconds per 50 m repeat.

A balanced stroke and good trunk rotation are keys to a strong freestyle technique.

This chapter provides valuable information for enhancing the stroke technique of sprint, middle-distance, and distance freestyle swimmers. Minimizing resistance is important for all events. By using the drill progressions in this chapter, the swimmer can improve stroke technique. Both the swimmer and the coach should use the checklist regularly to remind them of things that the swimmer should be practicing for freestyle.

Individual Medley

The individual medley (IM) should be the most important event for all 10-, 11-, and 12-year-olds, both in training and competition, to ensure all-round development. The 200 m IM should be a competition priority for 11-year-old swimmers. Within one or two years, following their 12th birthdays, the focus should shift to the 400 m IM to develop overall fitness and improve stroke efficiency. This event stimulates skill acquisition and skill enhancement in all four strokes and develops an aerobic background for each of the strokes. The event also provides variety and mental stimulus that will carry the athlete into successful senior swimming.

The individual medley is a unique event that should be considered an event in its own right.

IM work develops overall muscular and flexibility, prevents injuries, offers greater training stimuli, and offsets premature stroke specialization.

When planning the training for the individual medley swimmer the following should be taken into account:

- Between 800 m to 1000 m of butterfly work should be conducted in each session. The butterfly work can be a mix of swim, kick, drill, and so on. Butterfly training should be sprint-anaerobic based for the IM.

- Backstroke is an arm-dominated stroke in the IM. The swimmer should emphasize good trunk rotation to minimize resistance during this leg of the medley, working the stroke rate of the arms during the last 15 to 20 m of this section going into the changeover turn. Aerobic backstroke is a necessity for the IM swimmer. The IM swimmer should work on 5 × 800 backstroke, 8 × 400 backstroke, and 16 × 200 backstroke in preference to doing these types of sets in freestyle.

- Breaststroke in the IM should be leg dominated. Besides being leg dominated, this stroke needs to be efficient. Breaststroke plays a key role in the total percentage of the IM and is the largest section of the race.

- Freestyle should match the butterfly in time for the split (Sweetenham 1998h).

Test sets and the strengths and weaknesses chart for the IM are shown in chapter 2.

IM Drill Progressions

This IM drill progression is designed to have swimmers work on their weakest stroke to strengthen any weaknesses they may have. The progression also uses the minimum-maximum drill, as outlined in chapter 3, to have swimmers concentrate on efficiency with speed, an important aspect for IM swimmers. The progression also works on variable pace, another skill medley swimmers should learn for tactics in competitions.

IM DRILL PROGRESSION: PART 1

1 × 50 m	Freestyle, 15 m underwater streamlined kick, 20 m drill, 15 m sprint to finish.
1 × 100 m	IM minus weak stroke, 50 m of best stroke (freestyle not considered weak or best).
1 × 75 m	Weak stroke.
1 × 100 m	IM minus best stroke, 50 m of weak stroke.
11 × 25 m	Minimum-maximum drill (that is, maximum speed, minimum strokes) main stroke (any odd number of repeats).
4 × 50 m	Variable pace, build swims either 25 m easy and 25 m hard, or 25 m hard and 25 m easy.
4 × 100 m	Drills on main stroke or IM order. The first 75 m is three different drills, and the last 25 m of each 100 m is a repeat of the minimum-maximum drill, trying to hold efficiency rating achieved on the 11 × 25 m repeats of this progression.
Part 1 of this progression totals 1200 m.	

IM DRILL PROGRESSION: PART 2

4 × 100 m	IM switching drill format as follows: First 100 m as 50 m BF drill, 50 m BK drill Second 100 m as 50 m BK drill, 50 m BR drill Third 100 m as 50 m BR drill, 50 m FS drill Fourth 100 m as straight 100 m IM drill
4 × 100 m	Straight swim 100 m of each stroke with the second 50 m of each 100 m at 400 m IM race pace.
8 × 50 m	On 60 at 400 m IM race pace, two 50 m repeats on each stroke.
1 × 400 m	IM straight swim.
Parts 1 and 2 total 2800 m.	

(Sweetenham 1999c)

IM Planning

Training weeks for the individual medley swimmer must cover both conditioning and technique as required for swimming the event. A training week for the IM swimmer is outlined in table 8.1. Each session includes 800 m to 1000 m butterfly.

TABLE 8.1   IM WEEKLY PLANNING

	Monday	Tuesday	Wednesday	Thursday	Friday	Saturday
AM early season	FS	BK	BR	FS	BK, BR	IM
AM midseason	BF:BK 80:20	BK:BR 80:20	BR:FS 80:20	BF:BK 70:30	BK:BR 70:30	BF:BK 70:30
PM early and midseason	FS	BK, BR	FS	BK	BR, FS	
AM late season	BF:BK 70:30	BK:BR 70:30 (1)	BK:BR 30:70 (3)	BF:BK 70:30	BR	IM
PM late season	BF:BK 50:50	BK:BR 50:50 (2)	BR:FS 50:50	BK	BR:FS 30:70	

In the late-season plan, the aim is to swim to a ratio of 70:30, 50:50, and 30:70 backstroke to breaststroke in three consecutive workouts.

We suggest that the IM swimmer not do any significant amount of straight IM work until the last five weeks out from the competition.

IM Sets

The sets shown in this section are specifically designed for the IM swimmer. They focus on improving the swimmer's IM and developing physiological conditioning from the work done. This section shows many different sets, which include linking sets designed to help the IM swimmer transfer from one stroke to the next in races. Another important emphasis for the IM swimmer is the amount of work done on butterfly. This section shows examples of how to incorporate 800 m to 1000 m of butterfly within each training session.

100-Meter IM Sets

The swimmer can perform a set of 100 m IMs, swimming the sets as determined by the coach. Then the swimmer can progress to swimming 100 m IMs with backstroke pull and breaststroke kick, trying to hold the same time achieved on the 100 m IMs full stroke. The purpose of this set is to work the specifics of strong-arm domination in the backstroke and the kick importance in the breaststroke. Some 100 IM sets based on this philosophy are the following:

16 × 100 m as	Straight 100 m IMs, record times on 1:30
	(1600 m)

16 × 100 m as	4 × 100 m IM, straight on 1:30, holding average time from previous set 4 × 100 m IM, BK performed as pull, holding time from the first block of 4 × 100 m swims 4 × 100 m IM, BR performed as kick, holding time from the first block of 4 × 100 m swims 4 × 100 m IM, BK performed as pull and BR performed as kick, holding time from the first block of 4 × 100 m swims
	(1600 m)

16 × 100 m as	4 × 100 m IM, fast BF 4 × 100 m IM, BK performed as pull 4 × 100 m IM, BR performed as kick 4 × 100 m IM, fast FS maximum kick
	(1600 m)

16 × 100 m as	4 × 100 m IM, 25 m BF split timed 4 × 100 m IM, 25 m BK split timed 4 × 100 m IM, 25 m BR split timed 4 × 100 m IM, 25 m FS split timed
	(1600 m)

16 × 100 m as	4 × 100 m IM, 25 m BF split timed 4 × 100 m IM, 25 m BK split timed 4 × 100 m IM, 25 m BF split timed 4 × 100 m IM, 25 m BK split timed
	(1600 m)

16 × 100 m as	4 × 100 m IM, 25 m BR split timed 4 × 100 m IM, 25 m FS split timed 4 × 100 m IM, 25 m BR split timed 4 × 100 m IM, 25 m FS split timed
	(1600 m)

The swimmer could work the following set based on the IM principles outlined previously:

8 × 50 m, BF fast on 1:30.
4 × 100 m, BK pull last 25 m of each 100 maximum effort on 1:40
2 × 200 m, BR kick timed 3:30
1 × 400 m, FS negative split, kicking home hard

(1600 m)

IM Switch Training and Sample Sets

Switching sets help the IM swimmer learn smooth transfer from one stroke to the next. The swimmer should perform switching sets only in the order shown here to keep this set specific to the event.

Butterfly

Butterfly-backstroke

Backstroke

Backstroke-breaststroke

Breaststroke

Breaststroke-freestyle

Individual medley

Sample IM switching sets are as follows:

2 × 200 m BF
    200 m BF-BK
    200 m BK
    200 m BK-BR
    200 m BR
    200 m BR-FS
    200 m IM

                                                      (2800 m)

1 × 200 m BF
    400 m BF-BK
    200 m BK
    400 m BK-BR
    200 m BR
    400 m BR-FS
    400 m IM

                                                      (2200 m)

2 × 100 m BF
    200 m BF-BK
    100 m BK
    200 m BK-BR
    100 m BR
    200 m BR-FS
    200 m IM

                                                      (2200 m)

3 × 7 × 100 m as
    1 BF
    2 BF-BK
    3 BK
    4 BK-BR
    5 BR
    6 BR-FS
    7 IM

                                                      (2100 m)

An example of a switching set to incorporate swim-pull and kick is the following:

12 × 100 m on 1:40
1 and 7	25 m BF, 50 m BK, 25 m BR kick
2 and 8	50 m BK pull, 50 m BR kick
3 and 9	25 m BK, 50 m BR pull, 25 m FS kick
4 and 10	25 m BF kick, 50 m BK, 25 m BR
5 and 11	50 m BK kick, 50 m BR pull
6 and 12	25 m BK pull, 25 m BR kick, 50 m FS build

                                                      (1200 m)

The 12 × 100 m set just described can be done as follows on 200s:

12 × 200 m on 3:20
1 and 7	50 m BF, 100 m BK, 50 m BR kick
2 and 8	100 m BK pull, 100 m BR kick
3 and 9	50 m BK, 100 m BR pull, 50 m FS kick
4 and 10	50 m BF kick, 100 m BK, 50 m BR
5 and 11	100 m BK kick, 100 m BR pull
6 and 12	50 m BK pull, 100 m BR kick, 50 m FS build

                                                      (2400 m)

30 × 50 m as
10 BF-BK
10 BK-BR
10 BR-FS

(1500 m)

6 ×   3 × 50 m BF-BK, BK-BR, BR-FS
             1 × 100 m IM

(1500 m)

Butterfly Sets for the IM Swimmer

The following examples are useful in constructing butterfly sets for individual medley swimmers. The IM swimmer should do at least 800 m to 1000 m butterfly in each training session. The swimmer can do 800 m to 1000 m butterfly in many different ways, as the following examples suggest:

20 × 50 m butterfly on 60

(1000 m)

8 × 100 m minimum-maximum drill on 4:00

(800 m)

8 × 100 m descending in sets of four to race pace on the final 100 m swim on 4:00

(800 m)

16 × 50 m on 60 at 400 m IM race pace, holding racing stroke count and with racing stroke rate. Some swimmers may need to build up to holding 16 × 50 m repeats at this pace and may start by doing 8 × 50 m and increase to 16 × 50 m.

(800 m)

40 × 25 m at faster than 400 m IM race pace

(1000 m)

2 sets of 4 × 100 m drills, 100 m on each of the following drills: undulation, Biondi, Biondi plus one, minimum-maximum drill. Chapter 4 contains descriptions of each of these drills.

(800 m)

16 × 50 m kick on 60
        4 × 50 m front kick
        4 × 50 m side kick
        4 × 50 m back kick
        4 × 50 m choice of the above three types of kick

(800 m)

16 × 50 m pull on 60
        8 × 50 m with pull buoy
        8 × 50 m with band only

(800 m)

5 × 200 m kick

(1000 m)

5 × 200 m as 200 m pull, 200 m kick, 200 m drill, 200 swim, 200 IM hitting required BF split

(1000 m)

2 × 400 m as 150 m BF drills, 50 m swim holding 400 m race pace, racing stroke count, and racing stroke rate

(800 m)

Aerobic IM Sets

The sets outlined in this section can be amended in many ways. The coach can give different instructions, such as setting heart-rate levels to hold or stroke counts to hold.

3 ×   600 m FS
                 3 × 200 m IM
                 300 m MS
                 3 × 100 m weakest stroke

                                                                                    (5400 m)

800 m FS
2 × 400 m IM
600 m FS
2 × 300 m IM
400 m FS
2 × 200 m IM
200 m FS
2 × 100 m IM

                                                                                    (4000 m)

800 m, 400 m, 200 m, 100 m IM
600 m, 450 m, 300 m, 150 m FS
400 m, 300 m, 200 m, 100 m form-stroke choice mixture

                                                                                    (4000 m)

Following are some of the ways this set can be amended:

800 m IM on 11:30
7 × 100 m BF on 1:40
600 m IM on 8:30
5 × 100 m BK on 1:30
400 m IM on 5:40
3 × 100 m BR on 1:40
200 m IM on 2:50
1 × 100 m FS

                                                                                    (3600 m)

800 m BF on 14:00
7 × 100 m IM on 1:35
600 m BK on 9:30
5 × 100 m IM on 1:30
400 m BR on 6:40
3 × 100 m IM on 1:25
200 m FS on 2:30
1 × 100 m IM

                                                                                    (3600 m)

800 m FS on 12:00
7 × 100 m BF-BK on 1:40
600 m BR kick on 11:00
5 × 100 m BK-BR on 1:40
400 m BK pull on 6:00
3 × 100 m BR-FS on 1:35
200 m BF on 2:45
1 × 100 m IM

                                                                                    (3600 m)

200 m BF on 3:00
7 × 100 m BF-BK on 1:40
400 m BK on 6:00
5 × 100 m BK-BR on 1:40
600 m BR on 9:00
3 × 100 m BR-FS on 1:35
800 m FS on 11:00
1 × 100 m IM

                                                                                    (3600 m)

4 × 600 m IM as outlined
    300 m FS

First	600 m as 200 m BF, 200 m BK, 200 m BR
Second	600 m as 200 m BK, 200 m BR, 200 m FS
Third	600 m as 150 m drill each stroke
Fourth	600 m as 200 m IMs

        (3600 m)

3 × 400 m BK or BF on 6:20 BR on 7:00
3 × 300 m BK or BF on 4:30 BR on 5:00
3 × 200 m BK or BF on 2:55 BR on 3:15
3 × 100 m BK or BF on 1:25 BR on 1:35

        (3000 m)

Short-Rest Aerobic IM Sets

24 × 150 m as
    4 × 150 m BF
    4 × 150 m as 50 m BF, 100 m BK
    4 × 150 m BK
    4 × 150 m as 50 m BK, 100 m BR
    4 × 150 m BR
    4 × 150 m as 50 m BR, 100 m FS

        (3600 m)

5 × 100 m BF on 1:30
5 × 200 m as 150 m BK, 50 m BR on 3:00
5 × 100 m BR on 1:30
5 × 200 m as 150 m BR, 50 m FS on 3:00
5 × 100 m IM on 1:30

        (3500 m)

4 × 800 m IM as

First	200 m on each stroke
Second	2 × 400 m IM
Third	4 × 200 m IM
Fourth	8 × 100 m IM

        (3200 m)

200 m BF on 3:00, 100 m IM on 1:35, 6 × 50 m BF-BK on 50
200 m BK on 3:00, 100 m IM on 1:35, 6 × 50 m BK-BR on 50
200 m BR on 3:00, 100 m IM on 1:35, 6 × 50 m BR-FS on 50
200 m FS on 3:00, 100 m IM on 1:35, 6 × 50 m weakest stroke on 50
200 m IM on 3:00, 100 m IM on 1:35, 6 × 50 m main stroke (MS) on 50

        (3000 m)

400 m FS on 5:10, 200 m IM on 2:40, 100 m BF on 1:20, 50 m BF-BK on 50
400 m FS on 5:00, 200 m IM on 2:50, 100 m BK on 1:30, 50 m BK-BR on 50
400 m FS on 4:50, 200 m IM on 3:00, 100 m BR on 1:30, 50 m BR-FS on 50
400 m FS on 4:40, 200 m IM on 3:10, 100 m FS on 1:20, 50 m choice

        (3000 m)

4 × 50 m BF on 45	300 m as 100 m BF, 100 m BK, 100 m BR on 4:30
4 × 50 m BK on 45	300 m as 150 m BF, 150 m BK on 4:30
4 × 50 m BR on 45	300 m as 150 m BK, 150 m BR on 4:30
4 × 50 m FS on 45	300 m as 150 m BR, 150 m FS on 4:30

        (2000 m)

4 × 500 m	BF	BK	BR	FS
	50 m	100 m	150 m	200 m
	100 m	150 m	200 m	50 m
	150 m	200 m	50 m	100 m
	200 m	50 m	100 m	150 m

        (2000 m)

100 m IM
8 × 50 m BF
200 m IM
6 × 50 m BK
300 m IM
4 × 50 m BR
400 m IM
2 × 50 m FS

(2000 m)

100 m IM on 1:30
4 × 25 m best form stroke on 25
200 m IM on 3:00
4 × 50 m weakest form stroke on 50
300 m IM on 4:30
4 × 75 m IM switch (50 m, 25 m choice IM switch)
400 m IM on 6:00
4 × 100 m IM order

(2000 m)

8 × 250 m IM

1 and 5 as	100 m BF	50 m BK	50 m BR	50 m FS
2 and 6 as	50 m BF	100 m BK	50 m BR	50 m FS
3 and 7 as	50 m BF	50 m BK	100 m BR	50 m FS
4 and 8 as	50 m BF	50 m BK	50 m BR	100 m FS

(2000 m)

4 ×   50 m BF
             100 m BF-BK
             150 m BF-BK-BR
             200 m IM

(2000 m)

20 × 100 m as
4 × 100 m BK
     100 m as 25 m BK, 75 m BR
     100 m as 50 m BK, 50 m BR
     100 m as 75 m BK, 25 m BR
     100 m BR

(2000 m)

32 × 50 m IM order, rest 5 seconds every 50 m
BF   25 m four-right arm pulls, four left-arm pulls, two full strokes (4-4-2)
BK   25 m with 15 m underwater, then swim the rest of the 25 m
BR   Double underwater pull-out on the start
FS   No breathing between flags and wall

(1600 m)

8 × 200 m IM holding the stroke counts as outlined

1 and 5	3 BF	6 BK	3 BR	6 FS
2 and 6	4 BF	8 BK	4 BR	8 FS
3 and 7	5 BF	9 BK	5 BR	9 FS
4 and 8	6 BF	10 BK	6 BR	10 FS

(1600 m)

The above set is designed so that the swimmer has to work distance per stroke and efficiency in stroke technique. This swimmer can perform this set in reverse.

13 × 100 as
100 m	BF
100 m	75 m BF, 25 m BK
100 m	50 m BF, 50 m BK
100 m	25 m BF, 75 m BK
100 m	BK
100 m	75 m BK, 25 m BR
100 m	50 m BK, 50 m BR
100 m	25 m BK, 75 m BR
100 m	BR
100 m	75 m BR, 25 m FS
100 m	50 m BR, 50 m FS
100 m	25 m BR, 75 m FS
100 m	FS

(1300 m)

4 × 250 m IM as
1   100 m BF, 50 m BK, 50 m BR, 50 m FS on 3:45
2   50 m BF, 100 m BK, 50 m BR, 50 m FS on 3:45
3   50 m BF, 50 m BK, 100 m BR, 50 m FS on 3:45
4   50 m BF, 50 m BK, 50 m BR, 100 m FS on 3:45

(1000 m)

8 × 125 m as 100 m IM with an extra 25 m on the swimmer's weak stroke on 2:00

(1000 m)

8 × 125 m as 100 m IM with an extra 25 m on the swimmer's MS on 2:00

(1000 m)

Anaerobic Training Zone Sets for IM (Including Race-Pace Training)

The actual race pace can be determined by using the strengths and weakness chart shown in figures 2.14 and 2.15.

2 × 100 m BF at 400 m IM split pace on 1:50
200 m BF-BK, 100 m BK at 400 m IM split pace on 3:40
300 m BF-BK-BR, 100 m BR at 400 m IM split pace on 5:30
400 m IM, 100 m FS at 400 m IM split pace on 7:20
4 × 100 m, one on each stroke at 400 m IM split pace on 1:40

(1800 m at race pace, 2800 m total set)

Race-pace set, 400 m swims on 8:00
8 × 400 m alternate 400 m IM and 400 m FS recovery as follows:
1 × 400 m IM 10 seconds at the 200 m, target PB time plus four seconds
1 × 400 m FS at 50 BBM heart rate
1 × 400 m IM 10 seconds at each 100 m, target PB pace splits
1 × 400 m FS at 50 BBM heart rate
1 × 400 m IM 10 seconds at each 50 m, target PB goal pace
1 × 400 m FS at 50 BBM heart rate
1 × 400 m IM as 16 × 25 m on 20 at faster than race pace
1 × 400 m FS at 50 BBM heart rate

(1600 m at race pace, 3200 m total set)

3 × 50 m BF at 200 m IM split pace on 50
100 m BF-BK, 50 m BK at 200 m IM split pace on 1:40
150 m BF-BK-BR, 50 m BR at 200 m IM split pace on 2:30
200 m IM, 50 m FS at 200 m IM split pace on 3:20
4 × 50 m, IM order at 200 m IM split pace on 50

(1000 m at race pace, 2100 m total set)

100 m BF at individual checking speed
50 m BF at 400 m IM pace

50 m BF-BK at 200 m IM stroke rates
100 m BK at individual checking speed
50 m BK at 400 m IM pace
50 m BK-BR at 200 m IM stroke rates
100 m BR at individual checking speed
50 m BR at 400 m IM pace
50 m BR-FS at 200 m IM stroke rates
100 m FS at individual checking speed
50 m FS at 400 m IM pace
50 m FS at 200 m IM stroke rates
The swimmer does this set twice.

(800 m at race pace, 1600 m total set)

100 m BF at individual checking speed
50 m BF at 200 m IM pace
50 m BF-BK at 200 m IM stroke rates
100 m BK at individual checking speed
50 m BK at 200 m IM pace
50 m BK-BR at 200 m IM stroke rates
100 m BR at individual checking speed
50 m BR at 200 m IM pace
50 m BR-FS at 200 m IM stroke rates
100 m FS at individual checking speed
50 m FS at 200 m IM pace
50 m FS at 200 m IM stroke rates
The swimmer does this set twice.

(800 m at race pace, 1600 m total set)

Broken IMs at race pace
2 ×
50 m BF at 200 m IM split pace on 2:00
100 m BF-BK at first 100 m of 200 m IM split pace on 4:00
100 m BK-BR at middle 100 m of 200 m IM split pace on 4:00
100 m BR-FS at last 100 m of 200 m IM split pace on 4:00
50 m FS at 200 m IM split pace on 2:00

(800 m at race pace and 800 m total set)

High-Performance Endurance Sets for the IM

These sets are based on the principles outlined in chapter 1. The coach should monitor this high-intensity training closely to ensure that the swimmer works in the correct training zone. The swimmer should maintain the training pace throughout the set, being sure not to start the set at an intensity that would prevent him or her from maintaining the required pace throughout the set.

M$\dot{V}O_2$

For information regarding M$\dot{V}O_2$ training sets refer to chapter 1. Swimmers may perform these sets in many different ways. They can be stroke specific on just one stroke, switching order as outlined earlier in this chapter.

4 ×	400 m IM on 7:00	
	3 × 100 m on 1:15	50 m BF, 50 m BK
		50 m BK, 50 m BR
		50 m BR, 50 m FS
	200 m swim-down	

(2800 m main set, 800 m recovery = 3600 m total set)

6 × 3 × 100 m	2 sets as 50 m BF, 50 m BK on 1:15
	2 sets as 50 m BK, 50 m BR on 1:15
	2 sets as 50 m BR, 50 m FS on 1:20
200 m swim-down	
	(1800 m main set, 1200 m recovery = 3000 m total set)
5 × 3 × 100 m	1 set BF-BK on 1:15
	1 set BK-BR on 1:15
	1 set BR-FS on 1:20
	1 set FS on 1:10
	1 set IM on 1:20
200 m swim-down	
	(1500 m main set, 1000 m recovery = 2500 m total set)
4 × 3 × 100 m	1 set BF on 1:15
	1 set BK on 1:15
	1 set BR on 1:20
	1 set FS on 1:10
200 m swim-down	
	(1200 m main set, 800 m recovery = 2000 m total set)

Critical Speed

For information regarding critical speed training sets refer to chapter 1. The IM swimmer completes this type of training on single-stroke sets at appropriate training weeks as advised by the coach. Heart-rate levels during the sets are 20 to 10 beats below maximum. The swimmer's 200 m personal best times can also be used to set training paces. This method, outlined in chapter 1, is used for two strokes when the training set is based over two strokes such as an IM switching set.

30 × 100 m	13 BF-BK on 1:45, HR at 30 BBM	
	13 BK-BR on 1:45, HR at 20 BBM	
	4 IM on 1:45, HR at 10 BBM	
	Holding CS pace or HR levels as shown	
		(3000 m)
16 × 100 m	4 × 100 m BF on 1:50, HR at 20 BBM	
	4 × 100 m BK on 1:50, HR at 20 BBM	
	4 × 100 m BR on 1:50, HR at 20 BBM	
	4 × 100 m FS on 1:50, HR at 20 BBM	
8 × 100 m	IM on 1:50, HR at 20 BBM	
	Holding CS pace or HR levels as shown	
		(2400 m)
16 × 100 m	4 × 100 m BF on 1:50, HR at 20 BBM	
	4 × 100 m BK on 1:50, HR at 20 BBM	
	4 × 100 m BR on 1:50, HR at 20 BBM	
	4 × 100 m FS on 1:50, HR at 20 BBM	
	Holding CS pace or HR levels as shown	
8 × 50 m	2 × 50 m BF on 60, HR at 10 BBM	
	2 × 50 m BK on 60, HR at 10 BBM	
	2 × 50 m BR on 60, HR at 10 BBM	
	2 × 50 m FS on 60, HR at 10 BBM	
	Holding CS pace or HR levels as shown	
		(2400 m)

4 × 200 m IM on 3:30, HR at 30 BBM
8 × 100 m IM on 1:45, HR at 20 BBM
16 × 50 m IM, 2 each stroke on 60, HR at 10 BBM
Holding CS pace or HR levels as shown

(2400 m)

24 × 100 m on 1:45

     6 × 100 m BF-BK on 1:45, HR at 30 BBM
     6 × 100 m BK-BR on 1:45, HR at 30 BBM
     6 × 100 m BR-FS on 1:45, HR at 20 BBM
     6 × 100 m IM on 1:45, HR at 10 BBM
Holding CS pace or HR levels as shown

(2400 m)

IM Checklist

❏ Twice each week the IM swimmer should complete a backstroke resistance pull and breaststroke kick set at intensity.

❏ Incorporate 800 m to 1000 m of butterfly in all training workouts. This can be done in different ways, as shown in this chapter.

❏ The swimmer should work only in IM order for the strokes, that is, BF-BK, BK-BR, or BR-FS. He or she should not complete FS-BF on switching sets.

❏ Breaststroke technique in the 400 m IM is slightly wider and flatter than it is in the 200 m IM. The coach and swimmer will evaluate and alter technique to suit the individual, but the objective is to minimize resistance and increase efficiency rather than pursue speed.

❏ The IM swimmer should compete in all 200 m individual events and the 400 m, 800 m, and 1500 m freestyle events on a regular basis.

❏ The coach should compare the swimmer's race 200 m times in each stroke (second 100 m split) to the 400 m IM splits. For example, a swimmer with a 200 m freestyle PB of 1:59 and split 60 seconds for the second 100 m of this 200 m swim should have a 400 IM split of 60 seconds. Complete the IM strengths and weaknesses chart shown in figures 2.14 and 2.15.

❏ The swimmer should practice racing the middle or last 100 m of the 200 m form-stroke swims in his or her 400 m IM split.

❏ The IM swimmer should always sprint the last 15 m of all backstroke repeats in training sets.

❏ All IM swimmers should develop the arms in butterfly and backstroke, and the legs in breaststroke and freestyle.

❏ Coaches need to plan training to include HPE in all strokes, that is, IM link order and where possible in single strokes, until the last three to four weeks before the major competition.

❏ The IM swimmer should know his or her stroke count, stroke rate, and splits. Efficiency is important to the 400 m IM swimmer.

(continued)

(continued)

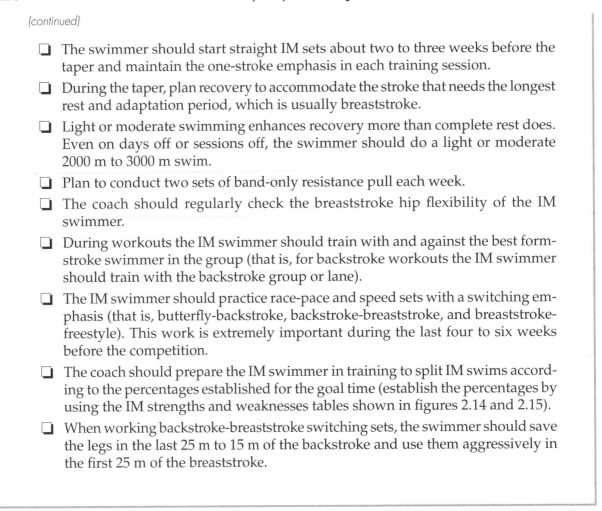

❏ The swimmer should start straight IM sets about two to three weeks before the taper and maintain the one-stroke emphasis in each training session.

❏ During the taper, plan recovery to accommodate the stroke that needs the longest rest and adaptation period, which is usually breaststroke.

❏ Light or moderate swimming enhances recovery more than complete rest does. Even on days off or sessions off, the swimmer should do a light or moderate 2000 m to 3000 m swim.

❏ Plan to conduct two sets of band-only resistance pull each week.

❏ The coach should regularly check the breaststroke hip flexibility of the IM swimmer.

❏ During workouts the IM swimmer should train with and against the best form-stroke swimmer in the group (that is, for backstroke workouts the IM swimmer should train with the backstroke group or lane).

❏ The IM swimmer should practice race-pace and speed sets with a switching emphasis (that is, butterfly-backstroke, backstroke-breaststroke, and breaststroke-freestyle). This work is extremely important during the last four to six weeks before the competition.

❏ The coach should prepare the IM swimmer in training to split IM swims according to the percentages established for the goal time (establish the percentages by using the IM strengths and weaknesses tables shown in figures 2.14 and 2.15).

❏ When working backstroke-breaststroke switching sets, the swimmer should save the legs in the last 25 m to 15 m of the backstroke and use them aggressively in the first 25 m of the breaststroke.

As stated at the beginning of this chapter the individual medley is a unique event that should be considered an event in its own right. Besides being considered the most important event for junior swimmers in training and competition, the individual medley is useful to youth and senior swimmers in training for variety and for a change of stimulus from their main training focus. Both swimmers and coaches should review the checklist regularly.

Sculling

Swimmers of all ages should practice sculling in their training to learn and improve their feel for the water, that is, their ability to put their hands and arms in the correct positions to maximize propulsion.

Before progressing to the sculling drills for each stroke, the swimmer should be able to perform wrist up (figure 9.1, a and b), flat wrist (figure 9.2), wrist down (figure 9.3), and midpoint sculling (figure 9.4, a to c).

FIGURE 9.1 Wrist up sculling.

FIGURE 9.2 Flat wrist sculling.

FIGURE 9.3 Wrist down sculling.

FIGURE 9.4 Midpoint sculling (c shows the side view).

Midpoint sculling action is performed with the swimmer on his or her front, with the chin on the water, performing a gentle freestyle kicking action. The elbows are forward of the shoulders and locked into place. The swimmer pushes in an inward and outward direction with the hands and lower arms. The swimmer must ensure that the elbows do not move during this drill.

Sculling Progressions

As with the stroke drill progressions for each of the competitive strokes, the sculling progressions should be specific for each of the competitive strokes. The aim of a sculling progression for each stroke is to commence with a basic sculling action, to progress to a more specific sculling action, and to finish the progression with full-stroke swimming.

Butterfly Sculling

Midpoint butterfly sculling action is performed with the fingers down with a high wrist position and elbows locked. The sculling action on this stroke scull is from the catch position of the stroke to an inward position of the hands almost touching under the belly button. The butterfly sculling progression is the following:

1. General midpoint scull, six to eight sculling actions
2. Butterfly midpoint scull, six to eight sculling actions
3. Butterfly full stroke, six to eight full strokes

Backstroke Sculling

The swimmer starts the drill in the lateral side kicking position with one arm extended and the opposite arm by the side. The extended arm is in the catch position and is sculling. The next step is to progress to midpoint backstroke scull. For this step of the progression the arm is in the water in the catch position as outlined earlier, the elbows bend and stay firm, and the hand then presses from the catch position to halfway, as shown in figure 9.5, a and b. The swimmer does not push through to the thighs.

The third step in the progression is shown in figure 9.6, a through c. The swimmer performs kick in the flat body position. As the swimmer rotates from the hip, he or she pushes through with the arm and hand and drives the hip around. Following this the swimmer returns to the flat kicking position, using only the right arm for an end-of-stroke push starting at midbody position. After working the right arm only, the swimmer progresses to using the left arm only and then the arms in combination.

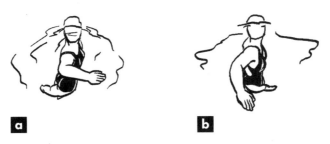

a   **b**

FIGURE 9.5 *Midpoint backstroke scull.*

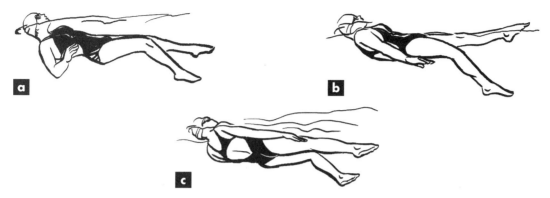

FIGURE 9.6   *End-of-stroke position for backstroke scull.*

Breaststroke Sculling

This progression starts with the swimmer performing midpoint scull with a high elbow position and gentle freestyle kick.

Breaststroke front scull is shown in figure 9.7. The wrist is higher than the fingertips and fixed. The swimmer presses outward from full extension, as he or she would do at the start of each arm stroke. The elbows do not bend during this action. The little finger is up during the outward scull, and the thumb is up during the inward scull. Breaststroke wide scull starts with the hands and arms at the widest point of the stroke with the palms facing outward (see figure 9.8). The palms then press, creating whirlpools as they scull. Again, the elbows stay locked during this sculling action. The little finger is up during the outward scull, and the thumb is up during the inward scull. Midpoint breaststroke scull starts in the wide position, and the elbows stay locked as they scull inward. Following this action they return to the widest point.

A breaststroke scull progression as shown in butterfly is the following:

1. General midpoint scull, six to eight sculling actions
2. Breaststroke midpoint scull, six to eight sculling actions
3. Breaststroke full stroke, six to eight full strokes

FIGURE 9.7   *Breaststroke front scull.*

FIGURE 9.8   *Breaststroke wide scull.*

Freestyle Sculling

For freestyle, the swimmer performs general midpoint scull and then progresses to a lateral side kicking position with one arm extended and one arm by the side working on catch position scull.

The swimmer progresses to single-arm lateral scull for freestyle as shown in the figure in step 2 of progression 1 in chapter 7 (page 100). The swimmer is in the side lateral position with one arm extended and the other by the side. The extended arm sculls from the catch position in a downward and outward action and then returns to the original starting position. The elbow stays locked in this drill and maintains a high position. The next sculling action is for the swimmer to work the normal midpoint scull.

Butterfly and Breaststroke Combination Scull

The swimmer performs midpoint scull for four, six, or eight presses and then immediately does four, six, or eight full strokes at race stroke rate. The swimmer concentrates on the inward scull for breaststroke, with the butterfly swimmer concentrating on that version of midpoint scull.

Individual Medley Mixture

For the individual medley swimmer or age-group athlete, the coach could introduce mixed sets of 25 m sculling and 25 m swim full stroke on all strokes as follows:

4 × 50 m as

1	25 m BF midpoint scull, 25 m full-stroke BF
2	25 m BK midpoint scull, 25 m full-stroke BK
3	25 m BR midpoint scull, 25 m full-stroke BR
4	25 m FS midpoint scull, 25 m full-stroke FS

Sculling practice develops the ability to maximize propulsions with correct hand and arm placement.

Sculling for Core Strength

Core strength training is one of the most important dryland training methods that swimmers can use to improve stability. With improved stability, swimmers will improve body position in the water and gain ability to maintain correct position through the duration of their races.

Core strength training and Swiss ball land routines are methods that are commonly used in programs to improve stability and teach swimmers how to hold and maintain their core strength. Chapter 15 covers specific dryland work for swimming.

To maintain correct body position when swimming, swimmers must have great core strength.

An often asked question is "How do we bring the core strength work done on land into the pool?" The following progressions are examples of how sculling can incorporate the swimmer's setting of core strength stability in the pool, as he or she has learned to do on land.

When the swimmer understands and can perform wrist up, flat wrist, wrist down, and midpoint sculling, he or she can do the following progressions, which incorporate body position, core strength work, kicking skills, and hand speed. The progressions should preferably be conducted immediately following a core strength or Swiss ball land-training routine.

The coach should initially teach each step in the progression as an individual skill. Later the swimmer combines all steps in the routine with no breaks and with the coach controlling the set.

The swimmer should perform each skill for 10 seconds, combining all steps for the first attempt. After becoming proficient at the activity, the athlete can increase to 20 seconds and so on. The time available could be the limiting factor for the total time spent on each action in the progression.

Before performing each skill in the progression the swimmer sets his or her core stability in the horizontal front scull with flat-wrist position and then performs the exercise.

On the steps of the progression that are single actions, the swimmer continues to perform that action for the duration of the time to be spent on that action. An example of this is step 5 in progression 1 (introduction level). If the swimmer is to work for 30 seconds, he or she performs as much of this action as possible in 30 seconds.

PROGRESSION 1: INTRODUCTION LEVEL

1	Horizontal front scull with flat wrist as shown in figure 9.2 on page 127. The swimmer returns to this skill after each progression.
2	Horizontal front scull wrist up as shown in figure 9.1, a through c, on page 127.
3	Horizontal front scull wrist down as shown in figure 9.3 on page 127.
4	Horizontal front scull wrist down, with maximum-effort kick. The swimmer can perform this step with a soft rubber inner ball bladder placed under the stomach for support.

5	Side lateral roll right. When rolling up to the side lateral position the hip comes up first and the shoulder second. The swimmer then performs the forward roll. One arm is extended, and the other arm is by the side. The side of the body that comes up out of the water is the side that has the arm by it, as shown in figures a through d.
6	Side lateral roll left.
7	Combination of side lateral right and left rotations.
8	Front somersault with a tight tuck. The swimmer starts in the flat-wrist sculling position and performs a double-arm pull, keeping the face in the water. After the front somersault the swimmer is in a streamlined position in the opposite direction.
9	Back somersault with a tight tuck. The swimmer starts in the flat-wrist sculling position and then performs a back somersault. After the back somersault the swimmer finishes in a streamlined position on the back. Figures a through c show the swimmer performing this step of the progression.
10	Choice of steps 1 to 9.

PROGRESSION 2: INTERMEDIATE LEVEL

11	The swimmer is on the back performing a tucked back scull. He or she lift the knees out of the water and brings them against the body. The swimmer is sculling in this position and staying on the same spot, as shown in figures a and b.

12	With the knees out of the water as in step 11, the swimmer rotates 360 degrees to the left.
13	With the knees out of the water as in step 11, the swimmer rotates 360 degrees to the right.
14	The flat-body rotation scull is shown in the figure below. The swimmer assumes the flat-body position and rotates 360 degrees to the left. During the rotation the swimmer should maintain body position. 
15	Flat-body rotation scull to the right.
16	The vertical freestyle kick is shown in the figure below. Hands go from the hips and lift above the head out of the water to the streamlined position in the air. The swimmer holds the streamlined position for a set period. 
17	Reverse vertical scull (arm-extended scull). The swimmer is upside-down in the water with hands toward the bottom and feet in the air. Figures a and b show the sculling action that the swimmer uses.  

18	Scull butterfly turn on the spot. The swimmer starts from the flat-scull position and performs a butterfly turn on the spot, as outlined in figures a through d. The swimmer finishes in the streamlined position, performing a butterfly kicking action.

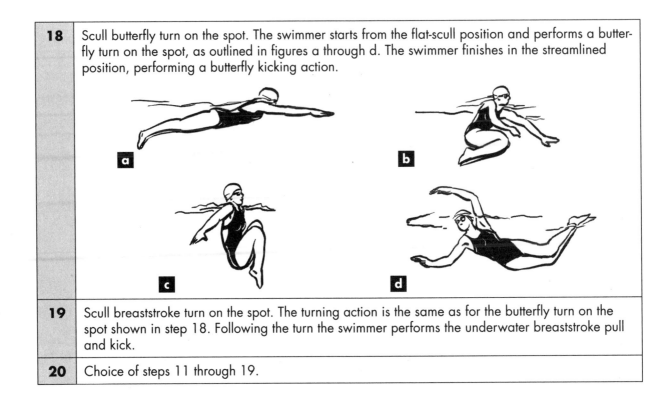

19	Scull breaststroke turn on the spot. The turning action is the same as for the butterfly turn on the spot shown in step 18. Following the turn the swimmer performs the underwater breaststroke pull and kick.
20	Choice of steps 11 through 19.

PROGRESSION 3: ADVANCED LEVEL

21	Scull butterfly to backstroke turn. The swimmer starts this progression in the flat-wrist sculling position and then performs the butterfly to backstroke turn on the spot finishing on the back in a streamlined position, performing a backstroke flutter kicking action. This is shown in figures a through c.

| 22 | Scull backstroke to breaststroke turn. The swimmer starts this step of the progression on the back with one arm extended, as he or she would be when hitting the wall for the turn. The swimmer then performs the turning action on the spot, tucking tightly for the spin. After straightening up, the swimmer performs the underwater pull and kick phase for breaststroke. Figure a shows the starting position, figure b shows the turning action, and figure c shows the straightening up following the turn. |

23	Scull breaststroke to freestyle turn. The turning action of this step of the progression is the same as that shown in step 18. The swimmer finishes in the streamlined position performing a freestyle kicking action.
24	Scull freestyle turn. The swimmer should turn as outlined in steps 5 and 6 of progression 1.
25	Scull breaststroke-to-breaststroke turn.
26	Scull butterfly-to-butterfly turn.

| 27 | Vertical butterfly kick as shown in figures a and b. Hands go from the hips and lift above the head out of the water to the streamlining position in the air. The swimmer performs the vertical butterfly kicking action. |

| 28 | Butterfly kick on the side as shown in figures a and b. The swimmer does the kick half the time on the right and then half on the left. |

| 29 | Combination of right and left rotations. |
| 30 | Choice of steps 21 through 29. |

Sculling is a great way for a swimmer to learn or improve feel for the water, which is important for all strokes. Sculling progressions are an excellent way to transfer the skills back into the full stroke. The progressions should be built into the swimmer's training program without compromising any other aspect of the program.

10

Starts, Turns, Finishes, and Relay Takeovers

Starts, turns, finishes, and relay takeovers can make the difference in the competitive performance of the swimmer. Although swimmers practice starts, turns, and finishes in every training session, the quality of the practice is what is important. Every set in training should start with a perfect competitive racing start to give the swimmer additional starting practice in each training week. Anything other than this reinforces less-than-perfect technique. Swimmers must do every turn correctly, regardless of the intensity of the training set. Similarly, swimmers must do every finish correctly throughout the training session. Relay takeovers are another specific skill that coaches and swimmers sometimes neglect. We believe that relays should be scheduled in workouts at least weekly to give swimmers an opportunity to practice the skill of takeovers.

Starts

Coaches need to ensure that swimmers work on starts throughout the season, not only in the week before the major competition. Every start that the swimmer performs in training should be a correct racing dive. At every workout the swimmer should start the warm-up and all sets with a racing dive. This is one way to have extra practice on starts. Whether the swimmer can do a racing dive in a warm-up at a competition depends on the rules that govern it. Before asking a swimmer to perform a racing start, the coach should test the swimmer in deep water and be confident that he or she is proficient in performing it.

© David Madison/Bruce Coleman, Inc.

Starts must be practiced throughout the season so that when competition rolls around the swimmer will have the technique mastered.

Grab Start

The grab start is one of the commonly used methods of starting in competitions. The feet should be slightly apart, just within shoulder-width, and the toes should be curled over the edge of the block for stability and control. As the swimmer bends forward on the block, the center of gravity will move from the sternum to the base of the spine. Bending the knees slightly will put as much of the upper body as possible over the block. The swimmer grips the front of the block firmly with the hands, either inside or outside the feet. The hips push up to shift the center of gravity back to the pit of the stomach; most of the weight will have now moved to the front of the block. In figure 10.1 the swimmer is gripping the block inside the feet, not using the handles of the starting block. In figure 10.2 the swimmer is using the handles of the block for the starting position. This method puts the swimmer in the correct position to drive the center of gravity through the hips.

Athletes must be able to get into these positions comfortably. They can do that by having great flexibility and range of movement.

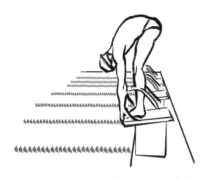

FIGURE 10.1 *Grab start position.*

FIGURE 10.2 *Grab start position, using handles.*

On the starting signal the swimmer pushes forward with the arms and brings the hips forward quickly, driving through the legs. The knees are slightly bent, giving the swimmer greater stability on the block. The swimmer needs to drive through the hips, not just the legs.

In figure 10.3a the swimmer is in flight following the start with the arms moving forward. In figure 10.3b the arms have reached their extended position, which occurs just before the head drops. In figure 10.3c the swimmer has progressed in the air and will enter the water in a piked position, which is clearly shown. The swimmer attained the piked position by dropping the head from the raised position, shown in figure 10.3b following the initial thrust off the block, to a position between the arms, shown in figure 10.3c.

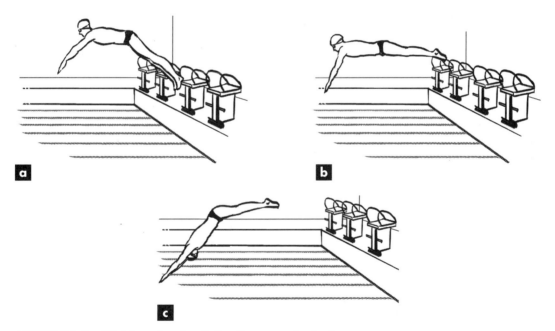

FIGURE 10.3 *Flight and entry following a grab start.*

Track Start

Another commonly used starting position is the track start. If you coach a swimmer who prefers to use this starting position, you will need to establish which foot the swimmer places at the front of the block. With the swimmer starting in a relaxed standing position, gently push the swimmer from behind without warning. Whichever leg goes forward to achieve balance is the leg the swimmer should have forward on the track start.

The track start has two variations: arms back, as shown in figure 10.4, and arms forward, as shown in figure 10.5, as the swimmer leaves the block. The swimmer can use the handles on the block if available when performing a track start.

The advantage of using the track start is that swimmers react faster off the block and therefore enter the water faster. This start will also give them a smaller angle on entry, which is advantageous when starting in shallow pools.

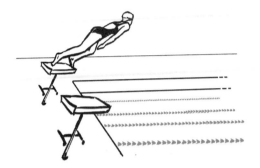

FIGURE 10.4   *Track start with arms back.*

FIGURE 10.5   *Track start with arms forward.*

Hoop Dives

A good drill for the swimmer to practice to ensure a clean entry on the start is hoop dives. One splash is what you should hear as the swimmer enters the water by traveling through a hoop placed (or held) on the surface of the water. The hands should enter the water first, followed by the wrists, elbows, head and shoulders, hips, legs, and feet. A reverse practice for this is a jump off the springboard in the diving pool (Sweetenham 1998i).

Checklists for the Start of Each Stroke

Every start in training must be a competition racing start. Butterfly kicking is used from the start on butterfly, backstroke, and freestyle. The reason for using the butterfly kicks is to maintain speed from the start, not for distance underwater.

Practice does not make perfect, perfect practice makes perfect.

A way of ensuring that swimmers practice starts is to insist that each new set of the training session begins with a racing start.

The coach and swimmer should consider the following points for each stroke when working on starts.

Butterfly Start Checklist

- To maximize speed off the dive, the swimmer should not begin butterfly kicks underwater immediately off the start. The swimmer holds the streamlined position until a point just before starting to slow. The butterfly kicks begin at this point. The first kicks are quite slow. As the kicks speed up, they become shorter and shallower than normal stroking, without excessive undulation. The swimmer should have a firm upper body.

- The swimmer maintains streamlining and underwater butterfly kicking for a maximum distance of 15 m. The swimmer who is not proficient at underwater butterfly kicking should work on this in training to attain proficiency rather than accept performing with a less efficient technique.

- The swimmer completes at least two strokes before breathing.
- The swimmer should aim to hit racing stroke rate from the first stroke.

Backstroke Start Checklist

- The swimmer grips the block at the front bar with the fingers over the top of the bar and the thumbs under the bar.
- The feet are positioned just under the water surface approximately shoulder-width apart.
- The swimmer can position one foot higher than the other to help prevent the feet from slipping down the wall during the start.
- The arms throw backward, aiming to carry the body and hips over the water. The swimmer drives through the hips.
- The entry into the water should be streamlined, with a lifting of the legs on entry. Figure 10.6a shows the swimmer in a streamlined position.
- Streamlining underwater is important, and the swimmer should keep the head between the arms during this phase.
- To maximize speed off the dive, the swimmer should not begin butterfly kicks underwater immediately off the start. The swimmer holds the streamlined position until a point just before starting to slow. The butterfly kicks begin at this point. The first kicks are quite slow. As the kicks speed up, they become shorter and shallower than normal stroking, without excessive undulation. The swimmer should have a firm upper body.
- The swimmer should maintain the streamlining and the butterfly kicks underwater for a maximum distance of 15 m. Butterfly kicks are shown in figure 10.6b. The swimmer who is not proficient at underwater butterfly kicking should work on attaining proficiency in training rather than accept performing with a less efficient technique.
- The swimmer makes a transition to a flutter kick just before breaking the surface and should not stop the leg motion, as shown in figure 10.6c.

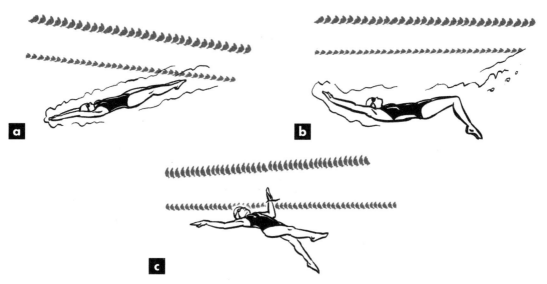

FIGURE 10.6   *Backstroke start shown underwater.*

Breaststroke Start Checklist

- The swimmer should streamline into the water following the dive to minimize resistance on entry.

- A powerful underwater pull and push-through are important. This underwater pull should be a keyhole (or hourglass) pattern, with the hands finishing the push-through by the side of the thighs. The elbows should be in a high fixed position during the outward and then inward sweep, as shown in figure 10.7a. This underwater pull should not begin immediately because the swimmer should develop maximum speed and distance off the wall while in the streamlined position.

- The head should stay in line with the body during the underwater phase and not drop out of alignment. Figure 10.7b shows the head staying in alignment during the underwater phase of the arm stroke. In this figure the hands and arms are about to start the push phase of the stroke. In 10.7c the pull phase has been completed and streamlining is maintained.

- As the hands and arms recover underwater after the pull and push, they stay close to the body with the elbows tight to the body to minimize resistance during this part of the underwater phase, as shown in figure 10.7c. The legs are recovering, ready for the kick phase of the underwater action.

- The swimmer performs a powerful leg kick as the arms extend forward past the head, as shown in figure 10.7d. The arms must be extended and streamlined to maximize propulsion from the kick by minimizing resistance.

- The head should break the surface of the water during the outward sweep of the first arm stroke to prevent any disqualification for two underwater pulls.

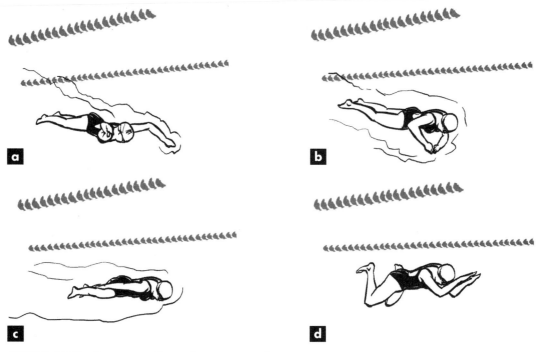

FIGURE 10.7   Breaststroke underwater action.

Freestyle Start Checklist

- The swimmer should streamline into the water following the dive to minimize resistance on entry.
- Butterfly kicks can be effective if the swimmer performs them well.
- To maximize speed off the dive, the swimmer should not begin butterfly kicks underwater immediately off the start. The swimmer holds the streamlined position until a point just before starting to slow. The butterfly kicks begin at this point. The first kicks are quite slow. As the kicks speed up, they become shorter and shallower than normal stroking, without excessive undulation. The swimmer should have a firm upper body.
- The swimmer should maintain the streamlining and the butterfly kicks underwater for a maximum distance of 15 m.
- Just before breaking the surface, the swimmer should change from a dolphin kick to a flutter kick, without allowing leg movement to stop.
- The swimmer should swim a maximum distance of 15 m underwater off the dive and turns.
- Swimming should begin before the first breath is taken.

Butterfly, Backstroke, and Freestyle Starts and Turns

The swimmer in conjunction with the coach needs to establish the distance that he or she should travel underwater from the start and out of the turn. Remember that butterfly kicks are performed to maintain and maximize speed off the start and turns. The swimmer must therefore practice starts and turns with different numbers of butterfly kicks to establish the approach that will result in the best race performance. Chapter 2 has a series of speed tests that the swimmer and coach should conduct to establish best practice for the swimmer on the starts and turns.

Backstroke Start Drill

The swimmer does a competition backstroke start and follows this with 10 butterfly kicks in the streamlined body position. Following the start and the 10 butterfly kicks the swimmer pulls through with the hands and arms to the side of the body and then slides the hands up the thighs until they reach as far down the lower legs as they can. The swimmer does this by sitting up through the action. While sliding the hands up the legs, the swimmer should be performing a maximum-effort kick.

The coach calls "Go" when the swimmer has reached the position described, and the swimmer then performs a backstroke start followed by 10 butterfly kicks before repeating the outlined sequence. The coach can control the amount of time the swimmer performs the maximum-effort kick before calling for the starting action.

Another way of doing this drill is for the swimmer to perform underwater dolphin kick in a streamlined position and a double-arm underwater pull on approaching the surface. As the hands get to the swimmer's side, he or she performs a double-arm throw back over the water and continues to perform the drill for the required distance.

BACKSTROKE START PROGRESSION

1	The swimmer should stand in the water, place the chin on the chest, and then jump high out of the water, aiming to land on the middle of the upper back. The arms are by the side. The water should be chest deep. This step of the progression is shown in figures a and b.
2	The next step is to perform step 1 over the lane rope. The swimmer can duck under to start and then jump back. The aim is to avoid touching the lane rope from the knees up. The hips should be high and the arms by the swimmer's side, as shown in figures a and b.
3	Like step 2, except the swimmer kicks out while going over the rope with the arms by the side.
4	This part of the progression is conducted in deep water (such as the diving pool). The swimmer starts by performing a backstroke start from the third step of the pool ladders. As the swimmer performs the start, the arms always stay by the side.
5	Like step 4, except the swimmer moves up one step on the pool ladders (in deep water such as the diving pool).
6	Like step 5, except the swimmer moves up to the top step.
7	The swimmer does a back dive from the edge of the pool with the arms by the side (reverse dive in deep water such as the diving pool).
8	The swimmer performs a normal backstroke start from a block.
Steps 4 to 7 must be conducted in deep water.	

(Sweetenham 1998i)

Freestyle Start and Turn Drill

This test can be used for starts, turns, finishes, and as a speed set, with or without a paddle. The swimmer wears a paddle on the weak arm for each pull out of the start and pulls into and out of the turns.

Competition start on command then
Sprint three strokes and turn, midpool
Sprint seven strokes and turn, at the wall
Sprint five strokes and turn, midpool
Sprint nine strokes and finish

or

Competition start on command then
Sprint five strokes and turn, midpool
Sprint nine strokes and turn, at the wall
Sprint three strokes and turn, midpool
Sprint seven strokes and turn

The swimmer will perform 24 strokes with the goal of traveling 50 m. The coach should mark the head position on each midpool turn to facilitate measurement of the distance swum. The distance swum added together should total 50 m. The swimmer should then do the set again, holding the distance swum and reducing the time for the test to as close as possible to personal best 50 m time. The younger swimmer may add two strokes to the previous values (that is, 7 strokes and turn, 11 strokes and turn, 5 strokes and turn, and so on) but continue to improve to the shown values.

This progression can also be adapted for use with the backstroke swimmer (Atkinson and Sweetenham 1999).

Turns

Every turn in training must be a competition racing turn, regardless of training intensity. The lower the training intensity, the greater the demand for skillfully executed turns.

Coaches should allow the swimmer to turn both ways in the training lane, training in a counterclockwise direction as well as a clockwise direction. Many stroke problems seem to develop because the swimmer always circles the lanes in the same direction. The coach may want to have the swimmer alternate lanes, swimming clockwise and counterclockwise during training sessions, or change directions from morning to evening sessions.

People will always debate the accepted standard of turns performed. As we all know, turns can make the difference between a good swim and a bad swim. Swimmers often learn how to perform turns correctly but then seem to fall into bad habits. To improve the effectiveness of turns, coaches have to look at the way they do things currently, in both teaching groups and coaching groups.

The progression through swimming lessons to the swimming club is a continuum. At times, coaching involves teaching something new. Although teaching can be described as helping someone acquire a new skill and coaching as aiding the development of that skill, all swimmers require a coach who can be part teacher.

From their first swimming lesson, young children are being taught the basis for advanced competition skills. The swimmer may arrive in the club with a bad habit of incorrectly pushing off the wall. The coach who allows the swimmer to continue the same bad habit reinforces it within a group environment. Coaches and teachers should work to ensure that swimmers arrive at the club with good habits so that time is not wasted by having to correct previously taught skills.

When swimmers are under the stress of a race and fatigued, they revert to habit! Telling swimmers before a race to streamline will have no effect on most of them because when they race they perform the way they have trained themselves to turn.

As a coach, you must never stand at the end of the pool and watch poor turns during training. You must be uncompromising in asking swimmers to raise themselves to high standards rather than let training standards fall to those of the worst swimmer in the group. If a swimmer has a problem, you should try to fix it.

How many times has your squad asked to practice turns? Swimmers usually want to practice turns by standing 10 m out from the wall and sprinting in to perform a turn when they are fresh! From time to time this type of turning practice is helpful, but how many turns are performed during training sets? Certainly, correct practice under pressure and when experiencing fatigue is closer to the real-life racing situation.

You will see more incorrect turns toward the end of the race when swimmers are stressed and fatigued than you will see at the beginning of the race. When you are conducting training sets in the high-performance endurance zone or as race-pace work or any other type of set, you should insist that swimmers perform perfect turns. If the coach insists on perfect turns from swimmers while they are under stress and fatigued, they will perform turns correctly under race conditions. The stressed, fatigued swimmer will return to habit (Atkinson 1998a).

Checklists for the Turn of Each Stroke

As already stated, every turn in training must be a competition racing turn regardless of training intensity. The lower the training intensity, the greater the application of skill and body control at the turn. Below are some points for each stroke that the coach and swimmer should consider when working on turns.

Butterfly kicking is used on butterfly, backstroke, and freestyle off the wall following the turn. The reason for using butterfly kicks is to maintain speed from the push-off, not to achieve distance underwater.

Butterfly Turning Checklist

- By being aware of how many kicks he or she performs on the start, the swimmer can hit the first turn on a full stroke.
- The knees should tuck tightly under the body as the two-handed touch is made to ensure that the rotation is fast.
- One arm pulls back under water and the other arm recovers over the water during the turning action.
- The recovering hand enters the water forward and slightly behind the head.
- As the swimmer drives off the wall he or she should have the hands together when exploding through the knees and hips to maintain streamlining.
- As the swimmer pushes off the wall he or she should be sure to maintain a streamlined position from the arms through to the pointed toes. The head should be between the arms, neither too high nor too low.

- While streamlining underwater the swimmer should perform the predetermined number of dolphin kicks to ensure hitting the next turn or the finish on a full stroke.
- The swimmer should stay underwater off the push and streamline to avoid the rough water. A head position that is too high or too low causes resistance.
- The dolphin kicks should be fast and vigorous, ensuring maintenance of a streamlined position.
- The swimmer should recommence swimming before taking the first breath.
- The swimmer should be able to turn both ways (left and right) and should practice this in training so that the skill is available for use in races.
- A time of 0.8 seconds or faster from the hands hitting the wall to the feet hitting the wall is an acceptable standard. The swimmer should achieve a time of 0.3 seconds from the feet touching the wall to the feet leaving the wall.

Backstroke Turning Checklist

- As the swimmer approaches the turn and rotates off the back, he or she should use the recovering arm by crossing over the body and entering the water while turning onto the front. The swimmer can then use the extended arm to pull into the turn.
- When turning, the chin goes to the chest with a minidolphin kick and the abdominal muscles tighten (by pulling the belly button to the backbone). The swimmer holds the chin on the chest and maintains it there until streamlining off the wall. The pull into the turn and the dolphin kick must be part of a continuous turning action.
- The knees need to tuck tightly to ensure that the rotation is fast.
- In pushing off the wall, the swimmer should be sure to maintain a streamlined position from the arms through to the pointed toes.
- While streamlining underwater the swimmer should perform the predetermined number of dolphin kicks to ensure hitting the next turn or the finish on a full stroke.
- The dolphin kicks should be fast and vigorous, ensuring maintenance of a streamlined position. This should transfer into a flutter kick as the swimmer starts the first arm stroke after the turn.
- The swimmer should stay underwater off the push and streamline to avoid the rough water. By maintaining a head position between the arms, neither too high nor too low, the swimmer minimizes resistance.

Breaststroke Turning Checklist

- The knees should tuck tightly under the body as the two-handed touch is made to a fast rotation.
- One arm pulls back under water, and the other arm recovers over the water.
- The recovering hand enters the water forward and slightly behind the head.
- The body rotates to the side of the arm that pulls back.
- Following the streamlined push-off, in which the swimmer maintains the head position between the arms, the swimmer starts the underwater pull. The shape of this pull is similar to that of used for butterfly (keyhole shape). During this pull the swimmer must maintain the level position of the head.

- The underwater pull will finish with both arms by the side of the thighs.
- The underwater recovery of the arms then commences as the legs begin to recover. To maintain streamlining, the hands and arms must stay close to the body during this recovery.
- As the arms stretch forward from underneath the face, the legs perform a breaststroke kicking action. The head stays in a downward position during this phase of the turn.
- Following the extension of the arms and the breaststroke kick, the head will break the surface during the outsweep of the pull. If the hands have started the insweep before the head breaks the surface, the swimmer will be disqualified.
- A time of 0.8 seconds or faster from hands hitting the wall to the feet hitting the wall is an acceptable standard. The swimmer should achieve a time of 0.3 seconds from the feet touching the wall to the feet leaving the wall.

Freestyle Turning Checklist
- When turning, the chin goes to the chest with a minidolphin kick and the abdominal muscles tighten (by pulling the belly button to the backbone). The swimmer holds the chin on the chest and maintains it there until streamlining off the wall.
- The swimmer kicks the heels to the butt while going through the turn.
- The swimmer should pull himself or herself into the turn. The swimmer should not finish the push-through with the arm that took the final stroke and then start the turn with both arms by the side of the body.
- Twisting does not occur on the wall. After hitting the wall, the swimmer pushes off and streamlines, twisting after the push.
- While pushing off the wall, the swimmer should maintain a streamlined position from the arms through to the pointed toes.
- The swimmer should stay underwater off the push, streamline to avoid the rough water, and maintain the head position between the arms. A position either too high or too low causes resistance.
- The dolphin kicks should be fast and vigorous, ensuring maintenance of a streamlined position. This should transfer into a flutter kick as the swimmer starts the first arm stroke after the turn.

IM Turns

When performing the butterfly-to-backstroke, backstroke-to-breaststroke, and breaststroke-to-freestyle turns in the individual medley, a time 0.8 second from the hands hitting the wall to the feet hitting the wall is an acceptable standard. The swimmer should achieve a time of 0.3 seconds from the feet touching the wall to the feet leaving the wall.

Turning Drills for Freestyle and Backstroke

Turning drills help the swimmer work on improving specific aspects of turns. This section will outline turning drills that are appropriate for all levels of swimmers. The drills can incorporate speed work with racing stroke rates to make them even more specific to the swimmer's requirements.

FREESTYLE LANE ROPE TURNS INTRODUCTORY PROGRESSION

When teaching the turn over the lane ropes, it is easy to use the lane ropes, keeping the following points in mind.	
1	The swimmer stands with the feet shoulder-width apart and then practices going over the lane rope. He or she grasps the lane rope with a thumb-under position, hands shoulder-width apart, and elbows slightly bent. The swimmer uses the lane rope to pull over the rope.
2	The swimmer performs step 1 quickly.
3	The swimmer pushes off the wall under the first lane rope and turns over the second lane rope as in step 2.
4	The swimmer pushes off the wall, goes under the first two lane ropes, and turns over the third lane rope as in step 2.
After the swimmer can achieve steps 1 to 4 he or she progresses to the following:	
5	The swimmer starts by facing the wall and kicking at maximum effort. He or she places the chin on the chest, holds for five seconds, and then pulls and turns. The pull is downward, not outward.
6	The swimmer repeats step 5, adding four dolphin kicks while pushing off the wall.
7	This step starts with the swimmer performing a jump turn in deep water. The swimmer jumps up and down on the T, at the bottom of the pool, and then explodes off the bottom, pushing the chin against the chest and performing a turn on the wall. The swimmer should practice this slowly before progressing to performing the turn at speed. Care should be used when practicing this turn in deck-level pools.
8	Practice of underwater turns prevents the legs from being too high through the turn. On reaching the backstroke flags, the swimmer goes into a streamlined position (head looking to the bottom), kicking to the wall and then turning, trying to cut down all resistance in a slow-motion turn during which no part of the body comes out of the water.
9	When the swimmer performs the kickboard turn, the coach should observe the speed of the kickboard. The kickboard should not stop moving once it has been released by one arm. A backward movement of the board means that the swimmer did not turn immediately on releasing the board with one hand or did not kick the heels to the butt.

After completing this progression, the swimmer should be ready to turn and go over the lane line without pulling on the lane line, as follows:

1. The swimmer starts with a kick or jump turn, pushes off the wall under the first two lane ropes, and turns over the third lane line using both arms to pull over the line.
2. The swimmer repeats step 1 using one arm to pull over the lane rope.
3. Like step 2, except that the swimmer pulls one arm back after the second lane rope, starts to turn by pulling the other arm back just before the third lane rope, continues the turn, and goes over the lane rope (on this third step the swimmer turns without using the hand on the lane rope).

Once the swimmer has mastered this he or she can progress to the lane-rope advanced-turning progression (Atkinson and Sweetenham 1999; Sweetenham 1998i).

FREESTYLE LANE-ROPE TURNS ADVANCED PROGRESSION

Three-two-one or one-two-three (3-2-1 or 1-2-3). This progression should be conducted in 2.5 m lanes. Juniors to try achieve the same times in 2 m lanes.

1	The swimmer starts by facing the side wall of the pool while kicking and then performs a kick turn. He or she then completes a turn and pushes off the wall as shown in figure a.
2	The swimmer follows the turn with underwater streamlined kicking, going underneath the lane ropes as shown in figure b.
3	The swimmer pulls one arm back after the second lane rope and starts the turn by pulling the other arm back just before the third lane rope, continuing the turn by going over the third lane line. In figure c the swimmer is pulling back with both arms. He or she would progress from this to pulling with one arm before the other. In figure d the swimmer is turning over the lane rope.
4	The coach can then position another swimmer holding a kickboard just beyond the third lane rope. The swimmer performs the steps as outlined earlier in steps 1 through 3, plants the feet on the kickboard, and returns underwater to the starting wall. Hitting the kickboard is called a "kickboard explosion."
5	Following the kickboard explosion, the swimmer returns underwater in a streamlined position to the wall, breathes, and turns off the wall. The swimmer streamlines to the second lane rope and turns over this second lane rope (performing a kickboard explosion) as outlined previously.
6	The swimmer again returns to the wall, breathes, and then turns and pushes off the wall. He or she goes over the first lane rope (performing a kickboard explosion) and returns to the wall.

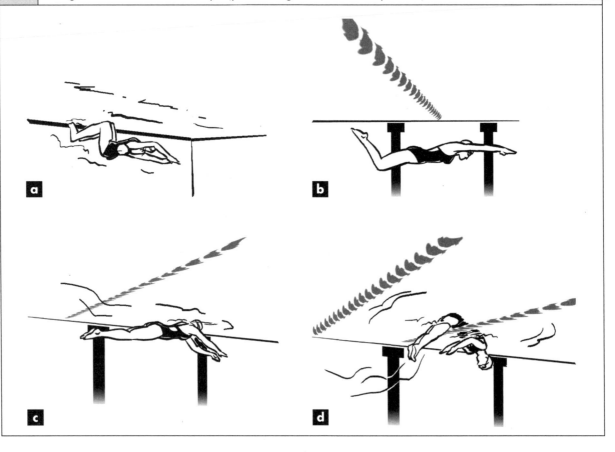

Target times to achieve from start to kickboard explosion are as follows, elapsed time to the feet hitting the kickboard:

Beyond the third lane rope is three and a half seconds.

Beyond the second lane rope is two and a half seconds.

Beyond the first lane rope is one and a half seconds.

The backstroke swimmer goes to the sixth lane rope (which equals 15 m), aiming to do this in six and a half seconds. This simulates 15 m push-offs, which the swimmer may use off each turn. The swimmer starts kicking at the wall and then turns and pushes from the wall on the back as shown in figure 10.8a. Figure 10.8b shows the swimmer working underwater on the back until reaching the point to turn from the back to the front and then over the lane rope, which is shown in figure 10.8c. Figure 10.8d shows the swimmer returning to the wall on the back following the turn over the lane rope (Atkinson and Sweetenham 1999).

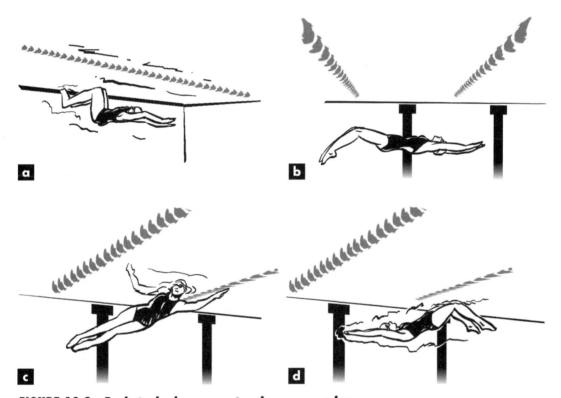

FIGURE 10.8   *Backstroke lane rope turning progression.*

When starting this progression the swimmer can do each section and stop after completing it. The swimmer aims to progress to doing the whole drill without a break. The target time for senior male swimmers to do the whole progression without stopping is 23 seconds or less; for senior female swimmers the target is 26 seconds or less.

When turning, the chin goes to the chest with a minidolphin kick and the abdominal muscles are tightened (by pulling the belly button to the backbone).

Target times can be adjusted to suit the individual requirements of the swimmer, but the swimmer should be training these skills above the current performance level (Atkinson and Sweetenham 1999; Sweetenham 1998i).

Slow-Motion Swim With Fast Turn Drill for Freestyle and Backstroke

A great drill for improving the rotation speed for freestyle and backstroke turns is slow-motion swimming with a fast turn that is timed from hand entry on the final stroke into the turn to the feet hitting the wall following the rotation.

The swimmer swims a set distance in slow motion. As the hand enters the water on the final hand entry before the turn, the swimmer must pull into the turn at faster than racing speed, tuck into the turn, and rotate onto the wall. The target time from final hand entry to the feet hitting the wall is 0.6 seconds.

To turn quickly, the swimmer must turn using the upper body and core strength; the advantage of the momentum of the speed from swimming is not available to help the swimmer turn quickly. This drill will help the swimmer improve the speed from hand entry to the feet hitting the wall.

Midpool Turns

To perform a midpool turn, a swimmer turns in the middle of the lane with no wall and swims back in the direction from which he or she started. Swimmers perform midpool turns at their individual desired racing stroke rate. Midpool turns can be done individually or as a group activity. Swimmers can do midpool turns in many ways and on all strokes. Practice should start with stationary midpool turns and progress to practice with double and triple spins and with training equipment before progressing to midpool turns performed at racing stroke rate.

Stationary Midpool Turns for Freestyle and Backstroke

The swimmer lies on the water with one arm extended. In slow motion the swimmer rotates from the hip and then the shoulder into a side lateral position. The swimmer then turns from the side lateral position. As the swimmer becomes more skilled, the speed of movement, that is, the speed of the turning action, should increase (Atkinson and Sweetenham 1999; Sweetenham 1998i).

Freestyle and Backstroke Midpool Turns

The swimmer starts from a horizontal sculling position. Any combination or single or triple turns can be used with or without hand paddles, with one hand paddle, or with fins, drag suit, weight belt, or other equipment (Atkinson and Sweetenham 1999; Sweetenham 1998i).

Freestyle Midpool Turning Tests at Race Pace

The swimmer starts this drill in the horizontal front sculling position in midpool and performs the following progression:

1   At 1500 m stroke rate, 2 or 3 strokes, turn, and scull back to center.
2   At 400 m–800 m stroke rate, 4 or 5 strokes, turn, and scull back to center.
3   At 400 m stroke rate, 6 or 7 strokes, turn, and scull back to center.
4   At 200 m stroke rate, 8 or 9 strokes, turn, and scull back to center.
5   At 100 m–50 m stroke rate, 10 or 11 strokes, turn, and scull back to center.

In a 25 m pool the number of strokes is cut in half.

Sculling back to the center is one of the options the coach may use with the swimmer. Other options are to have the swimmer turn and go straight into the next section or to turn and wait for the coach to start the next section.

The number of strokes taken before turning can also be changed; it could be 4, 8, 12, 16, or 20. Stroke rates will change accordingly. A mixture of stroke-rate changes can be used on midpool turning progressions (Atkinson and Sweetenham 1999; Sweetenham 1998i).

Freestyle and Backstroke Jump Turns

A freestyle jump turn is executed from a standing position in midpool. The aim is to go as high as possible out of the water, somersault, and land back on the same spot. As the swimmer performs this turn, the chin is tucked onto the chest. Figure 10.9, a through c, shows this turning action.

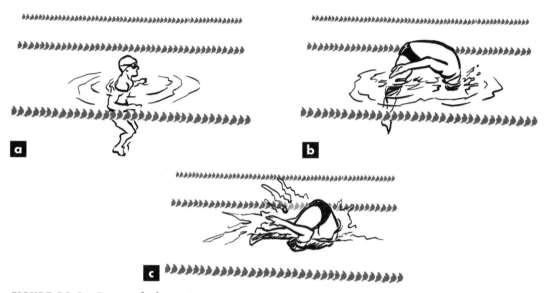

FIGURE 10.9   *Freestyle jump turn.*

When performing a backstroke jump turn, the swimmer tries to throw one arm over the opposite shoulder, tuck the chin, and somersault, as shown in figure 10.10, a through c.

Performing two, three, or even four or five jump turns in a row is excellent practice for tumble turn skills.

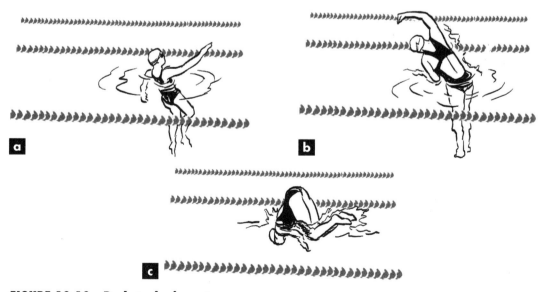

FIGURE 10.10   *Backstroke jump turn.*

Freestyle Kickboard Turns

During freestyle kick sets, the swimmer can be allowed to do a kickboard turn (that is, a tumble turn while holding the kickboard). As the swimmer approaches the turn, he or she pulls the kickboard back. The coach should watch the kickboard during the turn to monitor whether the turning action is smooth and unbroken. After the swimmer has pulled into the turn, the kickboard should not move toward the wall that the swimmer is turning on. If the coach sees the kickboard moving in that direction, there is a broken section in the turning action. Watched from the side, the turning action should reveal no stops (Sweetenham 1998i; Atkinson and Sweetenham 1999).

Turning Drills for Butterfly and Breaststroke

As with freestyle and backstroke, drills have been developed for butterfly and breaststroke to improve specific aspects of turning. This section will outline turning drills appropriate for all levels of swimmers. The drills can incorporate speed work with racing stroke rates to make them even more specific to the swimmer's requirements.

Midpool Turns

The progression is to have the swimmer perform stationary midpool turns before swimming at specific stroke rates. After mastering those turns, the swimmer can do the butterfly and breaststroke flags-to-flags turning drills.

Stationary Midpool Turns for Breaststroke and Butterfly

The swimmer should set core strength while sculling and kicking. He or she then brings the heels close to the buttocks to form a ball with the body and kicks out as if to turn. The target is to perform three turns in less than three seconds (Atkinson and Sweetenham 1999; Sweetenham 1998i).

Breaststroke and Butterfly Midpool Turns

The stroke count used in the individual medley can be used here. The swimmer starts at halfway in a horizontal sculling position and runs through the following for a 50 m pool. In a 25 m pool the number of strokes is cut in half.

- Midpool turn, 8 strokes swimming, midpool turn
- 8 strokes pulling only, midpool turn
- 8 strokes swimming, midpool turn
- 8 kicks (16 for butterfly), midpool turn

Continue by adding one stroke for the 200 m swimmer or two strokes for the 100 m swimmer on each set until the swimmer reaches one end of the pool or does not maintain the stroke rate.

For individual medley, breaststroke, and butterfly, the drill can start with any number of strokes and increase gradually (Atkinson and Sweetenham 1999; Sweetenham 1998i).

Breaststroke and Butterfly Flags-to-Flags Turning Drill

When the swimmer can attain three stationary midpool turns in three seconds or faster, he or she can progress to this turning drill. The swimmer starts in the front kicking sculling position (wrist down) underneath the flags (that is, the head would be at 5 m, and the swimmer would be facing the opposite end of the pool).

The swimmer performs a midpool turn underneath the flags on command from the coach. Following the turn the swimmer will be facing the wall where the turn will occur. The midpool turn is shown in figure 10.11a. The swimmer then swims three strokes to get to the wall, as figure 10.11b demonstrates for breaststroke (breaststroke could be one underwater pull and one stroke).

The coach can measure the time from the hands touching the wall to the feet hitting the wall. The goal is 0.8 seconds or faster. The feet should be on the wall for 0.3 seconds or faster. Figure 10.11c shows the turning action.

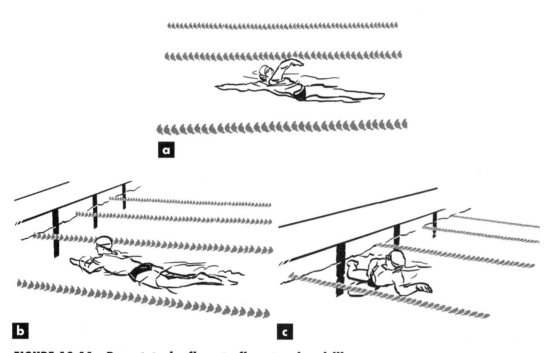

FIGURE 10.11   Breaststroke flags-to-flags turning drill.

As the swimmer hits the wall, he or she does one turn in the first instance and then pushes off the wall. The coach times this drill by starting the watch on "Go" as the swimmer is under the flags and stopping it as the head passes the flags coming out of the turn. The following targets apply to the four variations of the drill (Atkinson and Sweetenham 1999; Sweetenham 1998i).

One turn to start and one turn at the wall in 7 seconds or faster

One turn to start and three turns at the wall in 9 seconds or faster

Three turns to start and one turn at the wall in 9 seconds or faster

Three turns to start and three turns at the wall in 11 seconds or faster

Breaststroke and Butterfly Turn on an Up Drill

The swimmer swims into the turn and on reaching 5 m from the wall submerges underwater and performs streamlined kick. The swimmer gradually surfaces on approaching the wall, hits the turn on an up, performs the turn, and swims out (Sweetenham 1998i; Atkinson and Sweetenham 1999).

Finishes

Every finish in training must be a competition racing finish regardless of training intensity. The slower the training intensity, the greater the application of skill and body control at the finish. The finish is an important skill that all swimmers must perfect. The swimmer in the lead does not always win the race if he or she has a poor finish. The swimmer can develop the ability to perform a perfect finish when fatigued at the end of the race if the coach insists on perfect finishes on all sets in training. The checklists in this chapter will give the swimmer important points to work on in training.

Checklists for the Finish of Each Stroke

The following are some points for each stroke that the coach and swimmer should consider when working on finishes.

Butterfly Finishes Checklist

- The finish in butterfly may be affected by how the swimmer comes off the final turn because a reduced underwater turning distance will alter the stroke count on that lap. Consistent turning length and stroke count will ensure a proper finish.
- The swimmer must try to maintain distance per stroke on the final lap of the race. If the swimmer shortens the stroke, he or she may need an extra half stroke to hit the wall on the finish. The swimmer who needs to adjust the stroke for the finish should have worked that out before the final pull to the finish. The final stroke is shown in figure 10.12a.
- On a finish, the head and face should be between the arms to maximize the stretch to the wall. The swimmer should maintain propulsion from the kick during this streamlined finish. The upper body, arms, and head should all be streamlined to maintain speed.
- During the finish, the hands should be close to the surface, not above the surface.

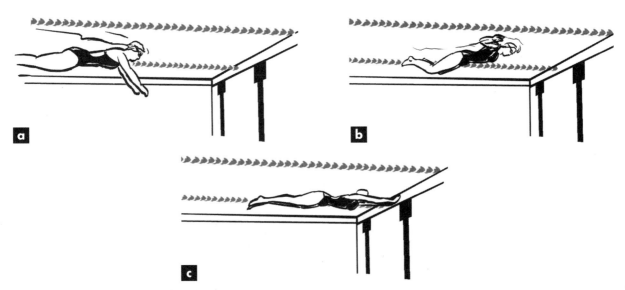

FIGURE 10.12 Butterfly finish.

- The butterfly swimmer should hit the finish with the arms extended, not on a half stroke. In figure 10.12b the arms are over the water with the face staying in the water. In figure 10.12c the swimmer hits the wall on a full stroke.

- If the butterfly swimmer is short stroked, he or she should streamline and kick rather than perform a small sculling action that could be considered a breast-stroke pull and underwater arm recovery. The small pull or scull will lead to a disqualification on the finish.

Backstroke Finishes Checklist

- The swimmer should count strokes to enable a finish on the wall with a full stroke.

- We suggest that the swimmer count strokes from the flags because they are a constant distance (5 m) from the wall. The backstroke swimmer should count strokes for the entire lap to avoid arriving under the flags midstroke and therefore misjudging the finish.

- The swimmer should also be aware that the number of butterfly kicks performed underwater off the start and each turn will affect the number of arm strokes required for that lap. If the swimmer normally takes eight fly kicks underwater and performs 30 strokes for the lap but takes only six fly kicks coming out of the last turn, that last lap will require more arm strokes. The swimmer must also maintain distance per stroke through the last lap to build consistency on every finish.

- The swimmer should roll toward the arm as it extends to hit the wall.

- While extending into the finish with the arm, the swimmer must be sure to maintain a strong kick onto the wall. Some coaches even suggest to their athletes that they perform a fly kick to keep the momentum moving to the finish, as shown in figure 10.13, a through c.

- The swimmer should be sure not to overreach to the finish. If the shoulders go past 90 degrees (relative to the water surface), the swimmer is technically off the back and may risk disqualification.

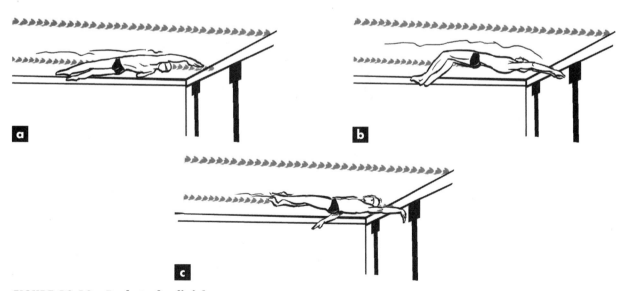

FIGURE 10.13   Backstroke finish.

Breaststroke Finishes Checklist

- What the swimmer does coming out of the final turn can also affect the finish in breaststroke. If the distance underwater is not consistent with the normal underwater pull, the swimmer may surface short and therefore be half a stroke short on the finish.
- The swimmer must maintain distance per stroke down the final lap. If stroke length shortens, the swimmer may need an extra half stroke to hit the wall at the finish.
- The breaststroke swimmer should focus on the wall in the approach to the finish. The finish is made with downward pressure from the hands with the arms extended, pushing the head down and forward to maximize forward stretch. The final stretch should occur as the legs are driving backward into the propulsive phase of the kick; this action will maintain the momentum into the wall. The upper body (arms and head) should be streamlined to maintain speed to the finish.
- As the arms reach forward for the finish, they should be near the surface, as shown in figure 10.14a, not above the water.
- The breaststroke swimmer should hit the finish with the arms extended as in figure 10.14b, not on a half stroke.
- If the breaststroke swimmer is short stroked, he or she should streamline in and get the most from the kick rather than start another stroke.

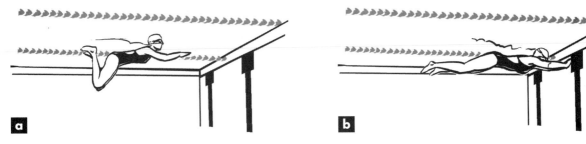

FIGURE 10.14   Breaststroke finish.

Freestyle Finishes Checklist

- The swimmer should never take a breath between the flags and the wall.
- On the last stroke into the wall, the swimmer should push the head against the arm that is extending and roll the body to gain maximum stretch. In figure 10.15a the swimmer is performing the final stroke. Figure 10.15b shows maximum stretch and rotation.

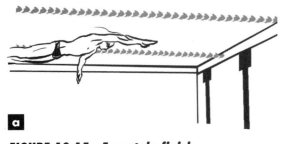 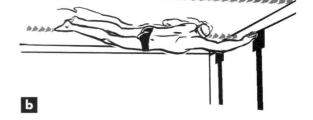

FIGURE 10.15   Freestyle finish.

- While extending the arm to the lateral position, the swimmer should be sure to maintain the kick to the wall.
- The swimmer should not lift the head until after the hand hits the wall.

Butterfly and Breaststroke Finishing Drill

This drill is similar to the butterfly and breaststroke turning drill. The swimmer starts with a midpool turn underneath the flags (5 m from the wall) and takes a maximum of three strokes to get to the wall for a finish, maintaining distance per stroke and finishing correctly on the final stroke (Sweetenham 1998i; Atkinson and Sweetenham 1999).

Start, Turn, and Finish Drill

This drill provides stimulus for sprint training. The drill itself may be practiced over distances from 10 m to 30 m. It may also be extended to a three-person relay drill aiming at a target of personal best 100 m time minus three seconds or to a three-person 25 m, 50 m, 25 m relay drill.

One person may do the drill, or swimmers may do it in teams against the clock for perfection. The order may vary with a kick or jump turn to start the drill, a finish, and a relay start.

Done with three swimmers, the drill has the first swimmer executing a racing start and sprinting a prescribed distance to touch the outstretched hand of the waiting second swimmer, who will sprint the distance to the wall, turn, and sprint back a prescribed distance to touch the outstretched hand of the third swimmer. The third swimmer then sprints into the wall for a racing finish. Swimmers can follow the outlined progression three times so that each member of the three-person relay performs a start, a turn, and a finish. By performing the same drill four times through with four swimmers, each would get extra rest on every fourth effort.

Relay Swimming

During training sessions a good challenge is to have swimmers pursue the following relay drill. The coach may choose to do this on a regular basis.

At the start of workouts when the athletes are reasonably fresh, the coach can conduct a relay of six or eight swimmers. This example uses a six-man relay. For a dive start 6 × 75 m relay, swimmers swim the 75 m at maximum speed, at race stroke rate. A push start 6 × 25 m relay follows.

Each swimmer adds together the times from the dive 75 m and the push 25 m. The two times added together should be faster than the swimmer's personal best 100 m time, and the distance should include fewer strokes and an enhanced stroke rate.

At the conclusion of another workout when swimmers are tired, the relay could be repeated in reverse format (that is, dive 6 × 25 m relay and push 6 × 75 m relay) with the same objective. The purpose is to do race-speed relay changeovers, perform quality turns and finishes, build teamwork, and work on 100 m racing skills.

The drill can be made more or less challenging by having fewer or more swimmers in each team. Instead of two teams of six swimmers, the coach can have four teams of three swimmers with one swimmer, a 200 m specialist, swimming twice, both leading the team and bringing it home.

The drill is even more difficult if swimmers do the 25 m push band only (arms only) or resistant pull (no pull buoy). These drills can be exciting coaching challenges. They are performance specific, and athletes find them exciting and motivational.

Another drill for relay swimming is to have each of three members of the relay team stand on a starting block, in lanes 1, 2, and 3. The fourth member of the team jumps into lane 2. The swimmer in lane 2 swims into the finish, and the three swimmers on the starting blocks perform a relay takeover. The swimmers do this three times before rotating. To rotate, the swimmer in the water gets out and goes to block 1, the swimmer on block 1 goes to block 2, the swimmer on block 2 goes to block 3, and the swimmer from block 3 gets into the water. The swimmers perform the drill until each has done three takeovers from each lane. By watching and comparing the takeovers performed by each swimmer, the coach gains information that is useful in deciding relay orders.

This chapter looks at the starts, turns, and finishes for all strokes. Coaches and swimmers should review the checklists and each day incorporate points from the lists into training. The training sets provide an ideal opportunity to practice the skills outlined in this chapter. In chapter 11 we discuss kick and pull training, which provides an opportunity for the swimmer to practice elements from this chapter while training isolated areas of the body.

11

Kick and Pull Training

This chapter looks at the importance of kick and pull training for all swimmers. We make suggestions for using flippers and hand paddles, which are either overused or underused in many training programs. Like training on full stroke, kick and pull training should be conducted as endurance work, as shorter quality work, and in speed sets. This chapter gives sample sets for the training of kick and pull as endurance, quality, and speed work.

Kick Training

Swimmers must try to gain every edge they can to improve performance. In the past, swimmers in middle distance and distance events may not have used the kick to its full capacity.

Today we see them able to use a strong kick throughout these swims. They must also be able to unload a big kick to make a break while maintaining stroke rate and stroke count, both during the sudden burst and after it. Having a strong kick can be a great tactical advantage when racing. To use a continuous kick or use the surge tactic in a race, swimmers must have well-conditioned leg muscles. Note that not all fit people have well-conditioned legs.

We also see swimmers using the powerful underwater dolphin kicking action more than ever before in butterfly, backstroke, and freestyle races off the start and turns. These efforts place more demands on the legs, which contain large powerful muscles (quads) that require large amounts of oxygen, especially if they are not well conditioned. For example, in the short-course 100 m backstroke event, the swimmer can travel up to 15 m underwater on both starts and turns, which can be 60 percent of the race.

© Sport the Library

Backstrokers who want to maximize their distance underwater on starts and turns can improve their propulsive force through kick training.

Training must condition the legs of the swimmers, and coaches should consider this when planning their programs. When swimmers find themselves in a race, they will race as they have trained. When swimmers whose legs are not conditioned put in a surge from the legs, they will not cope well. The coach should devise training sets so that swimmers get the most from their kicks. A backstroke swimmer who wishes to swim 15 m off the wall on all turns should train to do that. On certain sets the swimmer should aim to go even farther than 15 m. The swimmer should also know how many kicks it should take to reach 15 m and work to that.

The coach should time all kick sets in training regardless of the intensity of the set. This approach focuses the swimmer on the importance of what he or she is doing. Obviously, the rest interval in many cases will dictate the intensity level of the set. The coach must motivate the swimmer to work the kick, not just use the kickboard to stay afloat. Even when working a lower intensity kick set, the swimmer should be working and concentrating on technique, not chatting.

Coaches should check the types of kickboards that their squads use. They should be aware that the parents of junior swimmers often pick out kickboards for them. Parents often buy a full-size kickboard like those that the older adult-size swimmers in the squad use, with the hope that the child will grow into it. Junior swimmers should use small kickboards.

Kicking with Flippers

The coach should restrict the amount of work each swimmer does with flippers. Flippers can work well on short-rest repeats and sprint sets. A strong kick is extremely important to the sprint swimmer. The use of flippers should not exceed 50 percent of the total time spent on any activity.

A question for all coaches to consider is whether using flippers enhances the kicking ability of their swimmers. We believe that flippers provide stability for the upper-body part of the stroke. Another question for coaches is whether any proof exists that using flippers enhances kicking. We believe that resistance kick with a drag suit or belt will improve kicking ability.

We suggest that coaches build resistance kick into their programs and follow that type of work with speed kick with flippers. Kicking with flippers will allow swimmers to kick a greater distance in a shorter period, but we are not certain that doing so will improve swimmers' kicks.

Kick Sets

We suggest that swimmers and coaches frequently evaluate the kicking done in training, as they would evaluate all forms of training done in workouts. They should time all repeats, count the number of breaststroke and butterfly kicks done on sets, take the heart rate following all repeats, and compare this information on kick sets in all training workouts.

Endurance Kick Sets

1 × 1000 m FS kick, target to equal or beat PB 1500 m FS time
200 m swim-down
600 m FS kick, target to equal or beat PB 800 m FS time
200 m swim-down
300 m main stroke kick, target to beat PB 400 m time
200 m swim-down
150 m main stroke kick, target to beat PB 200 m time
200 m swim down

(2050 m kick, 2850 m total set)

1 × 600 m main stroke kick, target 9:00 or faster
200 m swim-down
400 m main stroke kick, target 6:00 or faster
200 m swim-down
200 m main stroke kick, target 3:00 or faster
200 m swim-down
100 m main stroke kick, target PB time plus 20 seconds

(1300 m)

In the following kick sets the repeats are timed and the average is worked out. The next time the swimmer does the set, the aim is to beat the average time recorded the last time he or she did the set.

20 × 100 m main stroke kick on 2:00, holding pace

(2000 m)

4 × 400 m FS kick on 8:00

(1600 m)

8 × 200 m main stroke kick on 3:30, holding pace throughout

(1600 m)

16 × 100 m main stroke kick on 1:50, holding same pace throughout

(1600 m)

2 × 800 m kick on 16:00, holding same pace throughout

(1600 m)

1 × 1500 m FS kick timed as fast as possible

(1500 m)

5 × 300 m kick aiming to beat PB 400 m time on 7:00

(1500 m)

8 × 150 m kick on 3:00, holding pace throughout

(1200 m)

Quality Kick Sets

2 × 200 m kick main stroke maximum effort on 4:00
     100 m easy swim on 1:40
     2 × 100 m kick main stroke maximum effort on 2:00
     100 m easy swim on 1:40
     4 × 50 m kick main stroke maximum effort on 60
     100 m easy swim

(1200 m quality kick, 1800 m total set)

4 × 100 m main stroke kick maximum effort on 2:30
     50 m main stroke kick faster than half of the 100 m kick on 1:15
     2 × 25 m main stroke kick faster than half of the 50 m kick on 45
     100 m swim-down

(800 m quality kick, 1200 m total set)

8 × 150 m main stroke kick on 3:00 as 50 m maximum effort, 50 m distance per kick
     (DPK), 50 m maximum effort

(800 m quality kick, 1200 m total set)

In the following kick sets the coach times the repeats and calculates the average. The next time the swimmer does the set, the aim is to beat the average time recorded the last time he or she did the set.

10 × 75 m kick holding PB 100 m swim time or faster on 2:00

(750 m quality kick)

6 × 100 m main stroke kick maximum effort on 4:00

(600 m quality kick)

2 × 100 m kick main stroke maximum effort on 2:00
     50 m easy swim on 50
     2 × 50 m kick main stroke maximum effort on 1:00
     50 m easy swim on 50
     4 × 25 m kick main stroke maximum effort on 30
     50 m easy swim

(600 m quality kick, 900 m total set)

10 × 50 m main stroke kick maximum effort on 2:00

(500 m quality kick)

8 × 50 m main stroke kick maximum effort on 1:30

(400 m quality kick)

6 × 50 m main stroke kick maximum effort on 1:10. Add all the 50 m swims together aiming at a target of the PB 400 m time.

(300 m quality kick)

Speed Kick Sets

The coach should again time the swimmer on these sets and work out the average. The next time the swimmer performs the set, he or she should aim to beat the average of the previous attempt.

20 × 25 m kick maximum effort on 45

(500 m speed kick)

16 × 25 m power sprint kick with fins on 45

(400 m speed kick)

4 × 50 m kick maximum effort on 60
4 × 25 m kick maximum effort on 60

(300 m speed kick)

| 10 × | 75 m DPK on 1:30 |
| | 25 m maximum kick on 60 |

(250 m speed kick, 1000 m total set)

| 10 × | 25 m maximum effort main stroke kick on 60 |
| | 75 m maximum effort DPK main stroke on 1:45 |

(250 speed kick, 1000 m total set)

| 10 × | 25 m from a push (FAP) as 15 m underwater back dolphin kick maximum effort, 10 m surface back dolphin kick |

(250 m speed kick)

| 10 × | 25 m from a dive (FAD) as 15 m underwater front dolphin kick maximum effort, 10 m surface front dolphin kick |

(250 m speed kick)

| 6 × | 50 m DPK on 1:30 |
| | 25 m maximum effort kick on 60 |

(150 m speed kick, 450 m total set)

Pull Training

The purposes of pull training are many and varied. Pull training can be leg floated and leg assisted by using pull buoys to fine-tune and isolate movement patterns of the hands, arms, and upper body. This form of pull training is known as technique-enhancement pull, in which the swimmer does not have to worry about the leg kick and can concentrate on head position, hand entry, pull patterns, and arm recovery in isolation.

Resistance pull training, which should always follow technique-based pulling, is a great way to convert strength gains from dryland training into specific swimming speed and power drills while simulating racing body position.

Coaches should avoid using pull buoys with their squads for pull resistance training. Pull buoys can be used for recovery or technique-enhancement pull sessions. Each swimmer should perform resistance pull sets on all strokes so that the sets are specific for his or her events.

No sudden increases should occur in either the volume of pull training or the amount of resistance. Swimmers should maintain quality of technique and proper trunk rotation on freestyle and backstroke pull sets.

In the sample pull sets, the coach and swimmer should record the times for the repeats and work out the average time from the set. The next time the swimmer does the set, the aim is to swim faster than the average of the previous set.

Endurance Pull Sets

3 × 1500 m FS pull
One with hand paddles and band
One with band only
One with pull buoy

(4500 m)

10 × 400 m FS pull with band and hand paddles on 5:30
Breathing three, four, five, six, seven through twice

(4000 m)

4 × 800 m FS pull on 12:00
One with hand paddles and pull buoy
One with hand paddles and band
One with band only
One with pull buoy

(3200 m)

20 × 150 m FS pull with bands and hand paddles on 2:15

(3000 m)

10 × 300 m FS pull with band and hand paddles on 4:00
Breathing three, four, five, six, seven through twice

(3000 m)

1 × 500 m BF pull
       600 m BK pull
       700 m BR pull
       800 m FS pull

(2600 m)

32 × 50 m FS pull holding rate and count on 45

(1600 m)

20 × 75 m with bands and paddles:
10 × 75 m FS breathing every three, four, five, six, seven through twice
10 × 75 m form stroke

(1500 m)

24 × 50 m form stroke pull holding rate and count on 60

(1200 m)

10 × 100 m form stroke pull with bands and hand paddles

(1000 m)

Quality Pull Sets

10 × 75 m main stroke pull, holding PB 100 m time or faster on each swim on 2:00
       25 m distance per stroke (DPS) pull on 60

(750 m quality pull, 1000 m total set)

2 × 150 m FS pull breathing every seven on 3:00
       50 m pull main stroke maximum effort on 40
       100 m FS pull breathing every eight on 2:00
       2 × 50 m main stroke pull maximum on 40
       50 m FS pull breathing every nine on 60
       3 × 50 m main stroke pull maximum on 40

(600 m quality pull, 1200 m total set)

3 × 100 m main stroke pull maximum effort with a band and hand paddles on 2:30
       50 m main stroke pull maximum effort with a band and hand paddles on 1:15
       25 m main stroke pull maximum effort with a band and hand paddles on 45
       25 m main stroke pull maximum effort with a band and hand paddles on 45
       100 m choice pull distance per stroke with pull buoy and hand paddles on 2:30

(600 m quality pull, 900 m total set)

10 × 50 m main stroke pull holding racing stroke rate on 1:30

(500 m quality pull)

6 × 50 m main stroke pull maximum effort on 1:00
Target to beat PB 400 m time when all 50s are added together

(300 m quality pull)

1 × 100 m BR pull with pull buoy, record time and stroke count.
100 m BK pull with band only, record time and stroke count.
50 m BK end of stroke pull (double-arm scull), count and record the number of sculling movements

(250 m quality pull)

Speed Pull Sets

On all forms of speed training, the formula shown in chapter 1 should be used to set goal times for repeats. The goal time should be the target for swimmers on the following sets.

16 ×   25 m maximum speed main stroke pull with band on 45
           75 m DPS main stroke pull on 1:45

(400 m speed pull, 1600 m total set)

16 × 25 m main stroke pull with bands and hand paddles, maximum speed sprints holding time and stroke count on 45

(400 m speed pull)

16 × 50 m pull on 1:30 done as four sets of 4 × 50 m repeats as follows:
4 × 50 m as 12.5 m maximum speed, 37.5 m DPS
4 × 50 m as 25 m maximum speed, 25 m DPS
4 × 50 m as 25 m DPS, 25 m maximum speed
4 × 50 m as 37.5 m DPS, 12.5 m maximum speed

(300 m speed pull, 800 m total set)

10 ×   75 m FS pull distance per stroke on 1:15
           25 m main stroke pull maximum speed on 30
           With bands and hand paddles

(250 m speed pull, 1000 m total set)

10 ×   50 m FS pull distance per stroke on 50
           25 m main stroke pull maximum speed on 30
           With bands and hand paddles

(250 m speed pull, 750 m total set)

10 ×   25 m FS pull distance per stroke on 30
           25 m main stroke pull maximum speed on 30
           With bands and hand paddles

(250 m speed pull, 500 m total set)

8 × 50 m main stroke with a band as follows on 60:
2 × 50 m as 40 m maximum speed, 10 m DPS
2 × 50 m as 30 m maximum speed, 20 m DPS
2 × 50 m as 20 m maximum speed, 30 m DPS
2 × 50 m as 10 m maximum speed, 40 m DPS

(200 m speed pull, 400 m total set)

8 × 25 m main stroke maximum speed sprints with hand paddles and a band on 60

(200 m speed pull)

Swimming With Hand Paddles

One of the most often asked questions concerns the type of hand paddle to use in training. Note that not every swimmer needs to use hand paddles. Some champions have preferred not to use them at all. Hand paddles should be selected to fit the need of the athlete at a given time for a particular fault.

Hand paddles are used for different reasons, which include correcting stroke faults and developing specific strength to power conversions in swimming. For instance,

The golden rule is to use any training aid for a maximum of 50 percent of the total volume on that activity.

finger paddles enhance the high wrist position, maintain feel for the water, and teach an early press into the catch position while not over-stressing the shoulder.

Swimmers can use oversized hand paddles on short sprints to develop power while maintaining specific stroke rates. Hand paddles can be molded to the hand for naked paddle sculling (without the wrist and finger straps) or naked paddle swimming. Swimmers should learn to use the hand paddles without the wrist strap to apply pressure with the correct pulling pattern. Care should be taken when using large hand paddles because they can exaggerate the dropped elbow position of the arm.

Each of the many available paddles serves a specific need. The selection of a paddle depends on the result being pursued. The coach should evaluate the strengths and weaknesses of the athlete, decide on the desired outcome, and then select the type of hand paddle that suits the circumstance. The coach should choose the hand paddle for the swimmer based on individual needs or consider designing and making one.

Swimmers should not swap pulling equipment—hand paddles, pull buoys, and so forth—with other swimmers. Substitution of equipment can cause injury and changes in technique. All swimmers should have their own equipment and not rely on others to provide them with equipment.

Clubs may choose to have hand paddles made in club colors. For example, a club with the colors blue and yellow could have hand paddles cut in those colors, with the left hand paddle being blue and the right hand paddle yellow. This distinction can be a good learning device with age-group swimmers, who could be given instructions to concentrate on, for example, their blue pulling pattern.

PART II

Workouts and Programs

12

Program Planning

For the successful coach and swimmer, every day is a rehearsal for the major championship competition. Swimming is a sport that requires both long-term and short-term training plans to help each athlete achieve maximum potential. Effective coaching methods allow each swimmer to peak at the relevant major competition, whether that be district, state, national, or international competition (depending on how far one's talent and dedication leads). Clearly, planning beyond a single season is required. Because the Olympic Games occur every four years, we commonly think in terms of quadrennial cycles.

Applied to a four-year plan, yearly training parameters (number of sessions, type of training performed, and training volume) follow a progression based on age (physical maturity), ability, and dedication to excellence. Each year the challenges of training and competition should build.

Swimmers, parents, and coaches should understand that the typical elite age-group or youth swimmer (12 to 18 years old plus or minus a year) should train for 48 weeks per year. The athlete should cover between 2100 and 2500 kilometers in 800 to 900 hours of swimming training, which equates to 400 to 450 two-hour swimming training sessions. Although this may sound like a lot of swimming, it breaks down to an average of 44 to 52 kilometers per week. These totals should be the goal for all age-group and youth swimmers and coaches. Middle-distance and distance athletes need to do more than this. Their goal should be 60 kilometers a week. Before attaining the above values, junior swimmers should build up their training volumes as outlined in this chapter. Senior athletes may cover the same distance or more depending on their event, and they do more work at higher intensity than age-group swimmers do.

Swimmers need to build up to achieving breakpoint volume. They cannot just start to swim 44 to 52 kilometers a week when they are 12 years old. This chapter will outline how swimmers build to achieving breakpoint volume.

Masters swimmers should consider the availability of training time and the number of training sessions available before planning seasonal plans and macrocycles. A masters swimmer can follow the training cycles recommended for the senior swimmer, although consideration must be given to the length of the training sets, repeat times, and recovery between hard sessions.

© David Sanders

Each practice prepares swimmers for the challenges of competition and the fulfillment of reaching their potential.

Triathletes obviously must consider the other sporting disciplines that make up their sport (running and cycling). The swim is generally the first leg of the triathlon event, and athletes use freestyle. To prevent injury, triathletes must be proficient on other strokes for use in training. We recommend backstroke for training sets to offset the work done on freestyle. Triathletes should also use backstroke in recovery-enhancement sessions.

Note that many competitive swimmers place highly in their school cross country running competitions and triathlons. But the reverse does not occur; runners do not have the skills of competitive swimmers. Swimming brings more to the triathlon than the other two sports do. The aerobic fitness from swimming enhances the athlete's recovery ability. Cycling and running skills do not enhance the swimming capabilities of the athlete.

With regard to the taper, age-group swimmers should generally follow a 7- to 14-day taper, worked out on an individual basis by the coach. Some age-group athletes require less than a 7-day taper, and some youth swimmers may taper for longer. For senior athletes, masters swimmers, and triathletes, the taper will vary depending on the length of their event and their physical build. The general rule is the shorter the event, the longer the taper. Chapter 14 covers tapering in detail.

Frequency of Competition

How frequently a swimmer should compete is a commonly asked question. A related issue is the definition of a competition.

We can describe a competition as any meet that requires two or more days of rest or any meet that includes an expectation of a personal best time. An event can also be considered a competition if it interferes with the training program of the athlete, either the week before the meet or the week following it. Coaches must ensure that swimmers do not miss training for club or team competitions.

We recommend that swimmers not exceed one competition per month, or 12 competitions per year. A competition generally occurs over three days. We try to avoid rolling meets, that is, competitions that take place on two or three weekends in a row. Twelve competitions of three days each translate to 36 days of competition per year.

If, as recommended, the swimmer aged 18 years or older performed within 3 percent of his or her best time in 12 competitions per year, the athlete would have 36 days of meaningful competition per year. The swimmer aged 17 years or younger uses a standard of performing within at least 1 percent of his or her best time to define meaningful competition. This athlete should also aim to compete at that level 12 times per year.

The recommended number of competitions is an absolute maximum. Some swimmers may compete significantly less often. Competing in a club-level meet that does not interfere with the training program of the swimmer should not be considered a competition.

Swimmers should compete in competitions at different levels. The following rules generally apply:

- Swimmers should compete at their own performance level in three competitions. The coach is critical of their results, expects them to be extremely competitive, and demands perfection.
- Swimmers should race in two competitions below their performance level. They could win while experimenting in performing the race in different ways.
- Swimmers should compete in one competition above their current performance level. In this competition they are out of their depth, and the coach praises the swimmers for their results.

This progression repeated twice in the year will give the swimmer 12 competitions. Competing too frequently is a problem within our sport. Good coaching can mean that swimmers need fewer competitions. Coaches should construct training to meet the needs of the swimmers they coach. The session for a 9-year-old will be much different from the session for a 20-year-old.

At a midseason meet, the less dedicated or less committed swimmer may have more success than the dedicated, committed swimmer. This occurs because the drop-off in training toward the end of the week for the less committed swimmer is not significantly different in stress from the first part of the week. In contrast, the hard-working athlete faces adaptation changes as soon as the workload decreases. The coach should structure the training week to build into the competition so that the dedicated athlete has suitable preparation.

The A track shown in figure 12.1 on the weekly cycle rewards the athlete who has low to medium work ethic and is less dedicated. The approach of resting into the meet offers little change in total stress, and the small rest offers great opportunity for the swimmer with low to medium work ethic. This approach, however, offers the dedicated athlete major changes in stress that can cause a disappointing result.

The B track shown in figure 12.1 is a better plan for the dedicated, committed athlete. This approach gives the athlete rest early in the week with a lighter work load building into the meet, providing the same training volume as the A track. It offers a much higher standard of quality for the committed athlete while being no different for the less committed athlete.

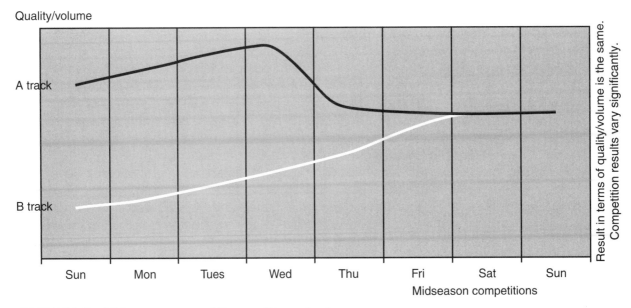

Quality/volume

A track

B track

Result in terms of quality/volume is the same.
Competition results vary significantly.

Sun   Mon   Tues   Wed   Thu   Fri   Sat   Sun

Midseason competitions

FIGURE 12.1   *Midseason competition quality and volume.*

Training Cycles

The terms *seasonal plan, annual plan, macrocycle, mesocycle,* and *microcycle* can be explained as follows. The seasonal or annual plan is the plan for the year. The coach and swimmer identify the main competition for the year and put the plan in place for the swimmer to achieve optimum performance at the targeted competition.

Macrocycles are the blocks of work that make up the seasonal or annual plan. These cycles are generally 12, 15, or 24 weeks in duration.

The macrocycle is divided into blocks, which are termed mesocycles. For example, a 12-week macrocycle could be split into three 4-week mesocycles. A 15-week macrocycle could be broken into three 5-week mesocycles or five 3-week mesocycles.

Each mesocycle is then broken down into microcycles. A microcycle can be each training week. For example, each four-week mesocycle may have four microcycles—that is, four weeks. Each microcycle (training week) should contain training from each of the zones. The percentage of each type of training changes within each microcycle. Some coaches may even work two microcycles in a training week.

Each mesocycle can be designed to have a major training emphasis, perhaps endurance or preparation or specifics. When planning the microcycle, placement of each main training set should be considered. This chapter includes examples of macro-, meso-, and microcycles. Another method of training is for the swimmer and coach to work to a rolling plan, which is the same from week to week. Each training session from week to week would have the same main emphasis.

Recommended Training Models

We recommend the following training models for swimmers. These models form the basis of the seasonal or annual plans.

Age-group and youth swimmers should be working to a long-term swimming career progression, not just for short-term gain. The coach should be committed to developing each swimmer to maximum potential, even if that means handing the swimmer to another training program after he or she has outgrown the current program. Swimmers need a physical profile. They must have portable technique and skills that they can take from age-group swimming to senior swimming.

With the examples of macrocycles shown, the length of the taper—usually one, two, or three weeks—can be adjusted to suit the swimmer. If the swimmer does not require a three-week taper, the additional weeks in this final preparation can be specifics weeks. Chapter 14 covers tapers in detail.

The section "Plans for Developing the Junior Swimmer" later in this chapter shows detailed training plans for junior swimmers.

Age-Group Swimmers

For the age-group swimmer the recommended plan is to split the year into two 24-week macrocycles to attain the 48 weeks of training. The 24-week cycle is also suitable for swimmers competing in distance events and triathletes. The two macrocycles making a 48-week training year are then broken into mesocycles. The example that follows has four mesocycles of six weeks in duration.

Each mesocycle has a different main emphasis. Adaptation weeks should not be scheduled into the mesocycles, so a policy of recovery on need should be followed. When a swimmer becomes overfatigued, the coach lowers the training intensity. We also recommend that swimmers not rest for every competition. The coach should monitor swimmers carefully to ensure that overexposure to any one training zone or energy system does not occur. In the following example the constant in the weekly microcycles is the training volume; the intensity of each week varies within the distance covered.

Age-Group Basic 24-Week Macrocycle

This age-group example shows a basic 24-week macrocycle broken into four mesocycles.

Week	Mesocycle	Emphasis	Distance	
1	1	Preparation week	45 kilometers	
2	1	Preparation week	50 kilometers	
3	1	Preparation week	55 kilometers	
4	1	Endurance week	55 kilometers	Competition
5	1	Quality week	55 kilometers	
6	1	Mixed week	55 kilometers	
7	2	Endurance week	55 kilometers	
8	2	Quality week	55 kilometers	Competition
9	2	Mixed week	55 kilometers	
10	2	Endurance week	55 kilometers	
11	2	Quality week	55 kilometers	
12	2	Mixed week	55 kilometers	Competition
13	3	Endurance week	55 kilometers	
14	3	Quality week	55 kilometers	
15	3	Mixed week	55 kilometers	
16	3	Endurance week	55 kilometers	Competition

(continued)

Week	Mesocycle	Emphasis	Distance	
17	3	Quality week	55 kilometers	
18	3	Mixed week	55 kilometers	
19	4	Endurance week	55 kilometers	
20	4	Quality week	55 kilometers	Competition
21	4	Mixed week	55 kilometers	
22	4	Mixed week	50 kilometers	
23	4	Taper week	45 kilometers	
24	4	Taper week	40 kilometers	Competition

In this example a 3-week preparation phase starts the 24-week cycle. Five types of training weeks are shown: preparation, endurance, quality, mixed (which is endurance and quality), and taper. Figure 12.2 shows the weekly volumes through this macrocycle.

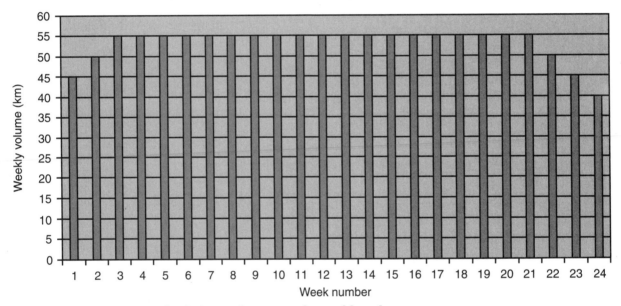

FIGURE 12.2   Age-group basic 24-week macrocycle weekly volumes.

The final four weeks are adjusted to suit the athlete concerned. In the model, competitions occur every fourth week of the macrocycle.

This example 24-week macrocycle done twice during the year gives the swimmer a maximum of 12 competitions. The competition placement shown here is ideal. Back-to-back weekends of competitions may occasionally be considered, but coaches and club committees must avoid scheduling their swimmers in events every weekend for an extended period.

Age-Group Varied 24-Week Macrocycle With Ascending Loading Sequence

The following age-group example shows a varied 24-week macrocycle broken into seven mesocycles.

Week	Mesocycle	Emphasis	Distance	
1	1	Preparation week	45 kilometers	
2	1	Preparation week	50 kilometers	
3	1	Preparation week	55 kilometers	
4	1	Endurance week	60 kilometers	
5	2	Quality week	50 kilometers	Competition
6	2	Mixed week	55 kilometers	
7	2	Endurance week	60 kilometers	
8	3	Quality week	50 kilometers	Competition
9	3	Mixed week	55 kilometers	
10	3	Endurance week	60 kilometers	
11	4	Quality week	50 kilometers	Competition
12	4	Mixed week	55 kilometers	
13	4	Endurance week	60 kilometers	
14	5	Quality week	50 kilometers	Competition
15	5	Mixed week	55 kilometers	
16	5	Endurance week	60 kilometers	
17	6	Quality week	50 kilometers	Competition
18	6	Mixed week	55 kilometers	
19	6	Endurance week	60 kilometers	
20	7	Quality week	55 kilometers	
21	7	Mixed week	50 kilometers	Competition
22	7	Mixed week	45 kilometers	
23	7	Taper week	40 kilometers	
24	7	Taper week	35 kilometers	Competition

This cycle is based on the basic 24-week macrocycle. The first mesocycle is four weeks in duration, each succeeding mesocycle is three weeks in duration, and the final mesocycle before the competition is five weeks in duration. The final mesocycle is descending volume into the major competition of the macrocycle.

This macrocycle includes an average loading of 55 kilometers per week, but the total varies each training week. An ascending loading sequence occurs throughout this macrocycle except in the final five weeks, which has a descending loading sequence. Figure 12.3 shows the weekly volumes through this macrocycle.

Each type of training week should contain all types of training. The percentage of each type of training changes within each week. Competitions occur at regular intervals within the macrocycle.

Age-group swimmers should be developed as multistroke, IM aerobic-based competitors. Backstroke is also an important stroke in the development of age-group swimmers, both for feel of the water and as a tool to prevent injury by offsetting all the work done on freestyle.

This macrocycle shows an ascending loading sequence built through the 24 weeks. The macrocycle can be arranged to show a descending loading sequence; following the first three weeks the sequence is 60 kilometers, 55 kilometers, 50 kilometers, and so on.

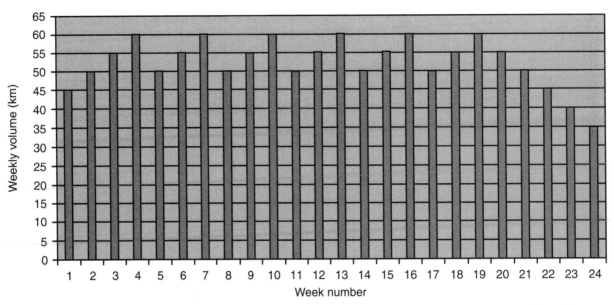

FIGURE 12.3 *Age-group varied 24-week macrocycle with ascending loading sequence weekly volumes.*

Youth and Senior Swimmers

For the youth or senior swimmer, we may talk in terms of 12- to 15-week macrocycles. The swimmer completes three blocks of training of around 15 weeks in duration. These cycles may also be suitable for triathletes and masters swimmers.

The macrocycles should be broken into shorter mesocycles and then into one-week microcycles. Each mesocycle will have its own emphasis, and adaptation weeks may be scheduled at regular intervals when required (adaptation on need).

Youth and Senior Early Season 15-Week Macrocycle

This example shows how the workload builds through the cycle, giving swimmers a preparation mesocycle to prepare for the work to follow. This macrocycle includes four mesocycles.

Week	Mesocycle	Emphasis	Distance
1	1	Preparation week	35 kilometers
2	1	Preparation week	40 kilometers
3	1	Preparation week	45 kilometers
4	1	Endurance week	50 kilometers
5	2	Endurance week	55 kilometers
6	2	Endurance week	55 kilometers
7	2	Endurance week	60 kilometers
8	2	Endurance week	60 kilometers
9	3	Endurance week	60 kilometers
10	3	Endurance week	55 kilometers
11	3	Quality week	50 kilometers
12	3	Specifics week	45 kilometers
13	4	Specifics week	40 kilometers
14	4	Taper week	35 kilometers
15	4	Taper week	30 kilometers

As with age-group swimmers, recovery on need is recommended, with no particular week being an adaptation week. If a swimmer requires an adaptation week, the volume would be maintained and the intensity lowered for the swimmer in question. Figure 12.4 shows the weekly volumes through this macrocycle.

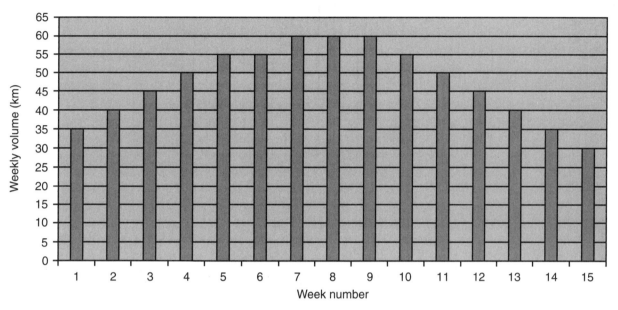

FIGURE 12.4　*Youth and senior early season 15-week macrocycle weekly volumes.*

Youth and Senior Midseason 15-Week Macrocycle

The swimmer may progress to this example following the early season example. This macrocycle is broken into four mesocycles.

The macrocycle does not include adaptation weeks, but they are used for individual swimmers if necessary. Adaptation weeks maintain volume at lower intensity and are only conducted as required by the swimmer. Figure 12.5 shows the weekly volumes through this macrocycle.

Week	Mesocycle	Emphasis	Distance
1	1	Endurance week	60 kilometers
2	1	Endurance week	65 kilometers
3	1	Endurance week	70 kilometers
4	1	Endurance week	70 kilometers
5	2	Quality week	65 kilometers
6	2	Quality week	65 kilometers
7	2	Quality week	60 kilometers
8	2	Quality week	60 kilometers
9	3	Specifics week	60 kilometers
10	3	Specifics week	55 kilometers
11	3	Specifics week	50 kilometers
12	3	Specifics week	50 kilometers
13	4	Specifics or taper week	45 kilometers
14	4	Specifics or taper week	40 kilometers
15	4	Taper week	35 kilometers

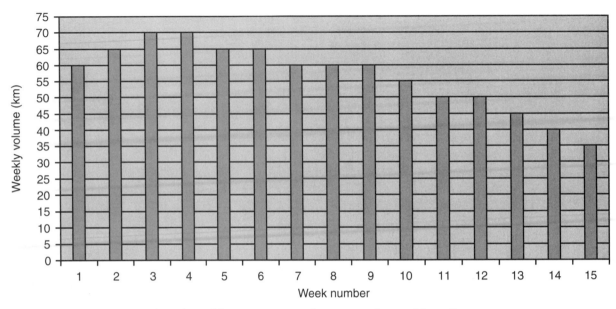

FIGURE 12.5 *Youth and senior midseason 15-week macrocycle weekly volumes.*

Youth and Senior Varied 15-Week Macrocycle

In this example the 15-week macrocycle is broken into five 3-week mesocycles. This cycle rotates through endurance, quality, and mixed training weeks. A descending loading sequence occurs in every mesocycle, from 65 to 60 to 55 kilometers. Figure 12.6 shows the weekly volumes through this macrocycle. A descending loading sequence is best suited to the sprint swimmer.

Week	Mesocycle	Emphasis	Distance
1	1	Endurance week	65 kilometers
2	1	Mixed week	60 kilometers
3	1	Quality week	55 kilometers
4	2	Endurance week	70 kilometers
5	2	Mixed week	65 kilometers
6	2	Quality week	60 kilometers
7	3	Endurance week	65 kilometers
8	3	Mixed week	60 kilometers
9	3	Quality week	55 kilometers
10	4	Endurance week	60 kilometers
11	4	Mixed week	55 kilometers
12	4	Quality week	50 kilometers
13	5	Specifics or taper week	45 kilometers
14	5	Specifics or taper week	40 kilometers
15	5	Taper week	35 kilometers

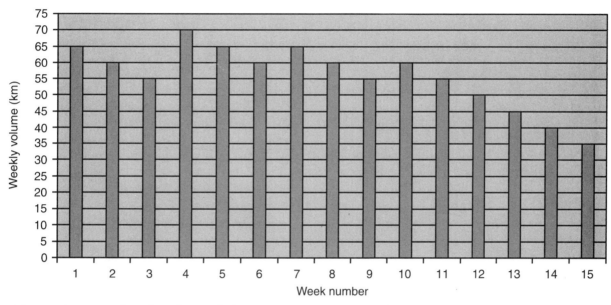

FIGURE 12.6   Youth and senior varied 15-week macrocycle weekly volumes.

Youth and Senior Distance Swimmers' Varied 24-Week Macrocycle

In this example the 24-week macrocycle is broken into four 6-week mesocycles. The first 6-week mesocycle has an ascending loading sequence, and the three remaining mesocycles have a descending loading sequence.

If adaptation weeks are required, the training volume would be maintained and the intensity would be lowered. Figure 12.7 shows the weekly volumes through this macrocycle.

Week	Mesocycle	Emphasis	Distance
1	1	Preparation week	55 kilometers
2	1	Preparation week	60 kilometers
3	1	Endurance week	65 kilometers
4	1	Endurance week	65 kilometers
5	1	Endurance week	65 kilometers
6	1	Endurance week	65 kilometers
7	2	Endurance week	70 kilometers
8	2	Endurance week	70 kilometers
9	2	Endurance week	70 kilometers
10	2	Endurance week	70 kilometers
11	2	Quality week	65 kilometers
12	2	Quality week	65 kilometers
13	3	Endurance week	70 kilometers
14	3	Endurance week	70 kilometers
15	3	Quality week	65 kilometers
16	3	Quality week	60 kilometers
17	3	Specifics week	55 kilometers

(continued)

Week	Mesocycle	Emphasis	Distance
18	3	Specifics week	55 kilometers
19	4	Endurance week	65 kilometers
20	4	Quality week	60 kilometers
21	4	Specifics week	55 kilometers
22	4	Specifics week	50 kilometers
23	4	Taper week	45 kilometers
24	4	Taper week	45 kilometers

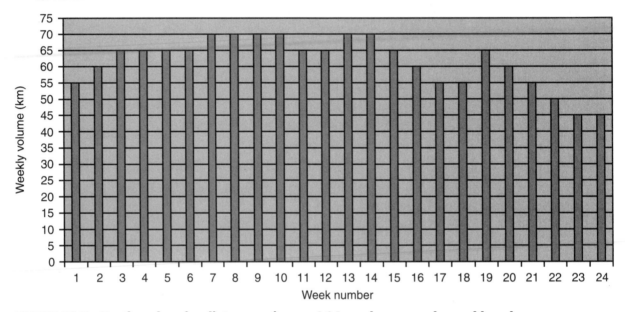

FIGURE 12.7 *Youth and senior distance swimmers' 24-week macrocycle weekly volumes.*

Youth and Senior Sprinters' 15-Week Macrocycle

In this sample macrocycle, the length of each mesocycle decreases to give swimmers additional recovery as they get closer to the competition.

This macrocycle also has a descending volume loading in each mesocycle. The volume descends through the mesocycles, which is a)n ideal way to load the work for sprinters. Figure 12.8 shows the weekly volumes through this macrocycle.

Week	Mesocycle	Emphasis	Distance
1	1	Preparation week	55 kilometers
2	1	Endurance week	55 kilometers
3	1	Quality week	50 kilometers
4	1	Specifics week	45 kilometers
5	1	Endurance week	55 kilometers
6	2	Quality week	50 kilometers
7	2	Specifics week	45 kilometers
8	2	Endurance week	55 kilometers
9	2	Quality week	50 kilometers

Week	Mesocycle	Emphasis	Distance
10	3	Specifics week	45 kilometers
11	3	Endurance week	55 kilometers
12	3	Quality week	50 kilometers
13	4	Specifics or taper week	45 kilometers
14	4	Taper week	40 kilometers
15	5	Taper week	35 kilometers

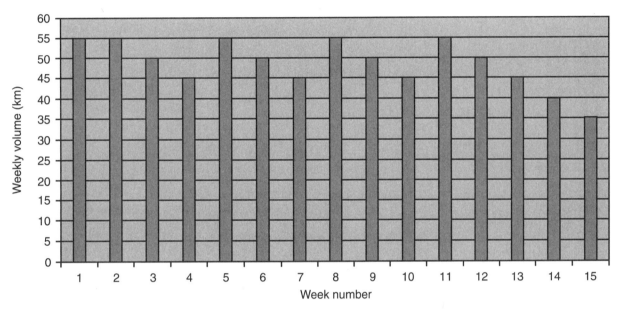

FIGURE 12.8   Youth and senior sprinters' 15-week macrocycle weekly volumes.

Youth and Senior Sprinters' Varied 15-Week Macrocycle

This macrocycle example is broken into five mesocycles, which decrease in length through the macrocycle. This example gives swimmers more rest and recovery as they get closer to the competition at the end of the macrocycle. The number of specific training weeks increases in this example. The workload also descends through each mesocycle, again suiting the sprinter. Figure 12.9 shows the weekly volumes through this macrocycle.

Week	Mesocycle	Emphasis	Distance
1	1	Endurance week	55 kilometers
2	1	Endurance week	50 kilometers
3	1	Quality week	45 kilometers
4	1	Quality week	40 kilometers
5	1	Specifics week	40 kilometers
6	2	Endurance week	50 kilometers
7	2	Quality week	45 kilometers
8	2	Specifics week	40 kilometers
9	2	Specifics week	40 kilometers

(continued)

Week	Mesocycle	Emphasis	Distance
10	3	Quality week	45 kilometers
11	3	Specifics week	40 kilometers
12	3	Specifics week	40 kilometers
13	4	Specifics week	35 kilometers
14	4	Taper week	30 kilometers
15	5	Taper week	25 kilometers

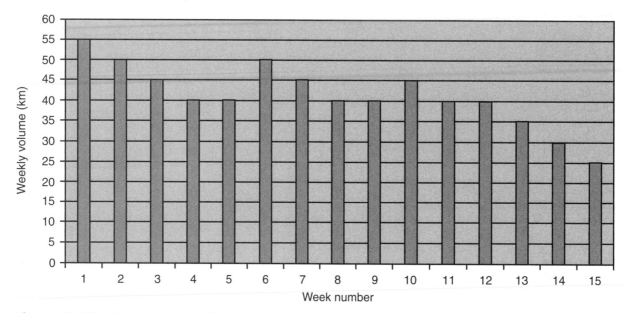

Figure 12.9 Youth and senior sprinters' varied 15-week macrocycle weekly volumes.

Senior Sprinters' 15-Week Macrocycle With Reverse Periodization

The aim of reverse periodization is to swim fast at the start of the macrocycle with very little aerobic work. No adaptation weeks are scheduled in the macrocycle. The program follows the principle of recovery on need.

Reverse periodization suits the senior sprint swimmer with around 10 years of training background in the sport. We do not recommend reverse periodization for age-group swimmers.

In a macrocycle, endurance work is normally the main type of work in the early mesocycles. The work emphasis gradually changes to quality and speed work during the specifics week. In this example the speed work and quality work occur early, reversing the normal planning sequence. We therefore use the term *reverse periodization.*

With mature senior athletes (postmaturation), those with 10 or more years of training background, we plan mesocycles with a stimulus different from what they normally receive. This macrocycle is designed for sprint-based events and is suited to good results for senior 50 m and 100 m swimmers. Success of reverse periodization with 200 m swimmers depends on the talent of the athlete; we therefore do not recommend it for most 200 m swimmers and we do not recommend it for 400 m and farther swimmers.

As a rule, the percentage of total volume for athletes training through this type of macrocycle is as follows:

• Aerobic (zone 1)—50 percent

- High-performance endurance and anaerobic threshold (zones 2 and 3)—20 percent
- Race speed and speed work (zones 4 and 5)—30 percent

The percentage of the total volume devoted to aerobic work is low compared with the percentage recommended for other types of swimmers (see table 1.1, page 4).

The first mesocycle, a preparation period, is for one week. All succeeding mesocycles are three weeks in duration, including a three-week taper period into the competition. Each training week is a specifics-type week, with the athlete gaining exposure to speed and race-pace work from week 2 of the macrocycle.

The aim is to maintain speed as the volume increases. Then, as the volume decreases after week 9, the swimmer gets faster. Figure 12.10 shows the weekly volumes through this macrocycle.

Week	Mesocycle	Emphasis	Distance
1	1	Preparation week	25 kilometers
2	2	Specifics week	30 kilometers
3	2	Specifics week	30 kilometers
4	3	Specifics week	35 kilometers
5	3	Specifics week	35 kilometers
6	3	Specifics week	35 kilometers
7	4	Specifics week	42 kilometers
8	4	Specifics week	42 kilometers
9	4	Specifics week	42 kilometers
10	5	Specifics week	35 kilometers
11	5	Specifics week	35 kilometers
12	5	Specifics week	35 kilometers
13	6	Taper week	30 kilometers
14	6	Taper week	30 kilometers
15	6	Taper week	25 kilometers

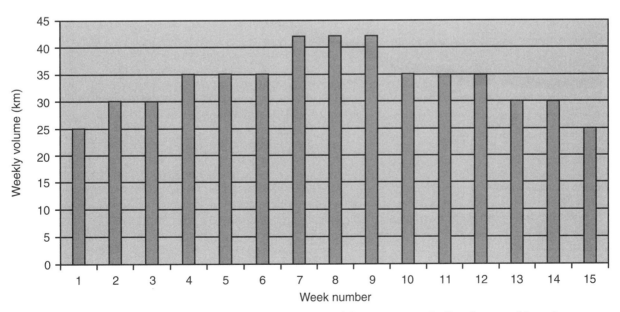

FIGURE 12.10 *Senior sprinters' 15-week macrocycle with reverse periodization weekly volumes.*

Masters Swimmers

The first example shown for the masters swimmer gives them built-in adaptation weeks. This approach is based on the theory that older athletes need more recovery. We have mentioned that senior swimmers require less time to achieve gains from conditioning work, but in our opinion masters swimmers require adaptation weeks in their training so that they have regular recovery from conditioning work. A recovery-on-need policy may be suitable for some swimmers.

Masters 15-Week Macrocycle

An adaptation week is scheduled every third week. Therefore, for every two weeks of hard training, the swimmer receives an adaptation week. This example comprises five mesocycles. Figure 12.11 shows the weekly volumes through the macrocycle. The volume is maintained during adaptation weeks, and the intensity is lowered. The number of adaptation training weeks varies for each swimmer and is based on recovery on need.

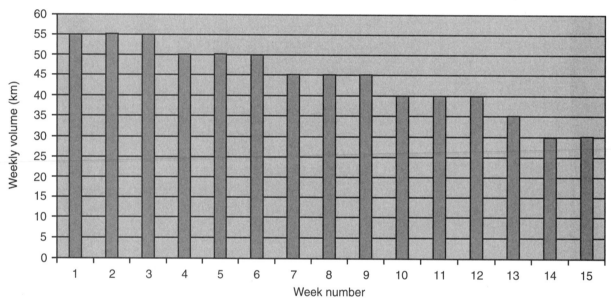

FIGURE 12.11   *Masters 15-week macrocycle weekly volumes.*

Week	Mesocycle	Emphasis	Distance
1	1	Endurance week	55 kilometers
2	1	Endurance week	55 kilometers
3	1	Adaptation week	55 kilometers
4	1	Endurance week	50 kilometers
5	2	Endurance week	50 kilometers
6	2	Adaptation week	50 kilometers
7	2	Quality week	45 kilometers
8	2	Quality week	45 kilometers
9	3	Adaptation week	45 kilometers
10	3	Quality week	40 kilometers
11	3	Specifics week	40 kilometers

Week	Mesocycle	Emphasis	Distance
12	3	Adaptation week	40 kilometers
13	4	Specifics week	35 kilometers
14	4	Taper week	30 kilometers
15	4	Taper week	30 kilometers

Masters 15-Week Macrocycle With Descending Mesocycles

In this sample macrocycle, the length of each mesocycle decreases, giving swimmers additional recovery as they get to the competition. Figure 12.12 shows the weekly volumes through the macrocycle.

Week	Mesocycle	Emphasis	Distance
1	1	Endurance week	55 kilometers
2	1	Endurance week	50 kilometers
3	1	Quality week	45 kilometers
4	1	Specifics week	40 kilometers
5	1	Adaptation week	40 kilometers
6	2	Endurance week	50 kilometers
7	2	Quality week	45 kilometers
8	2	Specifics week	40 kilometers
9	2	Adaptation week	40 kilometers
10	3	Specifics week	40 kilometers
11	3	Specifics week	35 kilometers
12	3	Adaptation week	35 kilometers
13	4	Specifics week	35 kilometers
14	4	Taper week	30 kilometers
15	5	Taper week	25 kilometers

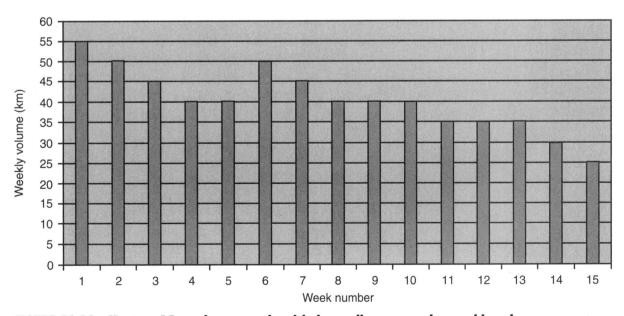

FIGURE 12.12   Masters 15-week macrocycle with descending mesocycles weekly volumes.

Triathletes

The following cycle takes into account the type of training required by triathletes. A competition may occur at the end of each mesocycle. To compete over 1500 m, the athlete must maintain volume throughout the macrocycle.

Triathletes' 24-Week Macrocycle

In this example the 24-week macrocycle is broken into four 6-week mesocycles. Figure 12.13 shows the weekly volumes through this macrocycle. Adaptation weeks can be scheduled as required.

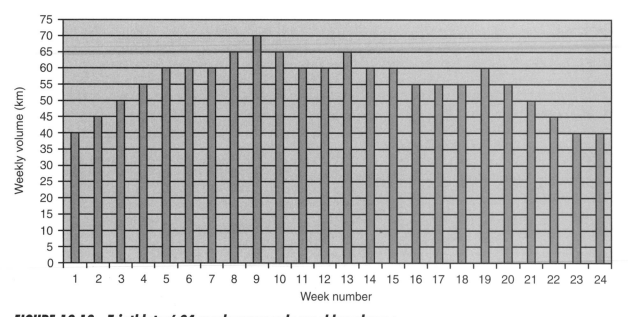

FIGURE 12.13 Triathletes' 24-week macrocycle weekly volumes.

Week	Mesocycle	Emphasis	Distance
1	1	Preparation week	40 kilometers
2	1	Preparation week	45 kilometers
3	1	Endurance week	50 kilometers
4	1	Endurance week	55 kilometers
5	1	Endurance week	60 kilometers
6	1	Endurance week	60 kilometers
7	2	Endurance week	60 kilometers
8	2	Endurance week	65 kilometers
9	2	Endurance week	70 kilometers
10	2	Quality week	65 kilometers
11	2	Quality week	60 kilometers
12	2	Endurance week	60 kilometers
13	3	Endurance week	65 kilometers
14	3	Endurance week	60 kilometers
15	3	Quality week	60 kilometers
16	3	Quality week	55 kilometers

Week	Mesocycle	Emphasis	Distance
17	3	Specifics week	55 kilometers
18	3	Specifics week	55 kilometers
19	4	Endurance week	60 kilometers
20	4	Quality week	55 kilometers
21	4	Specifics week	50 kilometers
22	4	Specifics week	45 kilometers
23	4	Taper week	40 kilometers
24	4	Taper week	40 kilometers

Sample Microcycles (Training Weeks)

The sample training weeks shown can be used with swimmers of all levels—age-group, youth, senior, masters, and triathletes. Notes within each sample microcycle apply to the individual medley swimmer.

Preparation Training Week (Microcycle)
- Generally, training weeks include 45 to 65 kilometers, depending on the placement of the week in the seasonal plan.
- No IM work is done as straight IMs. All squad members work single-stroke sets during these weeks.
- The week includes 42 to 48 HVOs (high-velocity overloads). The number in parentheses indicates how many HVOs the swimmers do in that training session. See table 12.1.
- Speed work conducted as HVOs can alternate between the start, middle, and end of training sessions. Swimmers can do this work as starts, turns, finishes, and swimming from a push.

Endurance Training Week (Microcycle)
- Generally, training weeks include 60 to 80 kilometers, depending on the placement of the week in the seasonal plan.
- The week includes 42 to 48 HVOs. The coach must maintain speed work with the swimmers during this microcycle. The number in parentheses indicates how many HVOs the swimmers do in that training session. See table 12.2.
- Speed work conducted as HVOs can alternate between the start, middle, and end of training sessions. Swimmers can do this work as starts, turns, finishes, and swimming from a push.
- Main sets of intensity for the week are shown in bold in the table.

Quality Training Week (Microcycle)
- Generally, training weeks include 50 to 65 kilometers, depending on the placement of the week in the seasonal plan.
- $M\dot{V}O_2$ and critical speed training are introduced as full sets during this microcycle.
- Swimmers do more IM work as straight IM sets.

TABLE 12.1 PREPARATION TRAINING WEEK

	Monday	Tuesday	Wednesday	Thursday	Friday	Saturday	Sunday
AM	A1 FS long swims BF skills and drills Quality kick Starts, HVOs (6)	FS descending to AT pace Endurance pull with finger paddles Turns	IM link set Endurance kick IM turns, HVOs (6)	Off	BF skills and drills BK skills and drills Endurance pull with finger paddles Turns HVOs (6)	A1-A2 FS 400 m work BR skills and drills with finger paddles FS skills and drills Starts, turns, HVOs (6)	Off
PM	BR swim and drills Endurance pull with hand paddles Turns Race-pace work	BK A1-A2 Speed kick Finishes, HVOs (6) Drills with fins	FS and IM descending to AT pace Endurance pull, no paddles BR skills and drills	A1 FS and IM Starts, HVOs (6) Quality kick	BK skills and drills with finger paddles BR skills and drills Turns, finishes, HVOs (6) Race-pace work Quality pull	Off	Off

TABLE 12.2 ENDURANCE TRAINING WEEK

	Monday	Tuesday	Wednesday	Thursday	Friday	Saturday	Sunday
AM	A1-A2 FS and BK sets as double-ups FS pull descending set with finger paddles Quality kick Turns, HVOs (10)	A2-A3 overdistance FS A1-A2 MS 50 m descending set to race-pace MS Drills with fins	**A3-AT FS 100 m and 200 m swims double-ups** Endurance overdistance kick Drills and skills form stroke with finger paddles	Off	A1-A2 IM and form double-ups Short rest FS set with finger paddles 50 m descending set to race-pace MS	Starts, HVOs (8) Overdistance A2-A3 FS Quality kick Fins drills	Off
PM	**AT FS set on 400 m swims** Endurance kick Drills and skills form stroke Starts, HVOs (8)	A1-A2 warm-up choice BF set 50 m and 100 m repeats Speed work with bands and paddles Overdistance band-only pull with paddles	A1-A2 warm-up swim IM mix BF drills and skills 50 m swims BK with paddles Speed BK as 25 m max, 25 m DPS Band-only pull mix FS and form	Aerobic FS overdistance 15 m or 25 m speed, HVOs (8) Turns work Quality kick 50 m swims fast band-only pull	Starts, HVOs (8) **AT FS 300 m swims and form 100 m swims** Overdistance kick Fins drills	Off	Off

190

- The week includes 60 to 80 HVOs. The number of HVOs increases during this microcycle. The number in parentheses indicates how many HVOs the swimmers do in that training session. See table 12.3.
- Speed work conducted as HVOs can alternate between the start, middle, and end of training sessions. Swimmers can do this work as starts, turns, finishes, and swimming from a push.
- The main set on the Saturday morning session works as follows: Week 1 is critical speed, week 2 is critical speed and race-pace mix, and week 3 is race pace. This example shows how to progress from critical speed to race-pace training.
- Main sets of intensity in the week are shown in bold in the table. The coach must monitor the recovery status of the swimmer in this phase. Some swimmers may need to reduce the amount of work they do at intensity, as determined by the coach.

Mixed Training Week (Microcycle)

- This week is a combination of the endurance and quality training weeks.
- The week includes 48 to 62 HVOs. During this microcycle the coach should maintain speed work with the swimmers. The number in parentheses indicates how many HVOs the swimmers do in that training session. See table 12.4.

TABLE 12.3   QUALITY TRAINING WEEK

	Monday	Tuesday	Wednesday	Thursday	Friday	Saturday	Sunday
AM	Overdistance IM and form **Critical speed MS 100 m repeats** (IM swimmers BF and BK) Starts, HVOs (10) Quality kick	A1-A2 FS Skill and drill work with finger paddles A1-A2 MS skills and drills	Starts, HVOs (10) Overdistance FS and form Short descending set of 50 m swims to race pace (IM swimmers BR and FS) Overdistance kick Fins drills	Off	A1-A2 FS double-ups Skills and drills (IM swimmers BK and BR) Band-only pull	Overdistance FS **Week 1 CS, week 2 CS and RP, week 3 RP 50 m and 100 m repeats event-specific MS** (IM swimmers BR and FS) Turns, HVOs (10)	Off
PM	Turns, HVOs (10) A1-A2 FS double-ups Skills and drills MS Fins drills	A1-A2 FS and MS mix A2 form-stroke set Band-only pull Starts, HVOs (10)	IM overdistance **Week 1 CS, week 2 CS and RP, week 3 RP 50 m and 100 m repeats event-specific MS** (IM swimmers BK or BR) Overdistance pull with paddles Turns, HVOs (10)	Starts, HVOs (10) Overdistance FS and form swim A1-A2 100 m 200 m swims MS (IM swimmers BF or BK) Quality kick A1 Pull	400 m repeats FS and form AT MS (IM swimmers BK or BR) Speed kick 25 m and 50 m repeats Fins drills Turns, HVOs (10)	Off	Off

TABLE 12.4 MIXED TRAINING WEEK

	Monday	Tuesday	Wednesday	Thursday	Friday	Saturday	Sunday
AM	Overdistance IM and form **Critical speed MS 100 m repeats** (IM swimmers BF and BK) Quality kick	A2-A3 overdistance FS A1-A2 MS 50 m descending set to race-pace MS Drills with fins Starts, HVOs (10)	A2 FS 100 m and 200 m swims double-ups Endurance overdistance kick Drills and skills form stroke with finger paddles Turns, HVOs (8)	Off	A1-A2 IM and form double-ups Short rest FS set with finger paddles 50 m descending set to race-pace MS	Starts, HVOs (8) **AT FS 300 m swims and form 100 m swims** Overdistance kick Fins drills	Off
PM	Turns, HVOs (10) A1-A2 FS double-ups Skills and drills MS Fins drills	A1-A2 warm-up choice A2 form set 50 m and 100 m repeats Speed kick 25 m and 50 m repeats Overdistance band-only pull with paddles	Aerobic FS overdistance 15 m or 25 m speed, HVOs (8) Turns work Quality kick 50 m swims fast band-only pull	Starts, HVOs (10) Overdistance FS and form swim **MV̇O₂ 100 m 200 m MS** (IM swimmers BF and BK) Quality kick A1 pull	A1-A2 swim-drill set Overdistance kick Fins drills Turns, HVOs (8)	Off	Off

- Speed work conducted as HVOs can alternate between the start, middle, and end of training sessions. Swimmers can do this work as starts, turns, finishes, and swimming from a push.

Specifics Training Week (Microcycle)

- These weeks are about preparing the swimmers in detail for the target competition.
- The week includes 40 to 55 kilometers of training, depending on the placement of the week in the seasonal plan.
- Swimmers do more IM work as broken IM sets.
- The week includes 60 to 80 HVOs. The number of HVOs stays constant during this microcycle. The number in parentheses indicates how many HVOs the swimmers do in that training session. See table 12.5.
- Speed work conducted as HVOs can alternate between the start, middle, and end of training sessions. Swimmers can do this work starts, turns, finishes, and swimming from a push.
- In table 12.5 the Monday morning, Monday afternoon, and Tuesday afternoon sessions of specific work simulate heats, semifinal swims, and final swims. The total length of the work on each set in this progression of three sessions is not

TABLE 12.5   SPECIFICS TRAINING WEEK WITH HEAT, SEMIFINAL, AND FINAL PROGRESSION

	Monday	Tuesday	Wednesday	Thursday	Friday	Saturday	Sunday
AM	A1 pull IM and MS **25s FAD timed starts (200 m of work)** (IM swimmers BF) Skills and drills Efficiency 50 m descending test	Overdistance FS A2-A3 FS band-only pull Turns, HVOs (10)	Starts, HVOs (10) A1 IM FS mix on 100 m repeats Skills and drills MS Fins drills with finger paddles	Off	A1 FS Band-only MS pull Skills and skills set	Prerace warm-up **Race-pace swims (broken specific sets 400 m to 600 m)** (IM swimmers do broken IM work) Fins skills and drills with finger paddles Turns, HVOs (10)	Off
PM	FS and form mix warm-up **Race-pace MS 100 m repeats (400 m of work)** (IM swimmers BK and BR) Quality kick Fins drills and skills with finger paddles	A1-A3 pull descending set Overdistance kick **Race-pace MS 50 m repeats (400 m of work)** (IM swimmers FS) 100 m swimmers 10 on 130, 200 m swimmers 16 on 60	A2 100 m swims Quality kick Fins skills and drills MS Starts, HVOs (10)	Prerace warm-up Starts, HVOs (10) **Race-pace swims 400 m to 800 m set depending on event of swimmer** (IM swimmers do all strokes) Turns, HVOs (10)	A1 IM mix A1-A2 pull MS and FS Quality kick	Off	Off

excessive. Swimmers do not perform this type of progression from week to week.

- With the example shown in table 12.5, a weekend competition can be extended to four days by having a three-session heat, semifinal, and final progression as outlined. If the coach uses the Friday of the previous microcycle in the same way, the meet simulation can be extended to five days.

- If the coach is not using the week as a competition simulation, one session of the three would include this type of work, as shown in table 12.6.

- If this week occurs close to the competition, the length of the main sets decreases.

- Swimmers start practicing their competition prerace warm-up, as discussed in chapter 14.

TABLE 12.6   SPECIFICS TRAINING WEEK

	Monday	Tuesday	Wednesday	Thursday	Friday	Saturday	Sunday
AM	Set descending to A3 A1 pull IM and MS Skills and drills Efficiency 50 m descending test	Overdistance FS A1-A2 FS band-only pull Turns, HVOs (10)	Starts, HVOs (10) A1 IM FS mix on 100 m repeats Skills and drills MS Fins drills with finger paddles	Off	A1 FS Band-only MS pull Skills and skills set	Prerace warm-up **Race-pace swims (broken specific sets 400 m to 600 m)** (IM swimmers do broken IM work) Fins skills and drills with finger paddles Turns, HVOs (10)	Off
PM	FS and form mix warm-up **25s FAD timed starts, leading into a race-pace set (200 m of work)** (IM swimmers BF) **Race-pace MS 100 m repeats (400 m of work)** (IM swimmers BK and BR) Quality kick Fins drills and skills with finger paddles	A1-A2 pull descending set Overdistance kick Skills and drills set on MS	Descending set to A3 100 m repeats Quality kick Fins skills and drills MS Starts, HVOs (10)	Prerace warm-up Starts, HVOs (10) **Race-pace swims 400 m to 800 m set depending on event of swimmer** (IM swimmers do all strokes) Turns, HVOs (10)	A1 IM mix A1-A2 pull MS and FS Quality kick	Off	Off

Taper Training Week 1 (Microcycle, Three Weeks to Competition)
- This week includes 60 to 65 percent of the seasonal highest weekly volume, or 40 to 50 kilometers, depending on the placement of the week in the seasonal plan and the volume worked in the highest-volume week in the season.
- This week includes 40 HVOs. The number in parentheses indicates how many HVOs the swimmers do in that training session. See table 12.7.

TABLE 12.7 TAPER TRAINING WEEK 1

		Monday	Tuesday	Wednesday	Thursday	Friday	Saturday	Sunday
AM		800 m mix of swim and drill Turns, HVOs (8) **3 × 50 m efficiency 50 m descending test** (IM swimmers do BF)	DPS technique set on FS and MS Starts, HVOs (8) Kick and pull set on 150 m repeats	A1-A2 drill swim warm-up Turns, HVOs (8)	Off	Prerace warm-up Starts **Critical speed** **8 × 100 CS** **3 × 100 SD** **8 × 50 CS**	Prerace warm-up Starts **Specific race-pace set 700 m with built-in swims-downs** DPS technique recovery work	Off
PM		A1-A2 drill swim warm-up **Critical speed** **8 × 100 m CS** **3 × 100 m SD** **8 × 50 m CS** (IM swimmers do 2 on each stroke)	A2 warm-up FS BK 12 × 100 m MS descending 1-3 to AT pace	Prerace warm-up Starts, HVOs (8) **Specific race-pace set 700 m with built-in swims-downs** Skills and drills set A1-A2	Starts, HVOs (8) Skills and drills A1-A2 with fins Kick and pull mix set	A2 drills and skills 9 × 100 m MS DPS technique set descending in 3s to A3 pace Kick and pull set Turns, HVOs (8)	Off	Off

- Speed work conducted as HVOs can alternate between the start, middle, and end of training sessions. Swimmers can do this work as starts, turns, finishes, and swimming from a push.
- The week includes 2400 m of critical speed work in two sets and 1400 m of race-pace work in two sets.
- The weekend before this week should be a weekend off for both the swimmers and the coach.
- For age-group swimmers, the maximum length of taper should generally be two weeks, depending on the athlete. This is the first week of the taper.
- Swimmers perform increased recovery and swim-down work between sets.
- The competition prerace warm-up is now a part of the training week. Swimmers should work to perfect the warm-up for the competition.

Taper Training Week 2 (Microcycle, Two Weeks to Competition)

- This week includes 50 percent of the seasonal highest weekly volume, or 30 to 35 kilometers, depending on the placement of the week in the seasonal plan and the volume worked in the highest-volume week in the season.
- This week includes 40 HVOs. The number in parentheses indicates how many HVOs the swimmers do in that training session. See table 12.8.

TABLE 12.8　TAPER TRAINING WEEK 2

		Monday	Tuesday	Wednesday	Thursday	Friday	Saturday	Sunday
AM		Mixed stroke warm-up Starts, HVOs (6) **3 × 50 m efficiency 50 m descending test** (IM swimmers do BF) **Critical speed** **5 × 100 m CS** **3 × 100 m SD** **8 × 50 m CS** (IM swimmers do mix on each stroke)	Prerace warm-up Starts **Race-pace set broken swims 400 m to 600 m** (IM swimmers do broken IM at pace) DPS skills and drills with fins	Prerace warm-up Turns, HVOs (6) DPS skills and drills with fins	Off	Prerace warm-up Starts **1 × timed swim race shorter than race distance and on another stroke** Swim-down	Prerace warm-up **Race-pace broken swims 200 m to 400 m** (IM swimmers do broken IM at pace) DPS skills drills	Off
PM		Prerace warm-up A1-A2 skills set DPS skills and drills with fins	Turns, HVOs (6) DPS technique set on FS and MS Kick and pull set over 100 m repeats	Prerace warm-up **Critical speed** **3 × 100 m CS** **3 × 100 m SD** **4 × 50 m CS** **4 × 50 m SD** **4 × 50 m CS** **4 × 50 m SD, amount of SD has increased** (IM swimmers do BK, BR, FS) DPS skills, drills with fins	A1-A2 DPS technique set on FS and MS Turns, HVOs (6)	A2 DPS fins skills and drills Starts, turns, and finish practice two on each, HVOs (6) Kick and pull set over 50 m repeats	Off	Off

- Speed work conducted as HVOs can alternate between the start, middle, and end of training sessions. Swimmers can do this work as starts, turns, finishes, and swimming from a push.

- The week includes 1800 m of critical speed work in two sets, with 50 percent of this work as 50 m repeats at the back end of the set. Swimmers perform more swim-downs between blocks of this work.

- The week includes 800 m to 1000 m of race-pace work in two sets, with more swim-downs between blocks of this work.

- For age-group swimmers, the maximum length of taper should generally be two weeks, depending on the athlete. This would be the final week of that taper. The Friday session will change if that is the case.
- Swimmers do more recovery and swim-down work between sets.
- Work on the competition prerace warm-up continues. By now swimmers should know this procedure well. They also practice postrace swim-downs.

Taper Training Week 3 (Microcycle, One Week to Competition)

- A three-week taper is used only with senior athletes. Therefore, this training week is used only with senior swimmers, not with age-group swimmers, females, or distance swimmers.
- This week includes 40 to 50 percent of the seasonal highest weekly volume, or 25 to 30 kilometers, depending on the placement of the week in the seasonal plan and the volume worked in the highest-volume week in the season.
- The week includes 20 HVOs. The number in parentheses indicates how many HVOs the swimmers do in that training session. See table 12.9.

TABLE 12.9   TAPER TRAINING WEEK 3

	Monday	Tuesday	Wednesday	Thursday	Friday	Saturday	Sunday
AM	Prerace warm-up Starts, HVOs (4) **3 × 50 m efficiency 50 m descending test** (IM swimmers do BF) **Critical speed 300 m to 400 m** (IM swimmers do BK, BR) DPS fins, skills and drills	Prerace warm-up **Distance swimmers: 24 × 50 m on 60 alternate controlled and race pace** **Middle distance: 12 × 50 m on 60 descending in sets of 3** (IM swimmers do a set of each stroke) **Sprinters: 12 × 50 m on 60 descending 1-4** Turns	Mixed-stroke warm-up swim Starts, HVOs (4) Kick and pull set over 50 m repeats	Off	Starts, HVOs (4) DPS skills, drills with fins	Prerace warm-up Specific pace work during the warm-up, small amount 100 m to 200 m DPS skills and drills	Off
PM	Prerace warm-up A1-A2 skills set DPS technique work on FS or MS	A2 DPS technique FS and MS Starts, HVOs (4)	DPS technique set MS and or FS Turns, HVOs (4) Kick and pull set over 50 m repeats	Prerace warm-up **6 × 50 m efficiency alternate DPS and descending to race pace** Starts, HVOs (4)	DPS skills and drills Turns	Off	Off

- Speed work conducted as HVOs can alternate between the start, middle, and end of training sessions. Swimmers can do this work as starts, turns, finishes, and swimming from a push.
- The week includes 600 m of critical speed work in two sets, with 50 percent of this work in 50s at the back end of the set. More swim-downs occur between blocks of this work.
- The week includes 200 m to 400 m of race-pace work in two sets and more swim-downs between blocks of this work.
- Swimmers perform more recovery and swim-down work between sets.
- Swimmers continue to do prerace warm-ups and practice postrace swim-downs.

Adaptation Training Week (Microcycle)

- If used, these weeks are positioned to help active recovery from the work conducted in the previous mesocycle.
- The intensity of the adaptation week is lower than it is in the previous weeks, but the volume stays the same.
- The volume of the adaptation week varies depending on the placement of the week.
- Speed work conducted as HVOs can alternate between the start, middle, and end of training sessions. Swimmers can do this work as starts, turns, finishes, and swimming from a push.
- Adaptation weeks are used as required by the swimmer.

Plans for Developing the Junior Swimmer

Coaches need to understand planning for elite age-group or youth swimmers and senior swimmers, but they also need to understand planning for junior-level swimmers. This section deals with the coaching and development of age-group swimmers.

Philosophy

We should develop swimmers younger than age 12 as 200 m individual medley (IM) competitors. Age-group swimmers aged 13 and 14 should be developed as 400 m IM, middle distance, and distance freestyle competitors. The theory behind developing younger swimmers as 200 m IM competitors is that they will develop four strong strokes and a good endurance base.

Talent Identification

Implementation of a talent-identification program is essential for both clubs and lesson programs. A swimmer identified as being talented should be moved from the group he or she is in at the lesson program straight to the competitive section of the club. This practice avoids the risk that the swimmer will drop out of swimming before reaching the competitive section of the club. Fast tracking the talented swimmer is important to his or her development. Successful clubs and squads have great talent-identification programs.

Club Squad System

All clubs need to have a grouping system. The groups in the club are called squads. Table 12.10 shows an example of how the squad system could be set up. The larger the number of members in the club, the more squads (levels) it generally has. To move

TABLE 12.10   SQUADS STRUCTURE

Squad level	Club system
1	Junior
2	Intermediate
3	Development
4	Junior national or club squad
5	National squad

from one squad to the next, the swimmer should meet set criteria, similar to those the club established for entry into the club program.

Squad levels 1 to 3 are progressive squads in which swimmers develop skills and learn how to train effectively. Movement from squad level 1 to squad level 2 encourages the swimmer to attain a higher standard, as shown in the sidebar on page 201.

The swimmer aiming at squad level 3 must attend the five available sessions in squad level 2 and be capable of swimming the criteria training sets outlined in the sidebar on page 202 before being considered.

The swimmer must make a decision about commitment on reaching the conclusion of squad level 3. The swimmer is directed into one of two squads at the next level, either the junior national squad or the club squad.

The late-developing swimmer in squad level 3 who has not made a state final or national age qualifying time by the age of 14 is directed to the club squad, regardless of training attendance. The 14-year-old swimmer who has the results but is not prepared to make the commitment to the program in the junior national squad or has not attended the five available sessions in squad level 2 is also moved to the club squad.

The talented swimmer in squad level 3 with a state final or a national age qualifying time who is prepared to attend to the required level in the next squad is moved to the junior national squad. This movement is based on the recommended training attendance for the swimmer's age in the next squad and attendance at the eight available sessions in squad level 3.

The junior national squad is for the swimmer who achieves his or her first national age qualifying time or a state or district final (between approximately ages 12 and 14). The swimmer achieves progression to the national squad by recording a senior national qualifying time, and he or she moves to the club squad if all the requirements (and commitment) are not yet in place. The national squad could contain age-group and youth swimmers and senior national swimmers. Depending on the numbers, pool space, and coaching resources, two squads could cater to the age group and youth swimmers and senior national swimmers (Atkinson 1992; Sweetenham and Goldsmith 1998). This section of the book will look closely at the first three squad levels.

Squad Level 1

When swimmers move to the first level at the club, they experience an increase in the amount of swimming they do. One session in squad level 1 may be equivalent to two swimming lessons. Swimmers are expected to attend two sessions per week when starting in squad level 1. After three to four weeks, when they have adapted to this level, they should start to attend three sessions per week. This squad includes the following work and expectations:

1. Stroke technique on all four competitive strokes, using coach-controlled sets and single-lap work.

2. Stroke drill progressions for all four competitive strokes, initially using fins to perform coach-controlled sets and single-lap work, taught as outlined in chapters 4 through 7.

3. Endurance and speed training to prepare swimmers for the next level.

4. Introduction to IM swimming.

5. Turns for all four competitive strokes and IM.

6. Starts on all four competitive strokes.

7. Relay takeovers.

8. Correct finishes of the four competitive strokes.

9. Sculling and games. The sculling teaches the difference between wrist-up, wrist-down, and flat-wrist sculling actions, as outlined in chapter 9.

10. Using a pace clock.

11. Training in a group environment and lane discipline.

12. Rules of the sport.

13. Club time trials on a variety of strokes and distances every sixth week.

14. Introduction to low-level competition.

15. Punctual start times for all sessions.

16. Introduction to basic stretching exercises.

17. The training equipment that swimmers need in the squad includes a kickboard, drink bottle, and flippers.

Even at this level a squad plan is needed to ensure that all areas of work are covered. Table 12.11 shows the simple squad level 1 plan. Three one-hour sessions are available each week. The volume of training is between 1000 m and 2000 m in each training session. Each box in table 12.11 shows the main set and secondary set of the session. Although not shown, the plan includes a warm-up and cool-down aspect.

To move to squad level 2, swimmers need to attain the criteria shown in the sidebar. The work covered in squad level 1 will give swimmers a base before their introduction to more training sets at the next squad (Atkinson 1992; Richards 1996; Sweetenham and Goldsmith 1998).

TABLE 12.11   SQUAD LEVEL 1, SIX-WEEK TRAINING PLAN

Session	Week 1	Week 2	Week 3	Week 4	Week 5	Week 6
1	BF technique and drills Relays	FS technique and drills Turns	IM and FS long swims Sculling	BF technique and drills Finishes	FS technique and drills Relays	All strokes, starts, turns, and finishes
2	BK technique and drills Sprints	IM 50 m repeats Finishes	BR technique and drills FS 100 m repeats	BK technique and drills Turns	IM 100 m repeats Sculling	All strokes, starts, turns, and finishes
3	BR technique and drills Sculling	FS technique and drills on 50 m repeats Sprints and turns	BK technique and drills FS long swims	BR technique and drills Sprints	FS technique and drills Relays	Timed swims

CRITERIA FOR MOVEMENT FROM SQUAD LEVEL 1 TO SQUAD LEVEL 2

1. 200 m FS with tumble turns and bilateral breathing.
2. 200 m BK with tumble turns and a bent arm pulling action.
3. 200 m BR with correct underwater pullouts.
4. 100 m BF with fins and correct turn.
5. 100 m IM and turns.
6. A competition racing start.
7. Correct finishes on the four competitive strokes.

Squad Level 2

When swimmers reach this level they are introduced to more types of training sets. Swimmers in this squad are steered toward swimming the 200 m IM as their main event. Five training sessions of one to one and one-half hours are available each week. Expectations of swimmers in this squad are the following:

1. Develop and improve stroke technique on all four competitive strokes.
2. Learn basic stroke drill progressions for all four competitive strokes. The swimmer is introduced to more complex stroke drill progressions, as outlined in chapters 4 through 7.
3. Monitor training using test swim, as shown in chapter 2.
4. Practice IM swimming sets.
5. Learn and perfect starts, turns, and finishes on all four competitive strokes and IM turns.
6. Learn and perfect relay takeovers.
7. Independently monitor training by using the pace clock.
8. Complete a well-balanced training program that includes varied pace swims (builds, negative split swims, descending sets, and so on), basic swimming speed, pacing, and overdistance swims.
9. Learn the rules of the sport.
10. Increase the distance covered in training sessions to improve endurance.
11. Participate in club time trials, performing a variety of strokes and distances.
12. Participate in local meets, carnivals, and scratch meets at a relevant level.
13. Learn the process of goal setting and working toward objectives.
14. Learn to keep a logbook of training and competition results as shown in the sample pages in chapter 16.
15. Learn and practice basic stretching and basic body-weight exercises including core strength work.
16. Take responsibility for training equipment required at each training session (pull buoy, drink bottle, and flippers).

Squad members should be able to cover between 2500 m and 4000 m during their one-and-a-half-hour training sessions. In a week of training, swimmers cover between

12.5 and 20 kilometers (Atkinson 1992; Richards 1996; Sweetenham and Goldsmith 1998). A typical six-week training plan includes the components shown in table 12.12. The criteria to move to squad level 3 is shown in the sidebar below.

TABLE 12.12   SQUAD LEVEL 2, SIX-WEEK TRAINING PLAN

Session	Week 1— Technique and drills	Week 2— Endurance and technique	Week 3— IM week	Week 4— Technique and drills	Week 5— IM and FS	Week 6— Skills and timed swims
1	BF technique and drills Starts	FS 100 m repeats and builds BK technique and drills	IM 50 m link set Starts	BR technique and drills Relays	IM 200 m repeats Fly drills and technique 100 m repeats FS	All strokes, starts, turns, and finishes
2	BR technique and drills Relays	FS 200 m builds BF technique and drills	BK and BR set Turns	FS technique and drills Sculling	FS 400 m negative split BK drills	IM set Starts and finishes
3	FS technique and drills Build swims	FS 400 m repeats negative split BR technique, drills, and sprints	BF and BK set Finishes Sculling	IM technique and turns Starts BF 25 m swims	100 m IM set BR drills	Timed swims All stroke turns
4	BK technique and drills Finishes	IM 100 m repeats Negative-split 100s FS	BR and FS set Turns	BK technique and drills Finishes	FS 100 m repeats and FS drills Descending swims	All stroke turns Sprints mixture
5	IM 100 m repeats and IM turns Relays and finishes	25 m repeats all strokes IM turns Sculling	All strokes mixture coach's choice and relays	FS technique and drills All stroke turns	25 m repeats all strokes Sculling and starts	Timed swims race night

CRITERIA FOR MOVEMENT FROM SQUAD LEVEL 2 TO SQUAD LEVEL 3

1. 10 × 100 m FS on 2:15 with correct turns.
2. 10 × 100 m IM on 2:45 with correct turns.
3. Be confident of swimming a 200 m IM in competition.
4. Attend the five sessions available in squad level 2 each week.

Squad Level 3

In this squad swimmers prepare to race at state or district age championship level or make their first national age qualifying time. The workload and expectations increase significantly in this squad. Swimmers are exposed to an increase in hours, distance, and level of competition. Within this squad some swimmers may show a preference toward specific events. The swimmer will have a favorite event but will be expected to compete in all events, especially the IMs.

Training frequency builds to training eight times each week, depending on age. Eight sessions a week should be planned for this squad, requiring two or three morning sessions. Eleven-year-olds are introduced to early morning training on Saturday and during school holidays. By the time swimmers are 12 years old they regularly attend one or two early morning sessions each week.

The coach might invite a talented and committed older swimmer to train with the next higher squad. Sessions should ideally be one and one-half to two hours in duration. Generally, the following progression will apply for training frequency and training volume:

11 years old	6 sessions per week	24 to 30 kilometers each week.
12 years old	7 to 9 sessions per week	30 to 38 kilometers each week, with distance swimmers covering up to 50 kilometers per week
13 years old and older	8 to 10 sessions per week	38-55 kilometers each week, with distance swimmers covering up to 60 kilometers per week

Swimmers at this level work to an eight-week program training and aim to peak at selected competitions throughout the year. A normal eight-week training cycle for this squad covers all types of training. The constant for this squad is the distance covered each week. Table 12.13 shows the eight-week training cycle. The intensity of individual sessions and weeks may change, but the distance covered remains relatively the same. The emphasis for this squad is building a strong aerobic endurance base.

Only when the swimmer has achieved a state or district age final or national age qualifying time is he or she considered for movement to the next level. Advancement depends on training attendance and attitude, which are just as important as ability.

In this squad the training focus and performance outcomes are the following:

1. Stroke drill progressions are continued and expanded, with the swimmer being exposed to more complex progressions, as described in chapters 4 to 7.
2. A variety of test sets are integrated into the program, as shown in chapter 2. The following tests are the initial tests introduced to the swimmers in this squad.
    a. 7×200 m step test
    b. Double-distance 400 m test
    c. Maximum heart-rate test
    d. 8×50 m efficiency test
    e. Cold-swim test
    f. High-performance endurance test-set progression
    g. Individual medley pace test
    h. Kick test set, 800 m, 400 m, 200 m, 100 m, 50 m, and 25 m
    i. Pull test set

TABLE 12.13 SQUAD LEVEL 3, EIGHT-WEEK TRAINING PLAN

Day	Week 1: Preparation week	Week 2: Endurance week	Week 3: Mixed week	Week 4: Endurance week	Week 5: Mixed week	Week 6: Endurance week	Week 7: Endurance week	Week 8: Endurance week
M	Individual checking speed BF 25 m repeats Kick test sets Pull set	IM efficiency Timed 2000 m as fast as possible Kick set IM link set 50 m repeats	Individual checking speed Kick test set BR drills and skills	IM efficiency 10 × 50 pacing test 50 m repeats kick set	Individual checking speed Timed 2000 m as fast as possible Pull set	IM efficiency Kick test set 400 m, 200 m, 100 m	Individual checking speed Timed 3000 m as fast as possible BK drill swim set	IM efficiency 10 × 50 pacing test Kick set
M	BK drill and swim set Kick set	FS aerobic 800 m repeats Pull set	FS high-performance endurance (HPE) set 100 m repeats kick set	400 m IM set aerobic Pull set	BF 75 m repeats Swim-drill and kick set	FS HPE set 2 100 m repeats pull set	BR 100 m repeats drill-swim set Kick set	FS HPE set 100 m repeats Pull set
T	BR 100 m repeats drill-swim set Pull set	100 m IM set Aerobic kick set	BF 50 m repeats Race-pace 50 m repeats Pull set	FS 200 m HPE set Kick set	BK swim and drill set Endurance pull	Aerobic 200 m swims negative split Kick set	FS drills and swim set Pull set	800 m repeats set aerobic and kick endurance
W	FS 200 m repeat set anaerobic threshold FS 200 m drills set Kick set	FS 400 m repeats anaerobic threshold and negative-split set Pull set	BK 75 m drill and swim set Aerobic 800 m repeats FS kick set	Aerobic mixed stroke 100 m repeats swim and drills Pull set	BR swim and drill set Endurance kick	FS 400 m repeats anaerobic threshold with negative split Endurance pull set	BF 100 m repeat swims and drill mixture Kick set	50 m FS repeats aerobic Pull set

W	BK 100 m repeats aerobic and drills Pull set	200 m repeats IM descending and build Kick and sculling	FS 400 m repeats anaerobic threshold with negative split Pull and drill set	FS aerobic drill 400 m swims 100 m IM set AT Sculling	BF 75 m repeats swim and drill mixture Endurance pull	200 m IM aerobic Kick set and sculling	BR swim set 200 m repeats Aerobic pull set	Anaerobic 50 m repeats set Kick set and sculling
T	BR 25 m repeats set mixture of skills and drills Kick set and sculling	200 m FS repeats slight negative split Pull set	BF 50 m set of repeats Kick set and sculling	Mixed-stroke set of 25 m repeats 800 m FS repeats Pull and swim set	BK swim 100 m repeats set Endurance kick Sculling	100 m IM aerobic set Race-pace set Pull set	FS drills Kick set and sculling	100 m anaerobic threshold set Pull set
F	BF 25 m set FS swim and pull set Relays	400 m IM set anaerobic threshold Kick set Starts	BR drills and swim set Endurance pull Relays	FS 200 m negative-split repeats at the anaerobic threshold Kick set Finishes	FS drills and swim set Endurance pull Relays	Anaerobic threshold 200 m IM set Kick set Starts	BK 200 m repeats set Pull set Turns	200 m aerobic kick set Finishes
S	FS AT 400 m repeat set Drills and kick set Starts	800 m repeats aerobic FS with a negative split Pull set Turns	BK drills and swim set Anaerobic threshold 100 m repeat set Finishes	IM aerobic 100 m repeat Pull set Relays	BR swim set Endurance kick set Starts	Aerobic long swims 800 m and 1500 m Pull set Turns	BF 100 m swim set Kick set Finishes set	Time trials
Session meters	6000-6900 m	6000-6900 m	6000-6900 m	6000-6900 m	6000-6900 m	6000-6900 m	6000-6900 m	5000-5600 m
Week total volume	48-55 km	48-55 km	48-55 km	48-55 km	48-55 km	48-55 km	48-55 km	40-45 km

    j. Speed tests

    k. IM and form stroke-count efficiency test

    l. Individual checking speed tests, 100 m, 200 m, 300 m, and 400 m

  The coach decides which tests to introduce to the program.

3. The following types of training sets are included in the overall training plan:

    a. Aerobic training zone

    b. Anaerobic threshold zone

    c. High-performance endurance training zone

    d. Anaerobic training zone (race-pace work)

    e. Speed work

    f. Negative split, build, descending, double-up sets

4. Female swimmers work on negative splitting their swims of 200 m and longer. Male swimmers work on even splitting the same swims.

5. Swimmers do equal amounts of work on pull and kick.

6. Speed work (short sprints) is programmed into the first part of the sessions to develop speed and programmed into the end of the session to develop race-specific endurance.

7. All swimmers learn the use of pace, stroke rate, stroke count, and training based on heart rates or perceived effort in conjunction with each other. Using pace, not heart rate, is the main way of setting training intensity. The swimmers will be introduced to heart-rate-controlled training sets.

8. Swimmers are responsible for their own training equipment (kickboard, pull buoy, band, hand paddles, drink bottle, and flippers) and self-monitoring recovery and adaptation.

9. Goal setting is formalized into a process that includes the coach and parents. Sample sheets are shown in chapter 16.

10. Logbooks are detailed and include recovery plans, strength and flexibility training, and time management (keeping up with school work).

11. Besides competing in local meets, carnivals, district championship meets, and state championship meets, swimmers also start to compete at open meets. They practice racing strategies, such as backing up fast heat swims with faster semifinals and even faster final swims. At this level they take part in about 12 competitions each year. These competitions should be of varying standards, with some meets below current standard, some at the standard, and some above it.

12. Stretching exercises and a land work circuit are part of the program, as shown in chapter 15.

13. Nutritional and drug education programs are available to both parents and swimmers.

14. The club referee should visit the training programs to check the legality of the swimmers' starts, turns, and swimming.

The training plan for this squad, which is based on eight swim sessions per week of two hours in duration, is shown in table 12.13. The main set and subsets are shown for each session, but the warm-up is not shown.

Criteria for movement from squad level 3 to the junior national is shown in the sidebar (Atkinson 1992; Richards 1996; Sweetenham 1998a; Sweetenham 1998c; Sweetenham and Goldsmith 1998).

CRITERIA FOR MOVEMENT
FROM SQUAD LEVEL 3 TO JUNIOR NATIONAL SQUAD

1. Attendance at training to required level as directed by the squad coach must be achieved.

2. An undertaking by the swimmer and parents to attend training in the next squad to the required level must be agreed.

3. A positive approach and attitude in training sessions must be shown in squad level 3.

4. Results in competition of a state final and/or national age qualifying time must be achieved.

Endurance Training Progression
for Maturation—Elite-Level Age Groupers

The progression of endurance training begins with an athlete who has learned rhythm of movement, control of technique, and breathing patterns that suit his or her individual strengths and weaknesses. These individual strengths and weaknesses depend on the athlete's core body strength and flexibility. The athlete must develop great technique and then be able to comfortably hold or maintain that skill under pressure for the length of a training session. Notice that we mention training session, not the athlete's particular event.

The athlete at this stage must love the sport, seek the challenge of competition, and be hungry for winning and the rewards that go with it. Continuous exposure to sprint training and sprint competition, however, tends to overdo this stimulus, promote stroke faults, and cause the swimmer to reach an early plateau in age-group performance.

The pursuit of endurance development must then progress into developing an aerobic and skill training base. Aerobic training is doing the most amount of work in the shortest possible time, with a minimum of rest during which the heart rate does not exceed 30 BBM and does not go below 50 BBM. The athlete maintains quality technique and recovers fully for the next workout.

Young age groupers and females, however, may and should frequently go harder than 40 BBM with this demand, changing over time as maturation sets in and as they identify and develop recovery skills.

This initial aerobic and skill-base training year should occur at approximately age 13 for female swimmers and age 14 for male swimmers. The model that should be used is a minimum of 2100 to 2500 kilometers of swim training in 800 to 900 hours over 48 training weeks per year (44 kilometers to 52 kilometers per week). Competition is in addition to this set of standards. Ideally, swimmers compete in one three-day competition per month.

With the exception of female 200 breaststroke swimmers and female and male 800 m to 1500 m swimmers, most competitive swimmers peak at 18 to 20 years of age. A limited window of opportunity is available for this development to take place. Because of lack of muscle mass and greater recovery skills, female swimmers can benefit greatly by having a much longer and more consistent aerobic training base. Lack of awareness of this point is a significant weakness in current coaching philosophies.

Most age-group athletes younger than 13 do not need to complete specific high-level endurance sets. Most training should be aerobic and focused on skill enhancement, with little need for critical speed training. Emphasis should be on short-rest and overdistance training with varying stimulus. People say that with aerobic training athletes become bored before they get tired. Good coaching, however, will make the difference.

Summary Points for Coaches

- Use more volume and intensity of aerobic training for the female swimmer.
- Swimmers should train down to high-performance endurance sets. That is, they should achieve 45 × 100 m on 1:20 at any heart rate and reduce to 30 × 100 m on 1:45 or 2:00 on a prescribed high-level heart rate of 20 BBM.
- Vary the stimulus—heart rate compared with speed, speed compared with heart rate, both compared with recovery, length of set, and repeats.
- Use negative-split training for repeats longer than 200 m, especially for female swimmers. Every swimmer should complete training sets with even-split training performances including feet-on-wall times.
- Hold back two endurance-based events for development should the athlete reach a plateau during maturation.
- Rather than have one-off weekly high training volumes, develop continuity of average volumes of training over an extended period. Continuity of training volume prepares athletes to train. Intensity prepares athletes to race and compete.
- Teach your athletes a progression of stroke counting, pacing skills, pacing with stroke counting, knowing their maximum heart rates, heart rate relative to speed, stroke rate and count relative to speed, and speed relative to heart rate.
- Efficiency at slow speed is a prerequisite for efficiency at high speed. Stroke and technique enhancement can be done at aerobic speeds at a young age.
- Most athletes benefit more by doing high-performance endurance sets at a constant speed or heart rate. Some outstanding talents may be able to get by with descending sets as high-performance endurance sets, but they are exceptions.

With the demands, obligations, and expectations of frequent and continuous competitions at senior and open level, and with the greater retention of senior swimmers through extended participation in the sport, we recommend that a secondary aerobic base and skills-enhancement phase of training take place for one year at the first year of open competition (from age 16 to age 17).

The goal, as already mentioned, is for swimmers to do at least 2100 kilometers and up to 2500 kilometers in 48 weeks of training (44 to 52 kilometers every week), in the similar but slightly shorter total number of training hours (800 hours). Training should continue over 48 weeks of every year, particularly during these two aerobic base years. Aerobic training must be used during the rest of the athlete's training life at approximately 70 percent of the total training volume, just as some speed and anaerobic training should be included in these aerobic overload phases (years).

Unless all this progression of development occurs, the high-performance endurance sets will produce short-term benefits and cause the athlete to reach a plateau. The athlete will not adjust to this specific stress.

Three Important Training Phases

We can describe the career of a swimmer by three phases of training: learning to swim, learning to train, and learning to achieve. Each of these phases teaches the swimmer important skills needed to achieve at the highest level of the sport. Long-term success as a mature senior swimmer is more likely to occur if the developmental process follows an established course.

Learning-to-Swim Phase

The learning-to-swim phase includes the years beginning with the first swimming lessons and progressing through mini-squad training. The primary objective is to learn the skills involved in swimming by developing each of the four strokes as well as the core elements of body control, feel for the water, and stable movement patterns. Swimming is a skill-dominated sport, particularly during the developmental period of early childhood. This period may begin at age 5 or 6 and continue through age 9 or 10.

Skill development is paramount. Therefore, the principles that guide skill learning are applied to the training of each swimmer. These principles include the application of distributed and mass practice techniques, the partitioning of skills into a sequence of learning components, and the linking of individual skills to overall

> Long-term development is more important than short-term competition results.

swimming technique. The quantity of practice (training) is always a consideration, but volume requirements are secondary to the level of skill. Normal physical growth and development during childhood will ensure that performance improves from one season to the next (Balyi 2002).

Learning-to-Train Phase

The second phase that each swimmer goes through is the learning-to-train phase. Typically, a swimmer enters this phase having mastered basic skills, and the demands of training take center stage. Swimmers must maximize their potential during the rapid increase of physical capacities during maturation. This period begins before the adolescent growth spurt (about age 10 or 11 in girls and age 12 or 13 in boys) and extends past maturation to about age 14 or 15 for girls and age 16 for boys. The starting and ending points vary because of individual differences in the timing and rate of maturation. During this period the objective is to extend the volume of training progressively. Training volume becomes a critical factor in long-term improvement. The quality of training is expressed in terms of maintaining efficient and effective technique over progressively greater seasonal loads. The debate over speed training versus training volume should not be an issue if the coach recognizes that swimmers can achieve both short-term and long-term training goals through a well-planned program. Speed is never ignored, but weight is given to the volume of training with respect to the portion of the training that is intense (Balyi 2002).

Learning-to-Achieve Phase

The third phase, learning to achieve, occurs after the swimmer has mastered the first two phases. This phase typically represents the later stages of age-group competition and the transition into open competition.

The first and third phases of the career of the swimmer occupy a considerable amount of the coach's attention. We feel, however, that many coaches have incomplete understanding of the importance of the second phase of development. Coaches make two common mistakes during the learn-to-train phase of development. First, they risk limiting long-term success by training the swimmer as if he or she were a mature adult swimmer. Second, they fail to establish a sufficient training base. Understanding the concept of breakpoint volume helps address the second point (Balyi 2002).

Breakpoint Volume

Breakpoint volume is a concept used to describe and plan training programs that seek to maximize individual training response based on annual training and competition demands of the age-group swimmer. These demands progressively change during the process of maturation. Breakpoint volume is also the optimum volume performed at optimum skill level achieved through participation in a maximum number of training sessions at controlled intensity. The training volume achieved at the end of the maturation period will essentially be the training volume an athlete will maintain for the remainder of his or her swimming career. We also believe that an athlete's recovery profile largely determines his or her future ability to handle intensive training situations (that is, a combination of high-performance training volume and intensity). Swimmers acquire the ability to absorb and adapt to training principally during the learn-to-train stage of their careers (Balyi 2002). Several important training relationships make a difference in the effectiveness of the program:

- Up to and through the maturation years, quantity counts more than quality (quality is defined as a high proportion of training performed under anaerobic workloads).
- After maturation, the proportion of quality within breakpoint volume is what counts. At this stage increases in quality have a significant effect.
- Recovery always counts.
- Quality technique and application of skills (such as turns, streamlining, starts, and so on) always count.
- Frequency of exposure to stimuli always counts.

Long-Term Development Program

Long-term development programs build slowly and steadily toward a breakpoint volume that swimmers achieve between ages 13 and 15. This volume may amount to 2100 to 2500 kilometers of training annually over 48 weeks and include about 400 training sessions (2500 kilometers in 48 weeks is 52 kilometers per week). The ideal progression is to achieve breakpoint volume at age 13 for girls and age 14 for boys, with flexibility and consideration for the influence of school, individual maturation rate, and training history. After age 17 (or the final year of school) the program maintains breakpoint volume (and the proportion of quality swim training) and uses the recovery profile of each swimmer to determine the increase in swimming intensity and land-based strength and fitness training (Balyi 2002).

Understanding the relationship between speed and effort is also important in planning optimum quality within a program. Athletes can give effort at any time, regardless of their state of fatigue. True speed training, however, requires that athletes practice 100 percent speed at 100 percent effort. Exerting 100 percent effort at high submaximal speeds (85 percent, for example) develops endurance. Performing at 100 percent speed with high submaximal effort (95 percent, for example) develops efficiency at speed. Understanding the difference between swimming fast and swimming easy is a vital skill that athletes must learn and continually rehearse at a young age. Swimming fast and easy is the key to maximizing talent.

Athletes and coaches must understand that swimmers can train and race too hard, but they can never train and race too fast. High speed at submaximal effort is the goal of every training or racing situation. For example, a swimmer can go out too hard in a given race, but not too fast. The ability to swim fast and easy during the early stages of a race improves the likelihood of a strong back end. These skills are teachable and controllable. Coaches familiar with the set of performance tests that we advocate will notice great emphasis placed on maximum speed at submaximal effort. Refer to chapter 2.

Improvement at and Following Maturation

As previously mentioned, some coaches overexpose immature athletes to training and racing demands that are beyond their maturation level. Overemphasis on racing in 50 m events before maturation creates a peak performance demand that is difficult to achieve. Peak performance in sprint events requires highly developed anaerobic capacity, core body strength, and efficiency. For swimmers of prematuration age, the majority of racing should be at 25 m and 100 m to 400 m distances, with a somewhat limited exposure to 50 m events.

If the athlete is to continue improving at or after maturation, the coach should be sure that the training program includes answers to these questions:

- Is the athlete still hungry for improvement because the coach has structured a continuum of goals and incentives?
- Is the athlete able to accept responsibility, accountability, and independence for results in competition?
- Does the athlete have great technique and racing skills in one stroke or in all strokes and IM swimming?
- Does the athlete have an opportunity to experience team success as part of a relay or club effort?
- Does the athlete have a balanced lifestyle?
- Has the athlete achieved breakpoint volume primarily at controlled swimming intensity?
- Has the swimmer developed a combination of speed and technique over short distances (that is, efficiency at speed)?
- Has the swimmer developed goals or motivations that support his or her involvement in training and competition?

A coach may employ a number of strategies to support continued success of swimmers through older age groups and ultimately to a transition into open swimming. Foremost among these strategies is the establishment of team (or squad) standards. For example, the coach may specify that everyone in the senior-age or open squad be capable of performing a standard training set (holding a specific time with a specific stroke count). A competition standard (for example, top 20 at the state or district championships) or a training attendance standard (minimum 98 percent, for example) offers something different. One is related to talent, the other to commitment. Skill and commitment can be assessed under a number of variables. The commitment of parents may also be an important consideration in future squad placement. The age of an athlete is perhaps the least important factor in advancing athletes from one training squad to another. Whatever criteria are used should be based on skill, commitment, and potential future achievement, not just past achievement (Sweetenham 1999d).

Winter Swimming

In the early to mid-1980s everyone involved in competitive swimming thought about a winter swimming season and a summer swimming season. This developed into the long-course season (summer) and the short-course season (winter).

Fortunately, we now accept training and competing for 11 to 12 months a year, with only short active rest breaks. This expanded schedule has led to continued improvement, fewer injuries (no major buildups starting from scratch), retention of the older athletes, and more frequent and consistent high-performance competitions.

We should therefore not consider that we have two different swimming seasons. Rather, we have three 15-week training cycles (and 3 weeks of active recovery) or two 24-week training cycles (and 2 weeks of active recovery).

Weather, hours of daylight, and heated pools are only a few of the factors that indicate which season we are in. Consider the following statements and coaching philosophies, which have a proven record of accomplishment in coaching age-group or youth swimmers during winter.

- Winter training cycles include less quality and more quantity, less racing and more training, more dryland training and cross-training on top of the swimming training, and more swimming workouts.
- Competition is based on the same events but has a different priority. Longer events are a higher priority. This idea is consistent with the training emphasis of the first point.
- Relay splits from the previous summer become the initial goals for both winter (short-course) and summer (long-course) individual events.
- Regular periods (annually) of illness or stress decrease with active rest, better nutrition, and higher vitamin intake.
- Swimmers should try to swim their long-course personal best time from a push but in a short-course pool.
- They can aim to see how high they can rank in the world rankings with their short-course times against the world's long-course times.
- Age-group swimmers should focus on open swimming competitions in winter and on swimming in their own age group in summer.
- Swimmers should get ahead in schoolwork to reduce interruptions to end-of-year competitions and training during exams.
- Swimmers should improve all weaknesses in winter and favor their strengths in summer.
- Athletes should do more than they have to, not so much in quantity, but in starting, turning, finishing, and so on.

In this chapter we looked at the planning that goes into a swimming season and offered varied and detailed plans for different groups of swimmers. The swimmer and coach can use the information in this chapter to plan the season and the content of individual training workouts. Chapter 13 looks in detail at training sets that the swimmer and coach can develop.

13

Sets for Training Zones

Training sessions should be structured so that each part of the workout flows into the next. When planning the session the coach needs to break it down into sections. A basic example is the following: warm-up, main set, secondary set, and cool-down.

Besides planning the session the coach must record what the squad actually did in the session and other information such as the microcycle that the session is part of (dates and week), date of the session, time and duration of the session, pool length, kilometers covered in the session, and aims of the session.

All this information can be recorded in a coach or swimmer training log. A completed example is shown in figure 13.1, and a blank example is shown in figure 13.2.

All swimmers should use recording boards in the sessions. They record the session and any training repeat times, stroke counts, training heart rates, and other relevant information. When presenting the workout to the swimmers, the coach should call the main set aloud to the swimmers, only once. They record it on their recording boards and then write the warm-up on the white board. Following the warm-up, the group can progress straight into the main set without having a long delay while the coach calls the main set. This way of presenting the session ensures that the warm-up links to the main set.

Zone 1—Aerobic Training Zone

Efficiency while swimming at slower speeds is a prerequisite to being able to swim efficiently at faster speeds. This training therefore forms the base from which other zones can be introduced. Swimmers should do stroke-technique enhancement at aerobic speeds first and then at faster training paces. Training on backstroke is highly recommended to develop an aerobic base, offset all the meters done on freestyle, and prevent shoulder injuries. When coaching age-group swimmers, coaches should plan

SAMPLE COMPLETED TRAINING LOG

Macrocycle details	Macrocycle 1, week 5
Day and date	Saturday, December 15, 2001
Time	6:00 to 8:00 AM, 2 hours
Pool length	LC
Length of session	5000 m (5 kilometers)
Session aims	FS aerobic development Main stroke technique enhancement
Warm-up 1200 m	200 m FS ICS on 3:30 4 × 100 m FS as 50 m kick streamlined, 50 m FS swim stroke counting 4 × 50 m FS as 15 m maximum speed, 35 m DPS on 4 × 100 m descending 1 to 4 on 1:30, as follows: 1 HR at 60 BBM 1 HR at 50 BBM 2 HR at 40 BBM
Main set 2000 m	10 × 200 m FS on 3:00 HR at 40 BBM for repeats 1 to 5 HR at 30 BBM for repeats 6 to 10
Secondary set 1000 m	10 × 100 m main form stroke drill progressions as outlined in chapters 4 to 7, on 2:00
Cool-down 800m	Swim-down protocol 400 m in the stroke the swimmer has just finished (combination of BF drill and FS for BF swimmers) as 4 × 100 m or a straight 400 m. 400 m going through all strokes, but to have 4 speed bursts of 10 m to 15 m in the stroke of the previous set. HR at 50 BBM.
Additional activity	Work on racing start practice

FIGURE 13.1   Example of a completed training log.

to train them on the same volume over an extended period rather than use one-off high-volume "hell weeks" (a hell week is a training week in which athletes push to achieve much more volume than they would normally complete).

Coaches should teach a progression of stroke counts, pacing, pacing and counts, and maximum heart rate using the following example:

10 × 50 FS on 60 holding 36 strokes on each 50 m
10 × 50 FS on 60 holding 34 seconds on each 50 m
10 × 50 FS on 60 holding 36 strokes and 34 seconds on each 50 m
Then establish the maximum heart rate

Many different sets can be used as A1, A2, and A3 sets if the swimmer is working at the correct intensity level. Some of the sets can be amended and made into anaerobic threshold training and M$\dot{V}O_2$ training sets.

COACHES'/SWIMMERS' TRAINING LOG

Macrocycle details	
Day and date	
Time	
Pool length	
Length of session	
Session aims	
Warm-up	
Main set	
Secondary set	
Cool-down	

FIGURE 13.2   *Blank coaches'/swimmers' training log.*

Overdistance and Continuous Training Sets

Overdistance work can be described as long repeats either in sets or as one long swim (longer than racing distance). Any distance longer than the race distance of the swimmer can be overdistance swimming.

1500 m	3 × 500 m
1200 m	3 × 400 m
900 m	3 × 300 m
600 m	3 × 200 m
300 m	3 × 100 m

This 9-kilometer session can be amended to work in many different ways.

(9000 m)

400 m, 800 m, 1200 m, 1600 m, 1200 m, 800 m, 400 m
Varied set construction can be used in this format.

(6400 m)

1500 m FS even-paced swim
500 m, 400 m, 300 m, 200 m, 100 m FS even-paced swims
1000 m FS pull, paddles and bands
400 m, 300 m, 200 m, 100 m breathing every three, five, seven, and nine
500 m form stroke even-paced swim
200 m, 150 m, 100 m, 50 m form stroke even-paced swims

(6000 m)

1 × 1500 m
3 × 500 m
5 × 300 m
15 × 100 m
This breakdown of distances can be amended in many ways.

(6000 m)

3 × 2000 m   1. Alternate 100 m FS and 100 m BK
                  2. As 100 m individual medley
                  3. Freestyle

(6000 m)

One-hour swim aiming at five kilometers

Five kilometers timed

5 × 1000 m on 13:00

(5000 m)

5 × 1000 m FS even paced breathing every three
          FS with paddles
          FS pull with a band, no paddles
          FS pull with bands and paddles
          FS even paced breathing every three
          On 12 minutes

(5000 m)

1 × 800 m FS pull on 14:00 breathing two, four, six
8 × 50 m on 55 kick with no kickboard
2 × 400 m FS pull on 5:20 breathing three, five, seven
4 × 100 m on 1:50 kick with no kickboard
4 × 200 m FS pull on 2:40 breathing two, four, six
2 × 200 m on 3:00 kick with fins
8 × 100 m FS pull on 1:20 breathing three, five, seven
1 × 400 m timed kick with no kickboard

(4800 m)

6 × 800 m on 10:30, 11:00, 11:30 through twice

(4800 m)

5 × 800 m on 12:00 (negative split and descending through all aerobic zones)

(4000 m)

10 × 400 m FS, RI (rest interval) 20 seconds

(4000 m)

20 × 200 m FS, RI 15 seconds

(4000 m)

5 × 800 m, first three with fins, mixture of drills and swim; last two swim DPS (distance per stroke)

(4000 m)

8 × 500 m   FS on 6:30 or 7:00 as two swims, four pulls, two swims

(4000 m)

4 × 400 m   One swim on 5:30, three pulls on 6:00
3 × 400 m   One swim on 5:20, two pulls on 6:00
2 × 400 m   One swim on 5:10, one pull on 6:00
1 × 400 m   One swim on 5:00

(4000 m)

6 × 600 m BR or BK, RI 15 seconds (fins optional)

(3600 m)

400 m IM, 800 m BF or FS, 1200 m FS, 800 m BF or FS, 400 m IM

(3600 m)

600 m, 300 m
500 m, 250 m
400 m, 200 m
300 m, 150 m
200 m, 100 m
100 m, 50 m
Many mixtures can be worked from this set.

(3150 m)

800 m FS, 400 m BF, 200 m FS, 100 BF, through twice

(3000 m)

3000 m straight swim (can be performed as a 2000 m swim)

T30—30 minutes of timed swimming as far as possible at a fast, even pace

3 × 500 m FS:
              500 m pull, with paddles optional
              500 m build
              500 m controlled breathing—100 m three, 100 m four, 100 m five,
              100 m six, 100 m seven
3 × 400 m FS technique as 50 m right arm only, 50 swim full stroke, 50 left arm only, 50
swim full stroke

(2700 m)

10 × 250 m or 300 m, RI 10 seconds

(2500 m)

1 × 600 m FS pull negative split
6 × 100 m on 1:20
1 × 400 m FS negative split
4 × 100 m on 1:20
1 × 200 m FS negative split
2 × 100 m on 1:20

(2400 m)

4 × 500 m BF or FS 500 m every fourth lap FS
                    500 m every third lap FS
                    500 m every second lap FS
                    500 m all FS

(2000 m)

4 × 500 m BR as 100 m kick, 100 m drill, 100 m pull, 100 m drill, 100 m swim

(2000 m)

Short-Rest Training Sets

After the swimmer has adjusted to the continuous overdistance work, he or she should
be introduced to short-rest sets as the next step. Rest intervals are 5 to 15 seconds.

500 m, 2 × 250 m, 5 × 100 m, 10 × 50 m, 20 × 25 m short rest

(2500 m)

250 m, 200 m, 150 m, 100 m, 50 m on the 40-second cycle
500 m, 400 m, 300 m, 200 m, 100 m on the 1:20 cycle
All swims are even paced and hold pace throughout the set.

(2250 m)

40 × 50 m FS on 40

(2000 m)

20 × 100 m as 50 m FS, 50 m BK on 1:30

(2000 m)

10 × 50 m FS on 40
    100 m BR on 1:40
    50 m FS on 40

(2000 m)

1 × 100 m on 1:20, 200 m on 2:40, 300 m on 4:00, 400 m on 5:20
     100 m on 1:20, 200 m on 2:40, 300 m on 4:00
     100 m on 1:20, 200 m on 2:40
     100 m on 1:20

(2000 m)

Holding even pace, that is, 1:10, 2:20, 3:30, 4:40
Many variations of the above set can be used.

2 × 50 m on 45, 100 m on 1:30, 150 m on 2:15, 200 m on 3:00
     50 m on 45, 100 m on 1:30, 150 m on 2:15
     50 m on 45, 100 m on 1:30
     50 m on 45

(2000 m)

Holding even pace, that is, 35, 1:10, 1:45, 2:20, and so on
Many variations of the above set can be used.

4 × 50 m, 100 m, 150 m, 200 m, switching strokes on each repeat every 50 m
Begin the first 50 m of each repeat on the same stroke.

(2000 m)

8 × 25 m on 25, 50 m on 50, 75 m on 1:15, 100 m on 1:40

(2000 m)

(Atkinson and Sweetenham 1999; Sweetenham 1990)

Varied-Pace Training Sets

Varied-pace training sets include a mixture of different training speeds. This work includes moderate or higher quality training speeds to provide better stimulation.

Swimmers can do this work in the form of a descending set, alternating set, or spike set that includes fast efforts or some short explosive efforts (HVOs).

6 × 600 m, 15 m   15 m dive start at maximum speed following each 600 m repeat

(3690 m)

6 × 500 m, 2 × 50 m   500 m on 6:30, 50 m on 1:30

(3600 m)

3 × 1000 m 1   As 250 m easy, 250 m minimum-maximum
            150 m easy, 150 m minimum-maximum
            100 m easy, 100 m minimum-maximum
       2   Descending × 250 m at 2:52, 2:48, 2:44, 2:40
       3   As alternating 50 m easy, 50 m minimum-maximum

(3000 m)

Five sets of 4 × 100 m FS   3 × 100 m of each set at aerobic speed
                      1 × 100 m of each set at $M\dot{V}O_2$ speed

(2500 m)

4 × 650 m   1   150 m hard, 150 m easy
             2   100 m hard, 100 m easy
             3   50 m hard, 50 m easy

(2400 m)

600 m, 450 m, 300 m, 150 m varied-pace work

(1500 m)

1500 m as 75 m DPS FS and 25 m main stroke minimum-maximum drill

(1500 m)

1500 m as   First 500 m   12.5 m fast to start each 100 m at speed training pace
             Second 500 m   25 m fast to start each 100 m at speed training pace
             Third 500 m   Alternate 50 m minimum-maximum drill and 50 m DPS

(1500 m)

Five sets of 4 × 100 m MS (main stroke), descending each set from aerobic pace to critical speed

(2000 m)

6 × 400 m FS in two sets of 3 × 400 m, descending each set of 3 × 400 m

(2400 m)

Double-Up Training Sets

Double-up sets are designed to improve the ability of the swimmer to maintain pace while increasing the distance, that is, 100 m 1:10, 200 m 2:20, 300 m 3:30, 400 m 4:40, and so on.

For reverse double-ups the swimmer starts with the 400 m and swims down to the 100 m. Descending double-ups are with descending time, rest, or distance, that is, 800 m, 700 m, 600 m, and so on. Ascending double-ups are with increasing distance, that is, 50 m, 100 m, 150 m, 200 m, and so on.

Sample Double-Up Sets

The swimmer should start with this type of training, holding a time on the repeats that he or she can easily achieve and thus learn the concept of this type of work. Times should be within the aerobic training zone of the swimmer. Suggested starting levels are 38 seconds per 50 m for 13-year-old girls and 36 seconds per 50 m for 14-year-old boys. When swimmers can achieve the training set and hold these times, they take off one second per 50 m and try to maintain that time for the set (Atkinson and Sweetenham 1999).

The swimmer progresses through the first sample set, adding 50 m on each subsequent section of the set. The swimmer starts with a 50 m repeat and concludes the set with a 400 m repeat, producing 1800 m for the set (Atkinson and Sweetenham 1999). A sample set is the following:

Example 1: Double-Up Ascending Distance

Distance	On	Target
50 m	1:00	0:38
100 m	2:00	1:16
150 m	3:00	1:54
200 m	4:00	2:32
250 m	5:00	3:10
300 m	6:00	3:48
350 m	7:00	4:26
400 m	8:00	5:04
800 m	16:00	10:08

(2600 m set)

Distance	On	Target
50 m	0:50	0:38
100 m	1:40	1:16
150 m	2:30	1:54
200 m	3:20	2:32
250 m	4:10	3:10
300 m	5:00	3:48
350 m	5:50	4:26
400 m	6:40	5:04
800 m	13:20	10:08

(2600 m set)

(Atkinson and Sweetenham 1999)

Example 2: Double-Ups With Ascending Distance and Cycle Time

Distance	On	Target
50 m	0:60	0:38
100 m	1:40	1:16
150 m	2:20	1:54
200 m	3:00	2:32
250 m	3:40	3:10
300 m	4:20	3:48
350 m	5:00	4:26
400 m	5:40	5:04
800 m	11:20	10:08

(2600 m set)

(Atkinson and Sweetenham 1999)

Example 3: Ascending Distance With Descending Cycle Time

Each 50 m added during this set would be one second faster than the 50 m swum before it, as outlined on the following example. This approach will ensure that each repeat over 100 m will have a negative split (Atkinson and Sweetenham 1999).

Distance	On	Target time and splits
50 m	0:40	0:38
100 m	1:30	1:15 (38, 37)
150 m	2:20	1:51 (38, 37, 36)
200 m	3:10	2:26 (38, 37, 36, 35)
250 m	4:00	3:00 (38, 37, 36, 35, 34)
300 m	4:50	3:33 (38, 37, 36, 35, 34, 33)
350 m	5:40	4:05 (38, 37, 36, 35, 34, 33, 32)
400 m	6:30	4:36 (38, 37, 36, 35, 34, 33, 32, 31)

(1800 m set)

(Atkinson and Sweetenham 1999)

The swimmer continues as far as possible through the set. The repeat times and target times can be adjusted for the individual swimmer.

Example 4: Ascending Double-Ups, Ascending Distances

When the swimmer can perform this set, he or she repeats, going the opposite way and holding 1:10 with the last 100 of each repeat being 1:08. Obviously, the times depend on the standard of the swimmer.

100 m on 1:30, holding 1:12, even split
200 m on 3:00, holding 2:24, even split

300 m on 4:30, holding 3:36, even split
400 m on 6:00, holding 4:48, even split
500 m on 7:30, holding 6:00, even split
600 m on 9:00, holding 7:12, even split
700 m on 10:30, holding 8:24, even split
800 m on 12:00, holding 9:36, even split

(3600 m)

(Atkinson and Sweetenham 1999)

Ascending Distance of Race Pace

8 × 400 m FS on 6:00
1. Last 50 m race pace for 800 m
2. Last 100 m race pace for 800 m
3. Last 150 m race pace for 800 m
4. Last 200 m race pace for 800 m
5. Last 250 m race pace for 800 m
6. Last 300 m race pace for 800 m
7. Last 350 m race pace for 800 m
8. 400 m at race pace for 800 m

(3200 m)

(Atkinson and Sweetenham 1999)

Zone 2—Anaerobic Threshold

Some of the sets shown in the aerobic training section can be done at anaerobic threshold pace. The swimmer should be able to work at the correct training paces, which are established by the method outlined in chapter 1.

Anaerobic Threshold Sample Sets

5 × 6 × 100 m on 1:30
    1 × 400 m on 6:00
At anaerobic threshold (AT) pace

(5000 m)

4 × 100 m FS descending 1 to 4 to AT pace on 1:40
6 × 100 m, 200 m, 300 m FS at AT pace on 1:30, 3:00, 4:30

(4000 m)

10 × 400 m FS at AT pace on 6:00

(4000 m)

20 × 200 m FS at AT pace on 3:00

(4000 m)

16 × 200 m FS at AT pace, four on each interval on 3:20, 3:00, 2:50, 2:45

(3200 m)

8 × 400 m FS at AT pace, two each on 4:45, 5:00, 5:15, 5:30

(3200 m)

Form or IM   4 × 100 m descending 1 to 4 to AT pace on 1:40
             4 × 100 m, 200 m, 300 m at AT pace on 1:30, 3:00, 4:30

(2800 m)

8 × 50 m form stroke on 50
8 × 100 m MS form stroke on 1:45
8 × 200 m MS form stroke on 3:30
At AT pace

(2800 m)

Form or IM   4 × 100 m descending 1 to 4 to AT pace
            10 × 200 m at AT pace on 3:50

(2400 m)

16 × 150 m at AT pace on 2:00

(2400 m)

12 × 200 m form stroke at AT pace on 3:30

(2400 m)

2 × 100 m, 200 m, 300 m, 400 m
At AT pace FS on 1:30, 2:50, 4:20, 5:00

(2000 m)

2 × 400 m, 300 m, 200 m, 100 m
At AT pace form stroke on 2:00, 3:30, 5:00, 6:30

(2000 m)

Zone 3—High-Performance Endurance

As mentioned in chapter 1, high-performance endurance training is high-intensity training. The swimmer must perform the set at the correct intensity. If the swimmer performs the set at too high a level too early, he or she will not sustain the required level for the full duration of the set. For further information about high-performance endurance training, see chapter 1.

Critical Speed Sample Sets

Critical speed (CS) training pace is established by using the methods shown in chapter 1. The swimmer's heart rate when performing these training sets should be 20 to 10 beats below maximum heart rate.

30 × 100 m FS on 1:45 holding CS pace

(3000 m)

15 × 200 m FS on 3:30 at CS pace

(3000 m)

3 ×   1 × 200 FS on 3:20
      2 × 150 m FS on 2:30
      3 × 100 m FS on 1:40
      4 × 50 m FS on 50
      Holding CS pace

(3000 m)

3 ×   8 × 100 m FS on 1:45 CS pace
      2 × 100 m FS on 1:45 as fast as possible maintaining stroke count

(3000 m)

4 × 100 m descending one to four to CS pace on 2:00
24 × 100 m form stroke on 2:00

(2500 m at CS pace, 2800 m total set)

4 × 100 m descending one to four to CS on 2:00
2 ×   1 × 200 m on 4:00
      2 × 100 m on 2:00
      4 × 50 m on 60

(2500 m at CS pace, 2800 m total set)

24 × 100 m front crawl on 1:45 holding CS pace

(2400 m)

12 × 200 m FS on 3:30 at CS pace

(2400 m)

```
3 × 1 × 200 FS on 3:20
    2 × 150 m FS on 2:30
    3 × 100 m FS on 1:40
Holding CS pace
```
                                                                    (2400 m)

```
3 × 6 × 100 m FS on 1:45 CS pace
    2 × 100 m FS on 1:45 as fast as possible maintaining stroke count
```
                                                                    (2400 m)

12 × 200 m form stroke on 4:00 at CS pace
                                                                    (2400 m)

```
4 × 200 m FS on 3:00
8 × 100 m FS on 1:40
16 × 50 m FS on 60
At CS pace, form stroke on 4:00, 2:00, and 1:15
```
                                                                    (2400 m)

```
2 × 2 × 200 m on 4:00 holding CS pace
    4 × 100 m on 2:00 holding CS pace
    8 × 50 m on 60 holding CS pace
```
                                                                    (2400 m)

```
2 × 1 × 200 m form stroke on 4:00
    2 × 150 m form stroke on 3:00
    3 × 100 m form stroke on 2:00
    4 × 50 m form stroke on 60
Holding CS pace
```
                                                                    (2000 m)

10 × 150 m FS on 2:30 at CS pace
                                                                    (1500 m)

Adjusting Training Sets

As a coach, what do you do when one of the following happens to the swimmer in your lane who is completing a critical speed set?

1. The times get slower, and the heart rate remains the same.
2. The times remain the same, and the heart rate gets higher.
3. The times get slower, and the heart rate gets higher.

The purpose of this type of set is to maintain critical speed. Therefore, the heart rate should rise toward the end of the set (Treffene 1994-1997). With the first scenario, slower times and a steady heart rate, you could increase the rest interval so that the swimmer continues to maintain the repeat time.

What should you do in the second case, when the times remain the same and the heart rate increases? You can expect a rise in heart rate if the swimmer is maintaining the required pace, so you change nothing and allow the set to continue.

With the third scenario, slower times and an increasing heart rate, you should be very careful. You could increase the rest in the hope that the swimmer can maintain the required pace. If this approach does not work you may need to amend the set rather than keep pushing the swimmer into a state of fatigue that may lead to overtraining. You can also amend the set by having the swimer swim the same pace over a shorter distance—for example, 75 m repeats instead of 100 m repeats.

Lactate-Removal Sample Sets

The term *lactate removal* indicates the purpose of the training set. The aim is for the swimmer to cope with and remove high levels of lactic acid through the training set.

For more details regarding lactate-removal training see chapter 1. This chapter offers sample lactate-removal sets based on the heart rate of the athlete. The swimmer completes the sets on his or her main stroke.

Male and female freestyle swimmers and male IM and backstroke swimmers do the following set three times (3000 m set). Male breaststroke and butterfly swimmers and female butterfly, backstroke, breaststroke, and IM swimmers do the following set twice (2000 m set).

4 × 50 m	On 60 swim Swims 1 and 3 at 200 m pace Swims 2 and 4 DPS moderate pace, 30 to 40 BBM
2 × 100 m	On 1:45 for FS and BK, on 2:00 for BR and BF Females holding HR at 10 to 15 BBM, males holding HR at 15 to 20 BBM
1 × 200 m	On 3:30 First 100 m at the same pace from 2 × 100 m swims and second 100 m holding HR at 10 to 15 BBM, not going above 10 BBM
2 × 100 m	On 1:45 for FS and BK, on 2:00 for BR and BF Females holding HR at 10 BBM, males holding HR at 15 BBM
1 × 200	On 3:30 First 100 m at the same pace from 2 × 100 m swims and second 100 m holding HR at 10 BBM

Swimmers record all repeat times and heart rates. Coaches observe the workout and add a small amount of additional rest on the second or third set if required. Swimmers should record stroke counts, and coaches should record stroke rates.

An aerobic workout should follow this workout. Swimmers should do the entire set on their main stroke.

24 × 100 m	10 × 100 m on 1:45, heart rate at 20 BBM 10 × 100 m on 1:45, heart rate at 15 BBM 4 × 100 m on 1:45, heart rate at 10 BBM

(2400 m)

2 ×	1 × 200 m on 3:30, heart rate at 20 BBM 2 × 150 m on 2:30, heart rate at 20 BBM 3 × 100 m on 1:30, heart rate at 15 BBM 4 × 50 m on 50, heart rate at 10 BBM

(2000 m)

2 ×	6 × 100 m on 1:50, heart rate at 20 BBM 4 × 100 m on 1:40, heart rate at 20 BBM 2 × 100 m on 1:30, heart rate at 20 BBM

(2400 m)

3 ×	1 × 200 m on 3:30, heart rate at 20 BBM 2 × 100 m on 2:30, heart rate at 15 BBM 4 × 50 m on 60, heart rate at 10 BBM

(1800 m)

M$\dot{V}O_2$ Sample Sets

M$\dot{V}O_2$ training pace is established by using the method shown in chapter 1. The heart-rate level during this type of training will be around 10 beats below maximum. Repeat distances are generally 100 m to 500 m. For more information refer to chapter 1.

    5 × 4 × 100 m on 1:10
         200 m swim-down, 3:00

(2000 m M$\dot{V}O_2$ pace, 3000 m total set)

4 × 300 m FS
    2 × 100 m on 1:10
    200 m swim-down, 3:00

                                (2000 m $\dot{M}O_2$ pace, 2800 m total set)

3 × 4 × 150 m on 1:45
    1 × 300 m on 6:00

                                (1800 m $\dot{M}O_2$ pace, 2700 m total set)

4 × 4 × 100 m FS holding 400 m pace on 1:10
    300 m swim-down, 4:30

                                (1600 m $\dot{M}O_2$ pace, 2800 m total set)

1 × 400 m FS on 4:40
    200 m swim-down on 4:00
    2 × 200 m FS on 2:20
    200 m swim-down on 4:00
    4 × 100 m FS on 1:10
    200 m swim-down on 4:00
    8 × 50 m FS on 35
    200 m swim-down on 4:00

                                (1600 $\dot{M}O_2$ pace, 2400 m total set)

5 × 300 m on 6:15
    200 m swim-down on 4:00

                                (1500 m $\dot{M}O_2$ pace, 2500 m total set)

3 × 100 m FS holding 400 m pace on 1:10 with a 200 m swim-down every set
Swimmers can repeat this set three to five times. When swimmers can cope with this set they can progress to a set of 300 m repeats on 6:00.

                                (1500 m $\dot{M}O_2$ pace, 2500 m total set)

Sample High-Performance Endurance Sets and Sessions

Following are sample sets for female endurance swimmers.

40 × 200 m
    5 on 3:15 choice (kick, pull, swim), at least 50 m kick
    5 on 3:00, at least 50 m BF
    10 on 2:40
    10 on 2:30
    10 at fastest possible interval or 10 seconds rest or 2:50 interval holding 400 m race pace

                                      (8000 m)

12 × 50 m FS on 45, stroke counting
12 × 100 m FS on 1:30, last four at 800 m race pace
12 × 200 m FS on 3:00 slightly faster than 800 m race pace
12 × 100 m FS on 1:40, last four at 400 m race pace
12 × 50 m FS, odds 200 m race pace, evens 400 m race pace on 50

                                      (6000 m)

3 × 500 m at 1500 m race pace
    400 m at 800 m race pace
    300 m at individual checking speed (ICS)
    200 m at 400 m race pace
    100 m at 200 m race pace
First two sets on 1:30 cycle per 100 m, third set on 1:40 cycle per 100 m

                                      (4500 m)

2 × 1 × 400 m on 5:30
    2 × 300 m on 4:30
    3 × 200 m on 2:30
    4 × 100 m on 1:30

Swimmers hold race pace on the last 100 m of each repeat.
Swimmers hold 1:10 average on repeats as follows:
400 m holding 4:40 (last 100 m at 1:06 pace)
300 m holding 3:30 (last 100 m at 1:06 pace)
200 m holding 2:20 (last 100 m at 1:06 pace)
100 m holding 1:06
No rest occurs between sets. Advanced swimmers can perform a more challenging set by doing the first and last 100 m at 1:06 and holding the same total times, by doing the last 150 m of each repeat at 1:39, or by doing a combination of both options.

(4000 m)

20 × 150 m FS on 2:15 at 800 m race pace, recording heart rates
20 × 50 m FS on 60 or 50 holding 400 m race pace

(4000 m)

5 × 800 m FS on 10:30 (all 800 m repeats are negative split)
Target times for first 400 m of each 800 m are as follows:

First 800 m	First 400 m split 4:50 on 10:30
Second 800 m	First 400 m split 4:45 on 10:45
Third 800 m	First 400 m split 4:40 on 11:00
Fourth 800 m	First 400 m split 4:35 on 11:15
Fifth 800 m	First 400 m split faster than the first 400 m splits on the first four 800 m repeats

Add 15 seconds of rest each time the swimmer achieves the standard.

(4000 m)

5 × 300 m FS (1500 m pace) on 4:30
    5 × 100 m FS on 1:10

(4000 m)

12 × 150 m, 100 m, 50 m on 45 cycle per 50 for the first eight sets and then 50 cycle for the next four sets. Hold the HR at 15 BBM for the 150 m and 100 m repeats. Hold goal 400 m pace for the 50 m repeats. All swims are even split.

(3600 m)

6 × 200 m minimum-maximum
    400 m at ICS
    2:00 per 100 m cycle or start next repeat when HR is 60 BBM, start ICS when HR is 40 BBM

(3600 m)

5 × 400 m at 800 m pace
    200 m at ICS
    2:00 per 100 cycle or start next repeat when HR is 60 BBM, start ICS when HR is 40 BBM

(3000 m)

4 × 200 m at 400 m race pace
    100 m at 200 m race pace
    50 m at 100 m race pace
    50 m easy
    50 m at 200 m race pace
    100 m at 400 m race pace
    200 m at 800 m race pace
    On 1:30 cycle per 100 m

(3000 m)

2 × 100 m, 200 m, 300 m, 400 m holding 38 seconds per 50 m pace
    2:10, 3:10, 4:10, 5:10
1 × 400 m, 300 m, 200 m, 100 m holding 38 seconds per 50 m pace
    5:10, 4:00, 2:50, 1:20

(3000 m)

This set can be adjusted by changing the repeat time that the swimmer must hold. If the swimmer can cope with 38, he or she may progress to holding a 37 cycle pace and so on.

> 1 × 100 m, 200 m, 300 m, 400 m holding 38 seconds per 50 m pace
>   2:10, 3:10, 4:10, 5:10
> 2 × 400 m, 300 m, 200 m, 100 m holding 38 seconds per 50 m pace
>   5:10, 4:00, 2:50, 1:20

(3000 m)

> 2 × 5 × 300 m at 1500 m race pace on 3:40, 3:50, 4:00, 4:10, 4:20

(3000 m)

> 4 × 400 m at 800 m race pace
>   200 m at 400 m race pace
>   100 m at 200 m race pace
> Start the next repeat when the HR is 50 BBM.
> Record time, HR, and rest period taken.

(2800 m)

> 1 × Set 1   16 × 50 m FS on 50
> Descend one to eight. On the first two 50 m repeats of each set of eight, the swimmer holds 38 seconds and descends by one second per 50 m repeat after that to 32 seconds on the final 50 m repeat of each set (38, 37, 36, 35, 34, 33, 32, 31).
>   Set 2   16 × 50 m FS on 40
> Descend one to four. On the first two 50 m repeats of each set of four, the swimmer holds 35 seconds and descends by one second per 50 m repeat after that to 32 seconds on the final 50 m repeat of each set (35, 34, 33, 32).
>   Set 3   ? × 50 m FS on 40
> The swimmer holds between 31.8 to 32.2 seconds per 50 m repeat, feet on the wall (? × 50 means as many as the swimmer can hold or a number determined by the coach). The swimmer rests one minute between sets. The times recorded must be exact. Record the number of 50 m repeats achieved in set 3 along with the stroke counts for each 50 m repeat. The goal for the swimmer is to achieve 40 × 50 m repeats on 40, holding 32.0 seconds exactly, with the same stroke count on each 50 m. The time is from the feet leaving to the feet touching the wall (the swimmer will finish each 50 m repeat with the feet). 32-second 50 m repeats are 16-minute pace for the 1500 m FS. Any other target time can be used.

(2400 m)

Another progression for female distance swimmers is to swim one of the following sets in a progression of a set each week on the same day each week.

> 40 × 100 m FS on 1:30 holding 1:06 to 1:08 per 100 m repeat. When the swimmer can achieve this, she moves to the next set.
> 30 × 100 m FS on 1:45, alternating odd-numbered swims on 1:06 and even-numbered swims on 1:03.5. Again, when the swimmer can achieve this, she moves to the next set.
> 30 × 100 m FS on 1:45, one swim holding 1:06, then two swims holding 1:03.50, and so on for the remainder of the set. Again, when the swimmer can achieve this, she moves to the next set.
> 30 × 100 m FS on 1:45, one swim holding 1:06, then three swims holding 1:03.50, and so on for the remainder of the set.

Progression can be set up in many ways, but the previous sets suggest how the coach and swimmer can progress the sets over a number of weeks.

> 2 × 5 × 200 m at 800 m pace on 2:30, 2:40, 2:50, 3:00, 3:10

(2000 m)

4 × 400 m on 5:00, 5:15, 5:30, and 5:45 holding 1500 m pace	Target 4:16
1 × 200 m at 800 m pace on 2:30	Target 2:08
3 × 400 m on 5:15, 5:30, and 5:45 holding 1500 m pace	Target 4:16
2 × 200 m at 800 m pace on 2:45	Target 2:08
2 × 400 m on 5:30 and 5:45 holding 1500 m pace	Target 4:16
3 × 200 m at 800 m pace on 3:00	Target 2:08
1 × 400 m at half 800 m pace on 6:00	Target 4:16
4 × 200 m at 800 m pace on 3:15	Target 2:08

Sample target times are for a swimmer with personal best times of 16:00 for the 1500 m FS and 8:32 for the 800 m FS

(6000 m)

4 × 300 m at 1500 m pace on 4:30	Target 3:12
1 × 100 m at 800 m pace on 1:30	Target 1:04
3 × 300 m at 1500 m pace on 4:30	Target 3:12
2 × 100 m at 800 m pace on 1:30	Target 1:04
2 × 300 m at 1500 m pace on 4:30	Target 3:12
3 × 100 m at 800 m pace on 1:30	Target 1:04
1 × 300 m at 1500 m pace on 4:30	Target 3:12
4 × 100 m at 800 m pace on 1:30	Target 1:04

Sample target times are for a swimmer with personal best times of 16:00 for the 1500 m FS and 8:32 for the 800 m FS

(4000 m)

6 × 400 m FS repeats at race pace as follows:

400 m	Split by 10 seconds at the 200 m split
	Target pace is current 400 m PB with an even split (2:08, 2:08)
400 m	Recovery drill and swim mixture
400 m	RI 10 seconds at each 100 m split
	Target pace is the season goal 400 m time (63.5, 63.5, 63.5, 63.5)
400 m	Recovery drill and swim mixture
400 m	RI 10 seconds at each 50 m split
	Target pace is next season's target 400 m time. (31.5, 31.5, 31.5, 31.5, 31.5, 31.5, 31.5, 31.5)
400 m	Recovery drill and swim mixture

Current 400 m FS personal best time 4:16, target PB 4:14, next season's target 4:12

(2400 m)

200 m race pace set

4 × 100 m	Descending one to four, final 100 m at second 100 m of 200 m pace (1:08.9, 1:06.9, 1:04.9, 1:02.9)
1 × 50 m	At 200 m pace (31.5)
3 × 100 m	Descending one to three, final 100 m at second 100 m of 200 m pace (1:06.9, 1:04.9, 1:02.9)
2 × 50 m	At 200 m pace (31.5)
2 × 100 m	Descending one to two, final 100 m at second 100 m of 200 m pace (1:04.9, 1:02.9)
3 × 50 m	At 200 m pace (31.5)
1 × 100 m	At second 100 m of 200 m pace (1:02.9)
4 × 50 m	At 200 m pace (31.5)

(1500 m)

The swimmer's target time is 2:06 for the 200 FS, split 1:03.1 and 1:02.9. The 50 m repeats are on 1:00, and the 100 m repeats are on 2:00. The swimmer descends on the 100 m repeats by two seconds on each repeat in the set, that is, 1:08.9, 1:06.9, 1:04.9, 1:02.9.

Zone 4—Anaerobic (Race-Pace Training)

As suggested in chapter 1, race-pace training is crucial to the swimmer's development in all events. The coach and swimmer should work together to develop training sets in this zone. This section will show examples of the many different ways to build training sets for this type of training. For more details on this type of training, refer to chapter 1.

Race-Pace Lactate-Production Sets

The first type of lactate training introduced in the swimming season is race-pace lactate production. In this section we outline sample training sets for the 400 m and farther swimmer, the 200 m swimmer, and the 100 m swimmer. The sets are based on repeat distances of 25 m, 50 m, 75 m, and 100 m.

400-Meter and Farther Swimmer

    4 × 100 m at 400 m pace on 2:00
         2 × 50 m at 400 m pace on 60
         200 m swim-down

                                                    (1200 m race pace, 2000 m total set)

    20 × 50 m at 400 m pace on 1:15

                                                    (1000 m race pace)

    6 × 100 m at 400 m pace on 2:30
         50 m at 400 m pace on 1:15

                                                    (900 m race pace)

    2 × 8 × 50 m on 60 at 400 m pace
         First 50 m of each set of 8 from a dive
         400 m swim-down after each set of 8 × 50 m

                                                    (800 m race pace, 1600 m total set)

    4 × 75 m on 2:00 at 400 m pace
         50 m on 1:30 at 400 m pace
         100 m swim-down on 3:00

                                                    (500 m race pace, 900 m total set)

200-Meter Swimmer

    5 × 50 m competition start at 200 m pace on 90
         50 m drill on 60
         100 m at second 100 m of 200 m pace on 2:00
         50 m drill on 60
         50 m push at final 50 m of 200 m pace

                                                    (1000 m race pace, 1500 m total set)

    3 × 5 × 50 m as dive, push, push, push, push on 60
         First 50 m at first 50 m of 200 m race pace
         Push start 50 m repeats at 200 m race pace
         400 m recovery every set

                                                    (750 m race pace, 1950 m total set)

    6 × 50 m competition start at first 50 m of 200 m pace on 60
         50 m push start at 200 m pace
         400 m recovery every set

                                                    (600 m race pace, 3000 m total set)

$5 \times$ 50 m on 40 at 200 m pace
     50 m on 2:20 at 200 m pace
     100 m swim-down on 3:00

(500 m race pace, 1000 m total set)

10×50 m at 200 m pace holding stroke count and stroke rate on 1:00 FS or 1:30 form stroke

(500 m race pace)

5×75 m on 5:15 with active recovery of 75 m after each swim at 200 pace

(375 m race pace, 750 m total set)

100-Meter Swimmer

$3 \times$ 4×25 m at one-quarter 100 m time on 30, 1×100 m swim-down
     2×50 m at second 50 m of 100 pace on 60, 2×100 m swim-down
     1×100 m as fast as possible, 3×100 m swim-down

(900 m race pace, 2700 m total set)

4×50 m at second 50 m of 100 m pace on 1:30
1×25 m maximum speed on 60
3×50 m at second 50 m of 100 m pace on 1:30
2×25 m maximum speed on 60
2×50 m at second 50 m of 100 m pace on 1:30
3×25 m maximum speed on 60
1×50 m at second 50 m of 100 m pace on 1:30
4×25 m maximum speed on 60

(750 m race pace)

4×50 m at second 50 m pace for 100 m on 1:30
1×25 m maximum speed on 45
3×50 m at second 50 m pace for 100 m on 1:30
2×25 m maximum speed on 45
2×50 m at second 50 m pace for 100 m on 1:30
3×25 m maximum speed on 45
1×50 m at second 50 m pace for 100 m on 1:30
4×25 m maximum speed on 45

(750 m race pace)

$6 \times$ 50 m competition start at first 50 m pace of 100 m pace on 90
     50 m push start at second 50 m pace of 100 m on 2:00
     400 m recovery every set

(600 m race pace, 3000 m total set)

$4 \times$ 50 m competition start at first 50 m pace of 100 m on 90
     50 m drill on 90
     50 m push start at second 50 m pace of 100 m on 90
     50 m drill on 90
     50 m push at second 50 m pace of 100 m on 90

(600 m race pace, 1000 m total set)

10×50 m at second 50 m pace of 100 m holding stroke count and stroke rate on 2:00

(500 m race pace)

$10 \times$ 50 m maximum effort at first 50 m of 100 pace from a dive
          50 m swim-down on 2:30

(500 m race pace, 1000 m total set)

$3 \times$ 25 m, competition start at 100 m pace on 45
     25 m, push start at 100 m pace on 45
     50 m, push start at 100 m pace on 90
     100 m swim-down

(300 m race pace, 600 m total set)

(Sweetenham 1990)

Race-Pace Lactate Tolerance Sets

Following the introduction of lactate-production training, the coach can introduce lactate-tolerance training sets. Again in this section we have outlined sample training sets for the 400 m and farther swimmer, the 200 m swimmer, and the 100 m swimmer. The sets are based on repeat distances of 50 m through 400 m.

400-Meter and Farther Swimmer

2 ×   2 × 200 m competition start on 5:00, 150 m swim-down at 400 m pace
     4 × 100 m competition start on 2:30, 150 m swim-down at 200 m pace
     4 × 50 m competition start on 1:15, 150 m swim-down at second 50 m of 200 m pace

(2000 m race pace, 2900 m total set)

2 ×   2 × 200 m, competition start on 5:00 at 400 m pace
     150 m swim-down
     4 × 100 m, competition start on 2:30 at 400 m pace
     150 m swim-down
     4 × 50 m, push start on 60 at 400 m pace
     300 m swim-down

(2000 m race pace, 3200 m total set)

12 × 50 m on 1:30 at 400 m pace
6 × 100 m on 2:30 at 400 m pace
2 × 200 m on 5:00 at 400 m pace

(1600 m race pace)

4 × 400 m on 8:00 at half 800 m pace

(1600 m race pace)

2 ×   400 m minimum-maximum on 5:00
     100 m swim-down on 2:00
     8 × 50 m alternating competition start 50 m on 60 and push start 50 m on 90 at 400 pace
     100 m swim-down on 2:00

(1600 m race pace, 2000 m total set)

6 × 200 m on 5:00   1 and 4   50 m on 60, 50 m on 60, 100 m on 3:00
                2 and 5   50 m on 60, 100 m on 3:00, 50 m on 60
                3 and 6   100 m on 3:00, 50 m on 60, 50 m on 60
Aiming to hold 400 m pace on the swims

(1200 m race pace)

3 × 200 m on 4:40 at 400 m pace
3 × 100 m on 2:30 at 400 m pace
3 × 50 m on 1:20 at 400 m pace

(1050 m race pace)

200-Meter Swimmer

4 ×   3 × 50 m as 50 m BF, 50 m BK, 50 m BR on 1:00 at 200 m pace
     2 × 50 m competition start 50 m, then push start 50 m on 1:30 at 200 m pace
     100 m IM on 2:00 at half 200 m pace
     1 × 50 m competition start 50 m BR on 2:00 at 200 m pace
     300 m swim-down on 7:00

(1600 m race pace, 2800 m total set)

3 ×   125 m at 200 m pace on 3:00
     100 m at 200 m pace on 2:30
     75 m at 200 m pace on 2:00
     50 m at 200 m pace on 1:30

(1050 m race pace)

3 × 100 m on 4:00 at 200 m pace
   75 m on 2:00 at 200 m pace
   50 m on 1:00 at 200 m pace

                        (675 m race pace)

4 × 50 m at 200 m pace on 1:20
2 × 100 m at 200 m pace on 2:00
1 × 200 m at 200 m pace broken × 10 seconds at each 50 m on 4:00
2 × 100 m at 200 m pace on 2:00
4 × 50 m at 200 m pace on 1:20

                       (1000 m race pace)

5 × 200 m as 2 × 50 m and 1 × 100 m on 1:30 and 2:30 at 200 m pace on 4:00

                       (1000 m race pace)

8 × 125 m at 200 m pace on 3:00

                       (1000 m race pace)

3 × 100 m at 200 m pace on 4:00
1 × 50 m at second 50 m of 100 m pace on 2:00
2 × 100 m at 200 m pace on 4:00
2 × 50 m at second 50 m of 100 m pace on 2:00
1 × 100 m at 200 m pace on 4:00
3 × 50 m at second 50 m of 100 m pace on 2:00

                       (900 m race pace)

6 × 150 m competition start on 7:30, targeting 150 m split of 200 m
   300 m swim-down between efforts

               (900 m race pace, 2700 m total set)

8 × 100 m competition start on 4:00, targeting 100 m split of 200 m

                       (800 m race pace)

5 × 200 m   First straight on 5:00
            Second as 150 m on 2:15 and 50 m at 200 m pace on 2:45
            Third as 100 m on 1:30 and 100 m at 200 m pace on 3:30
            Fourth as 50 m on 45 and 150 m at 200 m pace on 4:15
            Fifth straight on 5:00

              (400 m race pace, 1000 m total set)

100-Meter Swimmer

12 × 100 m   In four sets of 3 × 100 m
Each 100 m as competition start 75 m on 1:15 and push start 25 m on 30
Target to beat PB 100 m pace
4 × 50 m pull on 60 recovery following every set of 3 × 100 m

              (1200 m race pace, 2000 m total set)

8 × 50 m on 1:30 at 100 m pace
4 × 100 m on 2:30 minimum-maximum drill

                       (800 m race pace)

5 × 50 m MS at second 50 m of 100 m pace, BF, BK, FS on 55, BR on 60
1 × 100 m drill DPS on 4:00
4 × 50 m MS at second 50 m of 100 m pace, BF, BK, FS on 50, BR on 55
1 × 100 m drill DPS on 3:30
3 × 50 m MS at second 50 m of 100 m pace, BF, BK, FS on 45, BR on 50
1 × 100 m drill DPS on 3:00
2 × 50 m MS at second 50 m of 100 m pace, BF, BK, FS on 40, BR on 45
1 × 50 m drill DPS on 2:30
1 × 50 m MS at second 50 m of 100 m pace, BF, BK, FS on 35, BR on 40

              (750 m race pace, 1100 m total set)

6 × 100 on 2:30   1 and 4   25 m, 25 m, 50 m on 30, 30, 1:30
                2 and 5   25 m, 50 m, 25 m on 30, 30, 1:30
                3 and 6   50 m, 25 m, 25 m on 1:30, 30, 30
                Aiming to hold 100 m pace splits on this set

                       (600 m race pace)

4 × 50 m from a dive at first 50 m of 100 m pace 50 m on 1:30
    50 m from a push at second 50 m of 100 m pace on 1:30
    50 m from a push at second 50 m of 100 m pace on 1:30
    200 m swim-down

                                (600 m race pace, 1400 m total set)

(Sweetenham 1990)

Peak Lactate Training Sets

The swimmer produces peak or extremely close to peak lactate on each swim when doing peak lactate training. The swimmer therefore requires longer rest when doing peak lactate training than when doing tolerance work. An example is 4 × 100 m on 15 minutes, with active recovery between repeats.

The swimmer can perform this type of work over distances of 100 m to 400 m using straight and broken swims.

4 to 6 × 75 m	On 10:00 with 400 m to 500 m swim-down between swims
	100 m swimmer aiming at target 75 m split for the 100 m
	(300 to 450 m peak lactate)
4 × 100 m	On 20:00 with 1000 m swim-down following each 100 m
	100 m swimmer swims at maximum effort aiming to hit their target 50 m split of their 100 m event
	200 m swimmer, aiming to hit their target 100 m split for the 200 m event
	(400 m peak lactate)
3 × 200 m	On 30:00 with 1000 m to 1500 m swim-down following each 200 m
	400 m swimmer aiming at target 200 m split for the 400 m
	800 m swimmer aiming at target 800 m pace or faster on 20:00
	(600 m peak lactate)

Progression From Production to Tolerance Training

Early in the season the coach may introduce lactate-production training to the swimmer and then progress this to lactate-tolerance training over a period of a few weeks. An example of progressing to tolerance training from production training follows:

Week 1	12 × 50 m maximum effort on 2:30
Week 2	8 × 50 m, 2 × 100 m maximum effort on 2:30, 4:00
Week 3	6 × 50 m, 3 × 100 m maximum effort on 2:30, 3:30
Week 4	4 × 50 m, 4 × 100 m maximum effort on 2:00, 3:30
Week 5	2 × 50 m, 5 × 100 m maximum effort on 2:00, 3:30
Week 6	2 sets of 3 × 100 m maximum effort on 3:00

For a combination set that contains all areas of lactate training, the coach might use this set:

Production training: 2 × 50 m repeats on 2:00
Tolerance training: 4 × 150 m repeats on 3:00
Peak training: 2 × 50 m repeats on 5:00

That set progresses to the following set:

Production training: 4 × 50 m repeats on 2:00
Tolerance training: 6 × 150 m repeats on 3:00
Peak training: 2 × 50 m repeats on 5:00

Zone 5—Sprint

When training in this zone, the swimmer must never train to fatigue or compromise stroke length for speed (failing the back end of swims). Recovery when performing speed training is an individual skill. The swimmer and coach should understand the difference between maximum speed and maximum effort, as outlined in chapter 1.

Target times for speed training should be established for repeat distances of 10 m to 25 m using the method outlined in chapter 1.

Sprint Training Sets

3 ×	1 × 50 m	Minimum-maximum on 60
	1 × 100 m	Easy on 2:00
	1 × 25 m	Minimum-maximum on 30
	1 × 25 m	Easy on 60
	2 × 25 m	Minimum-maximum pull on 30
	1 × 50 m	Easy on 1:40
	1 × 25 m	Minimum-maximum kick on 30
	1 × 25 m	Easy on 60
	1 × 12.5 m	Maximum speed fast on 30
	1 × 12.5 m	Easy on 30
	1 × 12.5 m	Maximum speed fast on 30
	1 × 12.5 m	Easy on 30

(450 m sprint training)

4 × 25 m on 45	Explode the first and last 15 m on alternate 25 m repeats
4 × 25 m on 60	Competition start maximum speed to 15 m to 20 m
4 × 25 m on 45	Explode the first and last 15 m on alternate 25 m repeats
2 × 50 m on 2:00	Competition start maximum speed to 15 m to 20 m
4 × 25 m on 45	Explode the first and last 15 m on alternate 25 m repeats
1 × 50 m	Competition start fast for time, aiming to hit target 50 m split time for goal 100 m PB

(345 m sprint training)

20 × 25 m on 45	4 × explode the first 15 m of the 25 m
	4 × explode the last 15 m of the 25 m
	4 × with the first 15 m rating drill (at a high stroke rate)
	4 × with the last 15 m rating drill
	4 × explode the first 15 m of the 25 m

(300 m sprint training)

4 sets of 4 × 25 m on 45 or 60

Set 1	Competition start explode 20 m
Set 2	Push start explode last 15 m
Set 3	Push start explode first 15 m
Set 4	Turns 12.5 m in and 12.5 m out fast

(300 m sprint training)

Incorporating starts, turns, and finishes
3 sets of 5 × 50 m as follows:

Set 1, competition starts
Explode 3 to 4 strokes BR or BF and 6 to 8 strokes BK or FS. Do the remaining distance of the 50 m DPS on 2:00. Target distance 15 m to 20 m.

Set 2, turns

From 5 m out from at the wall, swim at maximum speed into the turn and at maximum speed for 10 m out of the turn on 2:00.

Set 3, finishes
Explode the last 15 m of each 50 m on 2:00.

(250 m sprint training)

4 × 15 m	HVOs on 40
1 × 200 m	Alt 50 m drill, 50 m swim on 4:00
4 × 15 m	Explosion kick on 50
1 × 200 m	Alt 50 m drill, 50 m swim on 4:00
4 × 15 m	Explosion pull on 50
1 × 200 m	Alt 50 m drill, 50 m swim on 4:00
4 × 15 m	Explosion finishes on 50
1 × 200 m	Alt 50 m drill, 50 m swim on 4:00

(240 m sprint training)

3 × 2 × 25 m on 60
    2 × 12.5 m on 60

(225 m sprint training)

1 × 50 m	25 m FS DPS, 25 m MS stroke drill on 60
1 × 50 m	15 m MS explosion, 35 m choice (CH) DPS on 60
1 × 100 m	50 m FS, 50 m MS stroke drill on 2:00
2 × 50 m	25 m explosion MS, 25 m CH DPS on 60
1 × 150 m	75 m FS DPS, 75 m MS stroke drill on 3:00
3 × 50 m	35 m explosion CH, 15 m DPS MS on 60
1 × 200 m	100 FS DPS, 100 MS on 4:00
4 × 50 m	Descending one to four on 60, final 50 m minimum-maximum drill

(220 m sprint training)

8 × 25 m competition start repeats timed with target pace the first 25 m of 100 m pace

(200 m sprint training)

2 sets of 4 × 50 m BR on 2:00 as follows:
50 m four underwater pull-outs, sprint the rest of that 25 m, then 25 m easy
50 m three underwater pull-outs, sprint the rest of that 25 m, then 25 m easy
50 m two underwater pull-outs, sprint the rest of that 25 m, then 25 m easy
50 m one underwater pull-out, sprint the rest of that 25 m, then 25 m easy

(200 m sprint training)

4 × 20 m starts, then swim distance per stroke to 25
4 × 20 m turns as 10 m in and 10 m out
4 × 25 m finishes with last 10 m maximum effort

(200 m sprint training)

2 sets of 2 × 50 m and 200 m swim-down:
50 m	25 m competition start maximum speed, 25 DPS on 60
50 m	Push start on 60 at second 50 m pace of 100 m
200 m	Swim-down on 4:00

(150 m sprint training)

3 × 50 m as 15 m fast, 35 m easy on 2:00
    50 m as 20 m fast, 30 m easy on 2:00
    50 m as 25 m fast, 25 m easy on 2:00
    50 m as 30 m easy, 20 m fast on 2:00
    50 m as 35 m easy, 15 m fast on 2:00
This set can be performed as pull, kick, swim, swim with fins, kick with fins, swim with paddles, or as a combo mixture.

(125 m sprint training)

6 × 20 m sprints with 30 m swim-down on 2:00

(120 m sprint training)

2 × 100 m	25 m competition start on 60
	50 m push, sprint turns 10 m in and 10 m out on 90
	25 m push, explode the last 15 m on 60

(90 m sprint training)

| 2 × 25 m | 25 m competition start maximum speed, 25 m swim-down on 2:00 |
| 1 × 50 m | 50 m push start on 60 at second 50 m of 100 m pace |

(75 m sprint training)

Short sprints can be built into the sessions following a high-intensity set to aid removal and recycling of lactate in the muscle system (Sweetenham 1990).

This chapter gives examples of training sets for all the training zones explained in chapter 1. Many of the sets here are examples of the training sets outlined in the sample weekly microcycle plans of chapter 12. By using both chapters 1 and 12, the coach and swimmer can begin to plan a detailed training program, using these sets or modifications of them.

© Human Kinetics

While training in zone 1, the swimmer becomes proficient in a skill at low speeds before building up to higher competitive-level speeds.

14

Tapering for Competition

Tapering is a component of training that must match the needs of the individual swimmer. No miracles occur with a taper or in the final race-preparation phase of the training cycle or season. Tapering is about an individual preparing physically and mentally to perform at the highest possible level.

A taper used by an entire team will not work equally well for all its members. Tapering is about refining skills and gradually reducing physical stress to allow the individual to develop peak fitness for a particular event on a given date. Tapering is about swimming fast and performing at one's best. Successful tapering is about being confident and feeling no pressure.

With those points in mind, the coach and swimmer should at least have a model to work with so that the taper contains as few variables as possible. The coach and swimmer should plan and record the taper in detail so that they can refine and repeat it. The swimmer does workouts each day but has the opportunity to taper only once or twice a year, usually in different conditions, so recording the process is important.

Planning the Taper

The swimmer and coach must understand that the swimmer requires less training to hold physical training gains than he or she originally needed to obtain them, so tapering need not lead to a loss of conditioning. A taper is a gradual reduction in physical stress and an increase in mental stress. The coach must mentally prepare and program the athlete and team by offering coping strategies that will allow the athlete to handle all situations, even unexpected ones. The coach should try to limit the mental stress and keep it under control.

In developing a model for tapering (race preparation) or considering a variation to a model, important factors include the athlete's age, muscular development, background, event, and psychological makeup. Tapering is about performing race-specific training along with adequate and increasing recovery and adaptation.

Intensity is the major training item in maintaining or improving fitness during the race preparation or tapering period. The appropriate level of intensity depends on the individual and the event. A suitable amount of critical speed work can be established in a convenient way by scheduling 100 m of such work for each day that remains until the meet. For example, 18 days out from the meet means 1800 m of critical speed work. Obviously, using this method means that quite a contrast in the level of effort is required. That is, a sprinter might descend training sets as follows: swim one 40 BBM, swim two 30 BBM, swim three 20 BBM, and swim four 10 BBM and broken at race pace. The distance swimmer might do 18 × 100 m at 20 BBM (the example is only in terms of the specific set).

Figure 14.1 shows a tapering chart model that starts five weeks out from the competition. A simple training mesocycle and microcycles that provide a good start for developing cycle training that is easy to taper from is shown in table 14.1.

For the age-group swimmer under age 15 (approximately), the coach can apply the tapering principles shown in figure 14.1 and table 14.2 (page 243), working down from 15 days out from the competition rather than 21 days out. For some age-group swimmers, however, a taper of only 10 days is appropriate in the initial stages of their careers. As athletes progress through the age groups and maturation, they progress to a 15-day taper and finally a 21-day taper. The event and the muscular development and training background of the athlete still dictate the type and amount of training

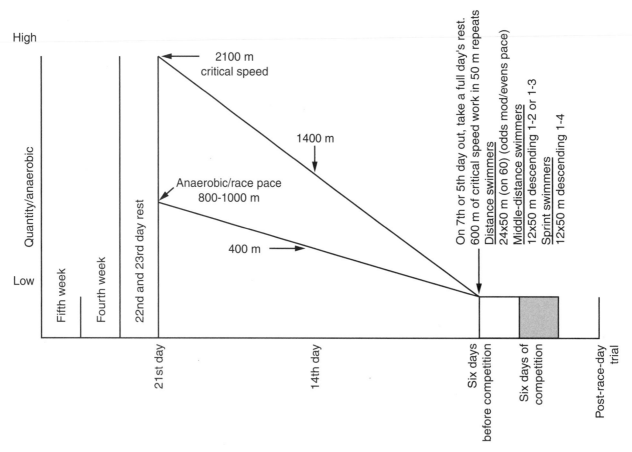

FIGURE 14.1 Tapering chart model.

TABLE 14.1   MONTHLY MESOCYCLE

Training week	Number of critical speed sets	Number of anaerobic/race-pace training sets	Weekly totals of HVOs to be conducted
Week 1	3	1	80
Week 2	2	2	60
Week 3	1	3	40
Week 4 (an adaptation week if required as taper rehearsal, or first week of taper)	2	2	40

completed during these progressions, but having an end product (model) and working backward from it is extremely helpful. An example is the following:

21 days as shown in this chapter (15 years and older)

15 days as shown by the last 15 days outlined (15 years and under, maturation)

10 days as shown by the last 10 days outlined (ages below maturation)

The tapering policy outlined in this chapter will help the coach and athlete handle "flat spots" or "taper blues" should they occur. If they occur, the swimmer should do aerobic work only, understand that this is a temporary adaptation, and use heart rate for intensity control, not repeat time.

In many instances flat spots occur because mental stimulation and challenge is absent from the workout environment. These flat spots rarely last longer than four to six days, but they can occur suddenly. In a taper, the coach should always seek to identify when the athlete experiences "real" speed. The swimmer should always perform faster at competition than when repeating at training. If this does not happen, the coach should look for overstress (physical or mental) or an adaptation plateau.

Both the coach and swimmer should have a notebook or training log at all meets of any importance (district, state, or national championships) and record their observations so that they can prepare a checklist for succeeding meets. From one championship to another can be 12 months. Remembering meet conditions that influence the athlete can be difficult. This idea also applies to pools, which a swimmer may use only once every four or five years.

Generally, the male swimmer tapers over a longer period than the female swimmer does. This distinction, however, is mainly due to the amount of muscle mass of each individual—the greater the muscle mass, the longer the taper. The breaststroker, because of the leg and arm stress of the stroke, may require a little more time to attain adequate rest or less volume of race-pace work during the same period of taper.

As a guideline for the last six days of the taper, the total daily yardage should not be more or less than the total daily yardage during the competition. Add up warm-ups, heats, swim-downs, semifinals, and finals and use that as a guideline.

The coach and athlete must develop the ability to focus on the next event and be ready for it, regardless of the outcome of the previous event.

Athletes must be practiced in drug-testing protocol and procedures. Besides knowing all the banned substances and what is expected of them in the testing procedure, athletes must know and be aware of their rights.

A set of 8 × 50 m MS on 2:30 (shown in chapter 2) starting eight weeks out from a meet descending one to eight and reducing the descent emphasis by one each week is a set we have found useful as a confidence builder for the swimmer. This means that the swimmer will eventually work from 400 m pace down to second 50 m pace of a 100 m swim by the seventh week out. In this set, the coach should record the time, stroke count, and heart rate (accurately) for each 50 m and compare these from one taper to the next. Each week, the swimmer drops the time of the first 50 m and repeats the time of the next 50 m.

We offer the following basic guidelines for coaches and swimmers to develop a model that might suit a team situation or individual, or challenge what the coach may be currently using as a model. A coach or swimmer following sound principles will find it difficult to detrain or lose form in the last 21 days, providing that the training progression has been adequate.

Four to Five Weeks From the Competition

Little difference in training occurs until five to four weeks before the competition. The individual medley swimmer begins to practice full IM work only during the final five weeks.

Race preparation starts five weeks out from the competition, in both morning and afternoon or evening training sessions. We suggest no increase in either the quality or amount of race-pace training. Race-pace training can be considered any training completed at 400 m pace or faster.

The swimmer and coach, having set clearly identified, realistic goals at the start of the last cycle of training, must rehearse and practice those goals by using broken swims during the last five weeks at the latest. The exact timing of each 50 m, taking into account the start, turning, stroke rate, and stroke count by 25 m or 50 m, must be rehearsed frequently as part of a race-pace training set, especially in conditions that simulate a race. We have learned, however, that a swimmer's ability to simulate race pace in broken swims should not be used as an indicator of form. Swimmers should also perform one-off race-pace work without the benefit of a pace clock. These broken events start approximately five weeks out with a short rest and build to long-rest swims closer to the meet.

The swimmer should reduce critical speed, lactate, all anaerobic, and quality work according to the model, an example of which is shown in figure 14.1. The swimmer must maintain kick sets through the taper for lower-body fitness but reduce them according to the chart. An increased component of critical speed sets should be swum in 50 m repeats at the end of the critical speed sets and keep at race pace or slightly slower.

Repeat 50 m swims done in a critical speed set at 15 BBM at the start of the set can tend to be anaerobic, and as such it can defeat the purpose of the set (maintaining race endurance) and complicate the more intense anaerobic sets in the rest of the weekly cycle. The 50 m repeats should therefore occur at the end of a critical speed set.

Swimmers should practice starts, turns, and finishes during the last five weeks with high demand and constant feedback, both positive and negative. With starts, they practice both reflex starts and command starts. For the first start, they concentrate on reflex and movement-reaction time. For second starts, they focus on being safe with concentration on command. Relay takeover practice is also important. Swimmers should practice starts, turns, finishing, and relay drills.

The amount of high-velocity overload swimming should not increase from five weeks out, but the sets should alternate from practice to practice, either after warm-up (speed enhancement) or before swim-down (race enhancement). The sets should also be done in swim, kick, resistance pull (race stroke rate), and speed drills. High-velocity overload work should vary from morning workouts to afternoon workouts, both after warm-ups and before swim-downs.

From five weeks out from the competition, the number of repetitions in dryland training and gym work should decrease. Athletes should lift slightly heavier loads with fewer repetitions. A significant increase should occur in both specific and nonspecific muscle strength and power during the taper period.

Swimmers should have a competition meal list and have the skills needed to prepare their own meals during competition. They should do this well before the competition. Five weeks before the meet, the coach should arrange a team meeting to review the meal list. Athletes should also be able to make wise selections from a buffet meal situation, which could naturally include both good and bad foods. Nearly all pasta dishes available at restaurants are made and coated with cheap fat-saturated sauces, so every high-performance athlete must be able to choose wisely or prepare his or her own food.

Training will differ only slightly from the fifth week to the fourth week out from the competition. Anaerobic training will be a little more intense or race specific. During the fourth week out, swimmers will focus more on racing skill refinement and intensity but will not increase the amount of race-pace work.

Starting five weeks out from the competition, athletes should do squat jumps or plyometrics on a daily basis. This workout should include approximately four sets of four jumps with long rest between sets (three to five minutes), decreasing to three sets by three weeks before

Make the environment work for you; do not become a victim of it.

competition, and then decreasing by one set each week. These workouts assist in starting and turning and replace leg exercises in the gym. Doing these workouts close to the competition will create an advantage.

Some coaches have a very hard endurance-anaerobic week about four weeks out from the meet based on the notion that this last hard week is either the last chance to make gains or a way to carry the swimmer through the last three weeks. This hard week can be counterproductive because it can confuse the body's adjustment before resting. It may be helpful, however, to add a little more aerobic work to the taper if the athlete is young or less muscular or has less background and may be unable to hold a three-week race preparation. Holding the volume of anaerobic work steady in the fifth and fourth weeks out and increasing the intensity in the fourth week out will usually produce more success.

Three Weeks From the Competition

During the last three weeks before a competition the swimmer will generally do fewer workouts to become fully rested going into the meet. The danger in this is that the athlete's body clock may change drastically during the last three weeks. The swimmer should have eight hours of sleep each night with two hours of rest during the day (reading, playing games, and so forth).

As a coach, encourage the athlete to take an afternoon off rather than a morning off so that he or she will, ironically, get more sleep. A morning off will sometimes mean that the athlete will stay up late, knowing that he or she can sleep in the next morning. This pattern must not be part of the high-performance athlete's preparation. The athlete must accept and practice the correct policy on rest at a young age. Resting the athlete in the pool and gym is pointless if the athlete subsequently increases other activities or has less quality rest during race-pace training periods, including the race-preparation phase. Quality rest and recovery is necessary for quality performance.

At 23 to 21 days out from the competition, every swimmer and coach should rest for 2 days so that on the 21st day the taper starts with a fresh athlete and coach.

On the 22nd or 23rd day out from the meet, the swimmer should review or prepare these items or points:

- Self-monitoring chart
- Competition checklists
- Vivid visualization skills
- Prerace warm-up (heats, semifinals, and finals)
- Relaxation skills
- Prerace plan (written)
- Race plan (written)
- Competition meal plan (menu)
- Familiarization with competition pool and environment

The training volume decreases in line with figure 14.1, which shows a tapering model from 21 days out from the meet.

After the 21st day out from the competition, the swimmer does no training faster than race pace, other than short (25 m or less) high-velocity overloads or, for the sprint swimmer, a small amount of sprint-assisted work. Race pace is determined as the second 50 m of the goal pace for 100 m or 200 m for each swimmer. All anaerobic work is now at race pace. Short sprints of six strokes, performed faster than race pace, are also of great value to the swimmer involved in 50 m or 100 m events. The ability to be at top speed in two or three strokes is of paramount importance for every swimmer, not just the sprinter.

Starting from 21 days before the competition, the athlete should fully recover from one workout or practice before performing the next one. That is, the athlete should not carry fatigue from one practice to the next. An increase in the amount or percentage of anaerobic or race-pace work in the last 21 days can result in overstress. Disregarding heart rates can also lead to a detraining effect.

Table 14.2 is an example of a three-week taper race-preparation phase descending from a monthly macrocycle. To bring this into line with the previously mentioned tapering philosophy, the fourth and fifth weeks out from the competition need to be balanced as equal weeks. All this means is that an additional critical speed set is added and a race-pace set is deducted from week 3 of table 14.1, or vice versa, depending on the athlete and the event.

The first week of taper (21 days to 14 days) should mirror exactly the adaptation weeks that have occurred throughout the season, if they have been used. Every time the seasonal program has an adaptation week, it should be a rehearsal of the first week of taper for a major meet.

For a minor but important meet (state or district championships) the same principal applies, with an exact rehearsal of the first two weeks of a taper (21 days from the competition to 7 days from the competition) from the seasonal program. This circumstance provides an opportunity to practice the second week of the taper. (Working the taper using 14 days from competition to the day of the competition, rather than 21 days from the competition to 7 days from the competition, has not been successful because the large drop in race-pace work has proved to be too dramatic.)

TABLE 14.2 FINAL THREE WEEKS OF RACE PREPARATION

Training week	Number of critical speed sets	Number of anaerobic/race-pace training sets	Weekly totals of HVOs to be conducted
Week 1 of taper	2	2	40
Week 1 of the taper is week 3 before the event and these sets are now down to 50-60% of highest weekly training volume while maintaining intensity.			
Week 2 of taper	1 (plus 1 pace set, mainly 50 m repeats)	1	30
Week 2 of the taper is week 2 before the event and these sets have continued to reduce in volume and become more race-specific (including more race pace).			
Week 3 of taper	1 (600 m, as per figure 14.1)	1 (single effort pace swims)	20
Week 3 is the final week of taper; rest and recovery is all important.			

Two Weeks From the Competition

At two weeks from the competition the taper may start for age-group athletes who require a 14-day taper. Some age-group athletes may require only a 7-day taper, but they could use a 14-day taper at another point in the season to see how it works. From 10 days out, athletes use broken and split swims at race pace. Throughout this period the coach and swimmer should be aware of diet and sleep patterns. Rest is important—no late nights.

Swimmers should perfect desired race stroke rates and do exact pace work from 10 to 6 days before the meet, in broken swims. They practice heat, semifinal, and final pace work and strategies.

Ten days before the meet, swimmers should perform a full-blooded swim at maximum effort in the morning. This swim should be over a slightly shorter race distance or with a different stroke; this, along with a race-specific broken swim in the afternoon practice, simulates race day. Athletes rehearse race and prerace plans along with prerace meal and warm-ups.

The coach should be extremely cautious with any anaerobic (lactate) training within 10 days of the meet. To keep athletes on edge and hold glycogen levels balanced, this type of training should not occur during the final 10 days. If in doubt, leave it out.

One Week From the Competition

You, as a coach, should conduct a team meeting two or three days before the meet to state your expectations and provide all available information about the meet. You should talk individually every day to each athlete and explain and define relay responsibilities and arrangements.

Prepare motivation strategies for the first day of the meet (big start) and for the difficult third day of the meet. Two days out from the main event help your swimmers relax. Encourage the athletes to do something that they get pleasure from, such as go to a movie or buy a new CD. Help them forget about the competition so that they feel less pressure.

Tapering Volumes

We suggest increasing, decreasing, introducing, or withdrawing only one thing at a time from a training program. Certainly, do not decrease the amount of training and increase the amount of quality work. That is usually a recipe for disaster.

An example of how to reduce the training volumes in a taper is shown in figures 14.2 and 14.3 for a program in which 75 kilometers is the highest seasonal week. Two weeks out from the competition the total volume is reduced to 50 percent, which is 37.5 kilometers.

The percentage of race-pace work (400 m pace or faster) in any given week should be around 10 to 15 percent of the total workload and should stay at that level or fall a bit during the taper period. Swimmers may benefit by dropping the amount (but not the intensity) of quality work by 5 percent per week in the last three weeks. Refer to figure 14.3.

Week 1 of taper: approximately 15 percent quality

Week 2 of taper: approximately 10 percent quality

Week 3 of taper: approximately 5 percent quality

For 400 m, 800 m, and 1500 m swimmers, the percentage of race-pace work should be slightly higher (about 5 percent to 7 percent) than those prescribed in figure 14.2. The same principles apply, but with slightly less volume, for the male sprinter.

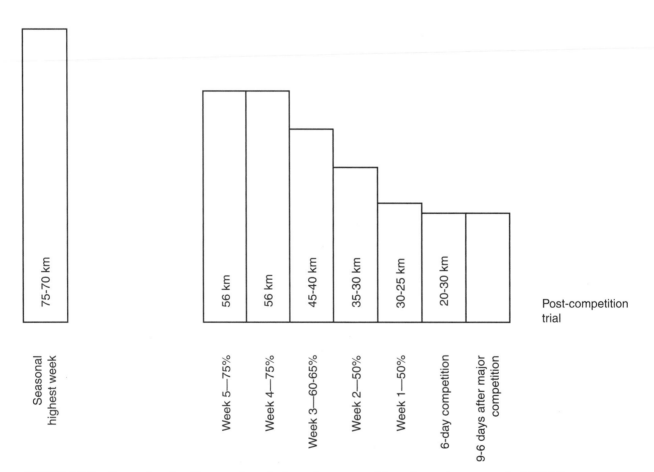

FIGURE 14.2 Example of a five-week cycle based on a weekly volume (pre-taper) of 75 kilometers.

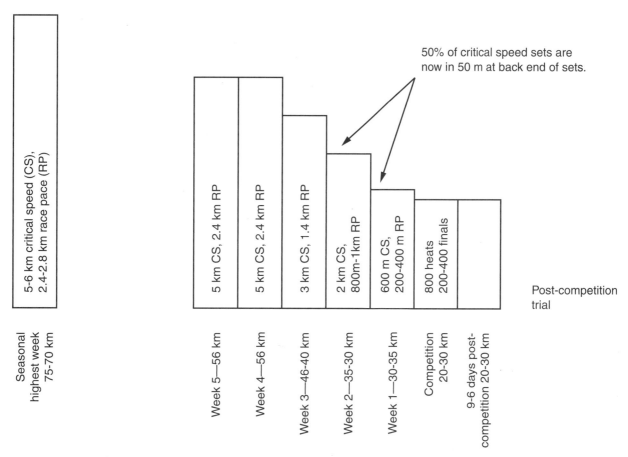

FIGURE 14.3   Five weeks to competition, showing amount of anaerobic/race-pace training versus critical speed and volumes.

The concern with intensity and stress during adaptation and race-preparation periods is that overexposure will result in a breakdown in muscle tissue (white fibers).

The total volume of training during the last three weeks drops to 60 percent and then 50 percent with the volume of race-pace training falling by approximately 5 percent per week. No reduction in the intensity of training occurs in this period, but avoiding lactate-tolerance and peak-lactate training in the last 10 days is important.

Both swimmers and coaches should record all variations during this race-preparation phase so that they can make adjustments for the next competition.

> *It is the coach's responsibility to provide the best opportunities and conditions for the best swimmers while retaining the confidence of the swimmers to perform at their best in the worst conditions. Do not be afraid as a coach to judge your program on the competition performance of the most talented and least talented athletes in your program.*

Warm-Up and Swim-Down Rehearsal

Swimmers should practice and experiment with the prerace warm-up and specific swim-downs, understanding that for an extended meet they will generally require slightly less quantity of warm-up and slightly greater quantity of swim-down. Heats usually require a more active and longer warm-up than finals do. Swimmers should practice this consistently throughout the year. While experimenting with the warm-up, swimmers should not change too much from one competition to another. Generally, the less rested the swimmer, the longer the warm-up needed.

The objectives of the warm-up are to prevent injury, increase blood circulation, provide a slight increase in heart rate and a slight rise in core body temperature, and prepare mentally. In conjunction with the warm-up, the athlete will have the choice of contrasting showers or massage to assist in preparation. The athlete must have a plan that will allow all this to happen, starting with morning heats. The athlete must have a program that allows fast heat swims, recovery, faster semifinal swims, recovery, faster finals, and then recovery again for the next morning's heats. In this regard, competition throughout the year must be treated as dress rehearsals of this process. In the interest of the continued improvement and future of the individual, the coach does not give the advanced age-group swimmer all the preparations and finesse that he or she gives the senior elite athlete. The age-group swimmer must remain hungry for winning and the rewards and benefits that go with winning.

The coach might need to plan with the athlete slightly different warm-ups for short course and long course or warm versus cold conditions. Note that the legs contain very large muscle groups that should not be overstressed with starting and turning practice in warm-ups. The swimmer must perfect warm-ups well in advance of the final taper. The coach should record all pace times swum in warm-ups for comparison from one meet to another.

Swim-downs are usually at least 1000 m in length, with a considerable amount of this at 50 to 60 BBM. The coach may ask the swimmer to swim four or five short bursts of 10 m to 15 m during the second 500 m of the swim-down to assist recovery.

CARBOHYDRATE INTAKE

Athletes must take in some carbohydrate fuel during the swim-down. Testing has shown that lactates must be significantly reduced in the swim-down and that about 1000 m is required to reduce them. If possible, lactates should be checked at the end of the event and the swim-down to learn about the individual in this situation and be certain that the lactates are reduced. A qualified person such as an exercise physiologist should take blood lactates. An individual checking speed swim should be conducted before the swimmer leaves the pool as a way to test recovery status.

The athlete should understand that carbohydrate intake must be substantial throughout the season. Carbohydrate loading in the last 7 to 10 days before a competition is not necessary. In fact, overdoing this can lead to fluid retention in muscle mass and have a detrimental effect. Carbohydrate loading is not necessary for swimming events unless the event lasts longer than 20 minutes.

Dual-Peaking Situation

For a dual-peaking situation, 2 to 3 days of low-intensity aerobic work should be followed by a repetition of training using the same number of days out from the competition. If another meet occurs in 9 days, the swimmer should do 3 days of aerobic training and repeat the last 6 days of training before the major meet. As a guide, spend about 25 to 30 percent of the total time on aerobic work for a dual-tapering situation for a meet within 15 to 18 days of the conclusion of the first meet.

We suggest that the swimmer do a follow-up time trial, preferably a swim meet after a full taper, to check the effects and accuracy of the taper. This should occur about six days after the major meet. This approach prepares the athlete to hold up for an extended meet similar to what may happen at future major games. It also assists in recovery from the taper. During these six days, training should occur just once per day with soft aerobic work but with some fast "spiking" work. This will establish a great attitude with the team in getting back up after meets.

Resting for Midseason Meets

With regard to resting for midseason meets, the hardest working athlete often experiences less than desired results while the less committed athlete experiences better results because of the differential between work and rest. A hard-working body can experience great physical change when exposed to rest, which initially causes a backward adjustment in fitness in the progress of adaptation.

Physical adaptations take place to a greater extent in the harder working athlete with rest (no matter how small, even two to three days) or fewer meters. Swimmers should learn to perform fast in solid training or take a full week of adaptation rather than take two or three days of rest before a meet. If there is no option, then the choice is either to keep the meters constant and decrease the intensity (preferred option) or to keep the intensity and decrease the meters. The coach should not allow this to be a negative influence on the better or harder working athlete in the program.

Tapering, which encompasses both mental and physical preparation, must be tailored to each athlete's individual needs to get them to their highest possible skill level.

Coping With Heats, Semifinals, and Finals

The reintroduction of heats, semifinals, and finals to international and national swimming competitions means that coaches have to prepare swimmers to cope with them at competitions.

The fastest swimmer does not necessarily win in the major competitions. The winner is often the best prepared swimmer, the one who has recovered best after a fast heat and semifinal. Most medal winners at recent international swimming championships went progressively faster through the heats, semifinals, and finals. The swimmers who were expected to do well but did not found it difficult to improve with each performance.

A way of incorporating the practice of heats, semifinals, and finals into workouts is to use the following progression for age-group and youth swimmers over three consecutive workouts. For open swimmers, the target could be set at an appropriate level.

Workout 1

Heat   200 m within 3 percent of the next higher age group at the national age championships.

Workout 2

Semifinal   200 m within 2 percent of the next higher age group at the national age championships. The 200 m is split at 100 m until the heart rate recovers to 40 BBM.

Workout 3

Final   200 m within 1 percent of the next higher age group at the national age championships. The 200 m is broken at 50 m until the heart rate recovers to 40 BBM. Record and measure time lapsed in heart-rate recovery time.

Swimmers do 30 to 40 minutes of active recovery and then swim the following.

Relay swim   A maximum-effort 100 m or 200 m aiming to swim within 3 percent of personal best time for the event. Swimmers need to be ready to perform relays.

This progression is a training tool that can prepare the athlete to perform at a high level, with progressively faster times through heats, semifinals, and finals. Only the exceptionally clear leader in any event will have the luxury of not having to learn this skill. A few might get away without it in the 50 m events.

This activity must be incorporated into the normal workout environment. Remember that the age-group swimmer will have to work hard at open national championships in the semifinals to get that sixth, seventh, or eighth position in the final. The swimmer should start working on it today.

Another method the coach can use to get swimmers to think about the heats, semifinals, and finals is to have them rock around the clock! Each swimmer should find three small, flat, smooth river rocks and print in permanent marker on each rock his or her goal time for the heat, semifinal, and final swims. The swimmers then put the rocks in their pockets along with their small change so that they can visualize their goals several times a day, select a rock at any time and challenge the goal at training, and tip all the rocks from their pockets and select the one nearest the edge for a workout challenge swim.

Swimming Down and Recovery

Recover fast to swim fast! This principle provides coaches and athletes with one of the most important aspects of today's competitive swimming. Recovery from one workout to the next and in the progression of heats, semifinals, and finals in multievent competitions or even from final to final at the same session of a meet can make the difference between swimming a personal best time in the final or not.

An athlete's recovery skill is just as important as sprint or distance capability.

How fast an athlete can recover under stress at a major competition depends on numerous factors in differing combinations.

What is the value of a swim-down? How long should it be and at what progression of intensity? Does it maximize mental relaxation? Is it a waste of time and effort? Following are several factors that affect swim-downs:

- Aerobic background of the athlete at prematuration (approximately age 13) and at the intermediate presenior level (first year of open swimming)
- Skill level of the athlete
- Mental strength of the athlete
- Current level of specific fitness
- Precompetition conditions (including events already swum)
- Result of the swim and the execution of the event
- Individual muscle mass and flexibility
- Any combination of the preceding factors

The variable that most needs to change with regard to swim-downs is the mental outlook of the athlete.

Calculating When a Swimmer Is Recovered

Most coaches do not have a 100 percent certain solution to knowing whether a swimmer has recovered. Coaches can use the following combinations of factors to calculate when a swimmer is recovered or back to normal:

1. The athlete should swim at the speed used in training for individual checking speed tests, which is personal best 100 m time plus 15 seconds for butterfly, backstroke, and freestyle and plus 20 seconds for breaststroke. The speed will be referred to as speed x.
2. The stroke count and stroke rate should be recorded while the swimmer swims at speed x.
3. The heart rate should be recorded while the swimmer swims at speed x with the stroke count and stroke rate from step 2.
4. The coach should observe the physical and mental state of the athlete.
5. Rehydration must take place. The intake of fluid and the time lapse before the athlete urinates should be measured. If medical assistance is available, urine samples can be taken.
6. If qualified personnel are available, they can take blood lactates.

Many coaches will not be able to use steps 5 and 6, but a coach can still gain valuable information and provide the athlete with quality coaching by using the first four steps.

Normally, the higher the lactate, the more effective the swim-down needs to be for the swimmer to come close to full recovery. The distance of the event is less important than the athlete's training background and lactate level following the event.

Another issue is whether temperature control with ice downs and contrast baths assists in this process. The coach and swimmer need to experiment with the process and rehearse before the competition. During the rehearsal they record what they do in detail to establish a process suitable for the swimmer.

Using the Individual Checking Speed Test in Swim-Downs

Having an individual checking speed value for each athlete will allow the athlete and the coach to evaluate the state of recovery following the swim-down. The coach can use the individual checking speed value to evaluate many things, including level of fatigue, injury, and illness, both in training and at competitions following the swim-down. The individual checking speed value also provides the coach with a guide to the aerobic and submaximal endurance fitness of the athlete from year to year, from the start of the year to the end of the year, and more important during midseason meets and tapering.

The checking speed test involves swimming 100 m in a time equal to personal best time plus 15 seconds for butterfly, backstroke, and freestyle and plus 20 seconds for breaststroke. Obviously, the swimmer may have to perform the test on more that one occasion to swim to the correct pace. Coaches should note that if the test results show different stroke counts of three or more or if the split times differ by two or more seconds, the swimmer would need to repeat the procedure. The coach then uses the values from the 100 m swim to establish the 200 m, 300 m, and 400 m speeds. Chapter 2 describes this test swim in detail.

The individual checking speed (ICS) can be used to monitor the swimmer's recovery status and preparedness for training. If the swimmer is ill or fatigued he or she will not be able to achieve the ICS values.

The coach can assess the recovery status of the swimmer by using an individual checking speed test at the end of a swim-down at a competition. The coach compares the values of the test during the swim-down at the competition with the test values from training. By having an individual checking speed, stroke count, stroke rate, breathing patterns, and heart rates, the test can be used effectively and with minimum supervision in precompetition warm-ups and postcompetition swim-downs. Using only one or two of the values will not allow adequate evaluation of the swim-down. Only when all values are constant and in line with training values can a coach or athlete assume that an effective swim-down has taken place (Atkinson and Sweetenham 1999; Sweetenham 1997b).

Competitive Swimmer's Competition Checklist

The swimmer should review this checklist 22 to 23 days before the competition.

❏ Try to arrange for your room to be away from noise and shielded from the afternoon sun or sunny side of motels or building so that your rest between workouts or heats, semifinals, and finals is as undisturbed as possible. Avoid rooms close to streets, over restaurants, or near lift wells. Choose an end-of-corridor room that will be generally free of traffic.

❏ If in a motel, request maid service for your room during heats or morning workouts. You will then not be disturbed during afternoon rest periods and will return from heats to a clean, tidy room.

❏ If traveling during this period, make as few changes as possible in your daily and weekly schedule and lifestyle. Avoid contact with people who have colds, sickness, or negative attitudes.

❏ If traveling, pack your swim-training equipment and uniforms on top of all other clothes for easy access so that you can get them quickly and easily because your coach will probably want you to swim either just before or just after you travel. Travel light—take only what you need to look professional but comfortable and to swim fast. Pack the basic swimming equipment in your hand luggage if traveling by air. If your luggage is delayed or lost, you can still train on arrival at the pool.

❏ From five weeks out from competition, train in nylon uniforms (perhaps one size too big) through to the meet with the exception of mock trials and one or two special race-pace sets.

❏ Shave only for major meets or selection trials. Do not shave during last five weeks until just before the main event. This recommendation applies to both males and females.

❏ Confirm that any medicine you are taking does not conflict with drug policy.

❏ If the meet is in a hot climate, fill the sink or tub with water to maintain moisture in the air because air conditioners tend to dehydrate the environment. Open a window if the air is clean; avoid colds caused by air conditioning.

❏ Keep a glass of water beside your bed and take a sip or drink each time you wake during the night if you are in air conditioning, either cooling or heating.

❏ Have a minimum of two drink bottles plus a postcompetition snack ready for each day. Keep your drink bottle clean and do not use anyone else's or allow anyone to use yours. If traveling to another country, take several boxes of your favorite breakfast cereal.

❏ Keep your sleeping habits the same as you do at home, especially if you are staying in a hotel or motel where you will not want to be distracted by your teammates or roommates or by constant television and other noise.

❏ Take a blow-up or foam mattress for comfortable resting at the pool during long meets or for added support if the accommodation bed is uncomfortable.

❏ Take your own pillow. This one item determines the quality of your rest and sleep, and using your own pillow allows you to avoid any allergies to the contents of other pillows.

(continued)

(continued)

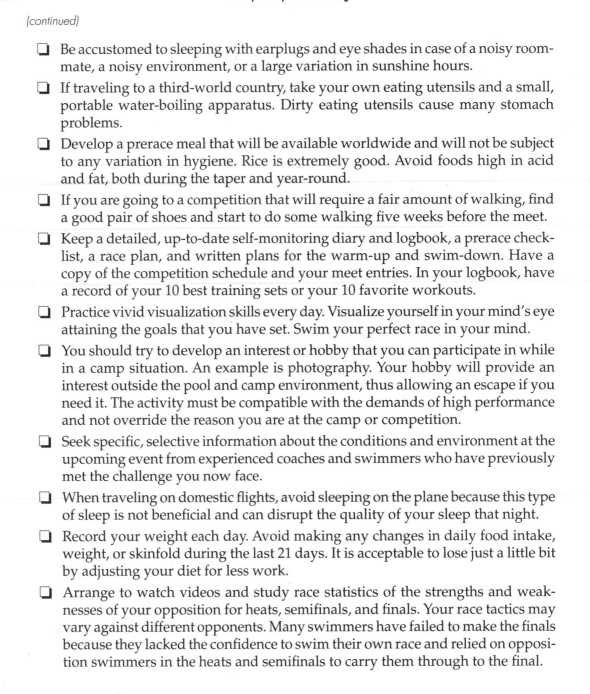

- ❏ Be accustomed to sleeping with earplugs and eye shades in case of a noisy roommate, a noisy environment, or a large variation in sunshine hours.
- ❏ If traveling to a third-world country, take your own eating utensils and a small, portable water-boiling apparatus. Dirty eating utensils cause many stomach problems.
- ❏ Develop a prerace meal that will be available worldwide and will not be subject to any variation in hygiene. Rice is extremely good. Avoid foods high in acid and fat, both during the taper and year-round.
- ❏ If you are going to a competition that will require a fair amount of walking, find a good pair of shoes and start to do some walking five weeks before the meet.
- ❏ Keep a detailed, up-to-date self-monitoring diary and logbook, a prerace checklist, a race plan, and written plans for the warm-up and swim-down. Have a copy of the competition schedule and your meet entries. In your logbook, have a record of your 10 best training sets or your 10 favorite workouts.
- ❏ Practice vivid visualization skills every day. Visualize yourself in your mind's eye attaining the goals that you have set. Swim your perfect race in your mind.
- ❏ You should try to develop an interest or hobby that you can participate in while in a camp situation. An example is photography. Your hobby will provide an interest outside the pool and camp environment, thus allowing an escape if you need it. The activity must be compatible with the demands of high performance and not override the reason you are at the camp or competition.
- ❏ Seek specific, selective information about the conditions and environment at the upcoming event from experienced coaches and swimmers who have previously met the challenge you now face.
- ❏ When traveling on domestic flights, avoid sleeping on the plane because this type of sleep is not beneficial and can disrupt the quality of your sleep that night.
- ❏ Record your weight each day. Avoid making any changes in daily food intake, weight, or skinfold during the last 21 days. It is acceptable to lose just a little bit by adjusting your diet for less work.
- ❏ Arrange to watch videos and study race statistics of the strengths and weaknesses of your opposition for heats, semifinals, and finals. Your race tactics may vary against different opponents. Many swimmers have failed to make the finals because they lacked the confidence to swim their own race and relied on opposition swimmers in the heats and semifinals to carry them through to the final.

Although the points in this checklist will help the swimmer attain a desired performance, the swimmer and coach must realize that success is a complex mixture of many variables. These points may seem complicated and sometimes unnecessary, but the swimmer should practice them to a point where he or she does them automatically as a normal part of the approach to camps and competitions. We have found that compromise is the beginning of the end. A compromised attitude or approach will provide a compromised result at best, just as a part-time commitment can produce only a part-time result.

Dryland Conditioning

Dryland training is important to the swimmer because it helps build strength and flexibility while offering variety in the training format. Dryland training should complement the work done by the swimmer in the water; under no circumstances should it replace water work. If swimmers are not attending swimming training to the required level because they are substituting dryland training for swimming training, the coach must get them off land and into the pool.

This chapter identifies specific dryland tests, exercises, and suggestions that are useful and easy to apply with swimmers of all ages and abilities. It details tests athletes can use to assess their core strength and flexibility, as well as specific exercises to work those areas. We will first look at warm-up and stretching exercises and their importance for swimming.

Warm-Up and Stretching

Many exercises can give athletes a good warm-up to their dryland program or pool session. The following general exercises and stretches can be combined in different variations. When stretching, athletes must be sure to avoid pushing past the point where they start feeling pain. They hold each stretch for 30 seconds, inhaling in the move to the stretch and exhaling in the move back to the starting position. The warm-up session should last about 15 minutes.

When warming up before the swimming session, the general warm-up exercises form the majority of the exercises that are performed, with certain stretching exercises incorporated to meet individual needs. The swimmer should stretch following any swimming or dryland training session to aid recovery from the work just done. The Swiss ball can be used in a stretching program, as shown in some of the stretches. The Swiss ball comes in different sizes. Before buying a ball, the swimmer should take advice from the store about which ball to buy. Generally, sitting on the ball should create a right angle between the thigh and the lower leg. The seat of the athlete should not be lower than the knees.

Arm Swinging, Backward and Forward

Standing straight with both arms swinging backward, the athlete can increase the speed of the swings as the warm-up proceeds. This exercise can then be repeated with the arms swinging forward. A variation on this exercise is to have the right arm swinging forward and the left arm swinging backward. The exercise is then repeated in the opposite direction.

Skipping Rope

Care should be taken to use a skipping rope of the right length. Many variations of skipping are feasible.

Double-Arm Skiing

The athlete bends forward, pushing the arms to the front, as shown in figure 15.1a, and then to the back, as shown in figure 15.1b.

FIGURE 15.1   Double-arm skiing.

Alternate Arm Crossing

The athlete bends forward, swinging the arms alternately in front. As one arm goes behind the body, the other crosses in front, as shown in figure 15.2.

FIGURE 15.2 Alternate arm crossing.

Arm Crossing and Swinging

The athlete bends forward, arms swinging from the side, as shown in figure 15.3a, and crossing in front of the chest, as shown in 15.3b.

FIGURE 15.3 Arm crossing and swinging.

Adductor Stretch

The athlete sits so that the soles of the feet touch. He or she grips the ankles and then uses the elbows to push down against the inside of the knees to gain maximum stretch, as shown in figure 15.4.

FIGURE 15.4 Adductor stretch.

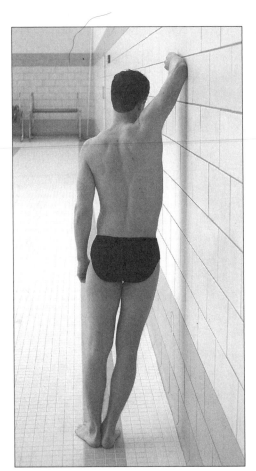

Combined Internal Rotation Elevation Stretch

The athlete stands side to the wall and lifts the arm so that the forearm rests on the wall, forming a right angle with the upper arm. He or she then gently leans toward the wall to feel the stretch underneath the arm, as shown in figure 15.5. The athlete performs this exercise on both arms.

FIGURE 15.5 Combined internal rotation elevation stretch.

Teres Stretch

The athlete stands and raises one arm, which then bends across the body, taking the hand past the opposite shoulder. He or she then grips the arm at the elbow and gently applies pressure into the stretch, as shown in figure 15.6. The exercise is performed on both arms.

FIGURE 15.6 *Teres stretch.*

Upper Trapezius Stretch

The athlete grasps the side of the head with one hand and gently pulls the head in that direction. Care should be taken not to place pressure on the neck while performing this exercise. While doing this, the athlete tries to press the shoulder down, as shown in figure 15.7.

FIGURE 15.7 *Upper trapezius stretch.*

External Rotators Stretch

The athlete stands and pushes one arm across the back. He or she then grips the elbow of that arm and pulls inward to gain maximum stretch, as shown in figure 15.8. The exercise is repeated on the other arm.

FIGURE 15.8   External rotators stretch.

Internal Rotators Stretch

Standing with one arm positioned behind the head (elbow up), the athlete reaches up with the other arm. The fingers grip, and the top hand pulls up while the bottom hand pulls down, as shown in figure 15.9. The athlete then switches arms.

FIGURE 15.9   Internal rotators stretch.

Triceps Stretch

Figure 15.10 shows the triceps stretch. The athlete raises one arm and then bends it behind the neck, placing the palm of the hand in the middle of the back. The opposite hand applies pressure to the stretch by gently pulling inward toward the center of the back and at the same time in a downward direction.

FIGURE 15.10   Triceps stretch.

Hamstring Stretch

The starting position for this stretch is lying on the back with the heel of one leg resting on a Swiss ball, as shown in figure 15.11. The opposite leg is held in the vertical position. The hands apply pressure as the leg is pulled back, maintaining a straight position. The exercise is performed on each leg.

FIGURE 15.11   Hamstring stretch.

Latissimus Stretch

An important stretch for swimmers, the latissimus stretch starts with the athlete lying on the side on a ball. The legs should be apart for balance. The stretch should allow the arms to stretch across the ball, as shown in figure 15.12.

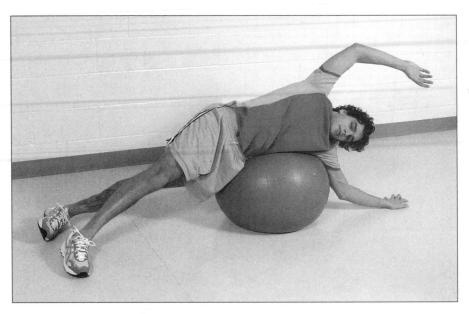

FIGURE 15.12   Latissimus stretch.

Pectoral Stretch

The starting position is to kneel with one arm on the ball and the other arm positioned so that the hand is flat on the floor giving support to the position. The athlete lowers body weight to attain the stretch shown in figure 15.13 and alternates between left and right sides.

FIGURE 15.13   Pectoral stretch.

Supine Stretch

The ball rests in the middle of the back, and the athlete reaches back with the arms to touch the floor with the hands, trying to stretch out with the legs as much as possible and maintain contact with the floor. This exercise is shown in figure 15.14.

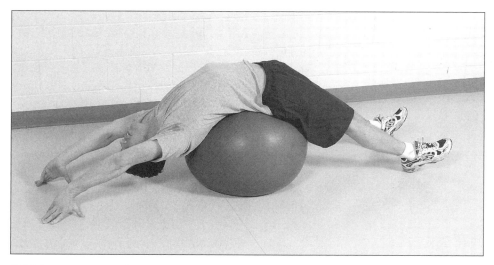

FIGURE 15.14   Supine stretch.

Core Strength Tests

As we know, the core strength of swimmers is important for maintaining correct body position during races. After assessing the core strength of swimmers using the tests in this chapter, the coach can plan a program of core strength training.

Push-Up Position Hold Test

The athlete holds the push-up position for a set period or until body position changes significantly. Generally, the aim is to hold the position for one to two minutes while maintaining perfect body position through the test.

The athlete assumes the push-up position, with the arms extended, back straight, and head in line with the body. The athlete should be looking toward the ground, not straight ahead, as shown in figure 15.15. The athlete holds the position for the duration of his or her main event.

The push-up position should be performed on

FIGURE 15.15   Push-up position hold test.

a flat surface, with the hands in a comfortable position under the shoulders and the fingers pointing forward. The athlete is timed while holding the position. The watch is stopped when significant changes occur in body position, and the time is recorded.

Push-Up Test With Shoulder Blades Together

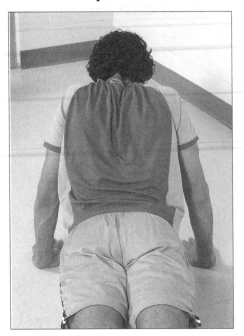

Following the push-up position hold test, the athlete performs the same test while holding the shoulder blades together, as demonstrated in figure 15.16.

As with the previous exercise, the athlete holds the position without allowing significant deviation. In this test, deviation will occur when the athlete cannot hold the shoulder blades together. While holding the push-up position, the athlete sets core stability at the point of holding the shoulder blades together.

As in the previous test, the athlete performs the test on a flat surface with the hands in a comfortable position under the shoulders and the fingers pointing forward. Again, the athlete is timed while holding the position. The watch is stopped when significant changes occur in body position, and the time is recorded.

FIGURE 15.16   Push-up test with shoulder blades together.

Lumbar Hold

To start this test, the athlete lies face down in a streamlined position on a flat surface. The arms and legs extend, and the face looks downward. When performing this test, the athlete may use exercise mats.

On command, the athlete raises both legs and holds the position for one to two minutes or until significant changes occur in body position. The knees should be held well clear of the ground, as shown in figure 15.17. When the swimmer attains this position, the timing of the test starts. The watch is stopped when significant changes occur in body position, and the time is recorded.

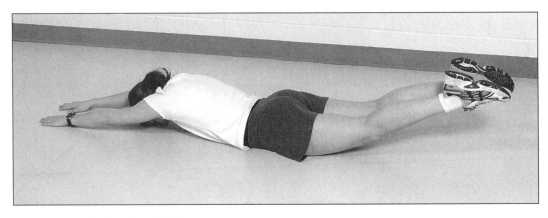

FIGURE 15.17   Lumbar hold.

Front Abdominal Hold

The athlete attempts to perform the front abdominal hold for one to two minutes. The starting position is shown in figure 15.18a. The athlete is on his or her back with the legs bent 90 degrees, feet flat on the floor, and arms held in front of the body. As the athlete sits up, the back rises off the floor and the arms extend forward, as shown in figure 15.18b.

As with the previous tests, the hold is timed until a significant change occurs in body position. The time is recorded.

FIGURE 15.18 Front abdominal hold.

Swim Bench Test

A biokinetic swim bench is required for this test, which evaluates the power rating of the swimmer.

The swimmer is weighed in a swimsuit before the test. A reliable and accurate set of scales is required.

The swim bench is set to a zero setting. The swimmer performs 10 butterfly pulls, and the score is recorded. The swim bench score divided by the swimmer's body weight yields a second score. On that scale, four is considered acceptable, and six is considered a sprint score. All swimmers performing this test are ranked. Swimmers who score less than four require further core strength training and more power.

Advanced Core Strength Bench Test

The swimmer lies on three benches or chairs, as shown in figure 15.19, in the supine position. The benches are placed underneath the head-neck area, buttocks, and heels and feet. When the swimmer assumes the supine position, he or she sets the core, with the arms behind the head.

As the swimmer sets core stability, the middle bench or chair is removed. The athlete should be able to maintain the position for one to two minutes. The athlete is timed

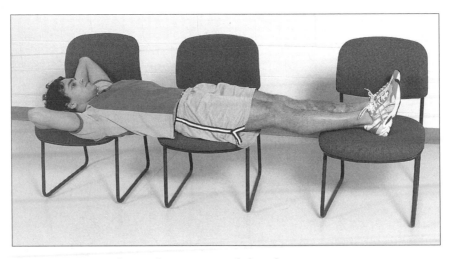

FIGURE 15.19   *Advanced core strength bench test.*

while holding the position. The watch is stopped when significant changes occur in body position, and the time is recorded.

Flexibility Tests

To swim the strokes efficiently, swimmers need specific flexibility and range of movement. The tests shown in this section evaluate flexibility. Once flexibility has been assessed, a stretching program can be recommended.

Upper-Body Flexibility Test

The athlete grips each elbow with the opposite hand above the head and pushes upward, as shown in figure 15.20a. A gap should be present between the lower arms and the head. A large space between the top of the head and the lower arm indicates that the athlete will be able to attain an early catch and high elbow position in the propulsive phase of the stroke.

The next step of the test is shown in figure 15.20b. The athlete bends forward and maintains that position, which more closely simulates the position of the body in the water.

Lower-Body Flexibility Test

The athlete folds the arms behind the knees with the hands gripping the elbows, as shown in figure 15.21a. The legs have a slight bend at this stage. The athlete then pushes upward through the hips in an attempt to straighten the legs while maintaining the arms-folded position and the grip on the elbows, as shown in figure 15.21b. Hamstring flexibility is important to the swimmer, particularly for starts and turns.

Exercises for Starts and Turns

To develop specific leg strength and power for swimming starts and turns, the swimmer must perform dryland training. Strength in the legs is essential for the swimmer's starts and turns. We have selected some straightforward exercises that athletes of all ages can perform. Any swimmers with knee problems or injuries should ask for advice from a dryland trainer or swimming coach before attempting any of the leg exercises.

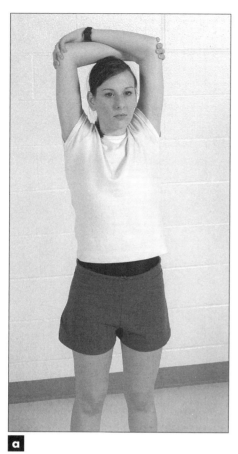

FIGURE 15.20   Upper-body flexibility test.

FIGURE 15.21   Lower-body flexibility test.

Lunges

The athlete starts this exercise standing in a streamlined position, steps forward into a lunge, holds the position shown in figure 15.22, and returns to the streamlined position. He or she alternates lunges from one leg to the other.

FIGURE 15.22   Lunge.

Squat Jumps

The athlete starts this exercise in a standing position with the hands behind the head. He or she squats as shown in figure 15.23a, being careful to maintain a straight back and alignment through the head and neck. The athlete then jumps upward from this position, maintaining the positioning of the hands and the alignment of the body, as shown in figure 15.23b.

FIGURE 15.23   Squat jump. **a**

(continued)

FIGURE 15.23 (continued) b

Plyometric Jump

Before doing the plyometric jump and leg power drill, the swimmer should have worked through a program of lunges and squats to build strength in the legs, working at a program of all-around conditioning for a set period determined by the dryland coach.

The swimmer stands on top of a stable chair or gym bench, jumps down off the chair, lands in the starting position, and then jumps forward as far as possible. The coach measures and records the distance traveled. The athlete performs the drill three times, trying to increase the distance traveled. This exercise is shown in figure 15.24.

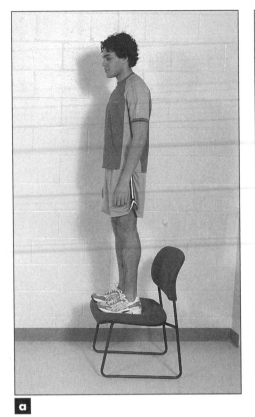 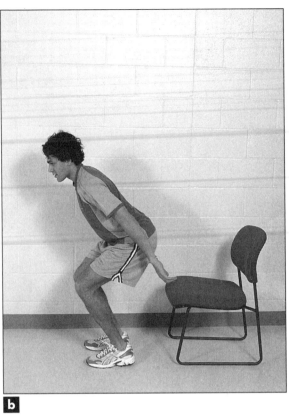

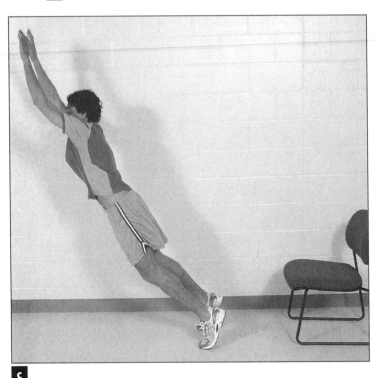 

FIGURE 15.24 Plyometric jump.

Leg Power Drill

As mentioned earlier, the athlete must have worked through a program of lunges and squats to build all-around strength in the legs before progressing to this type of exercise.

The swimmer starts this drill from a stable chair or gym bench. He or she jumps down off the starting platform and then jumps two hurdles (gym benches can be used) in a row. After jumping the second hurdle, the athlete jumps forward as far as possible. The coach measures and records the final jump. The swimmer performs this sequence three times, trying to get farther forward on each jump. The positioning of the feet and legs in each jump is the same as that used for the start. This drill is shown in figure 15.25, a through c.

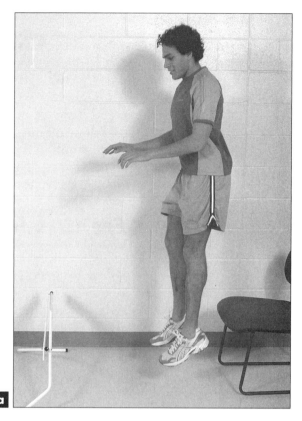

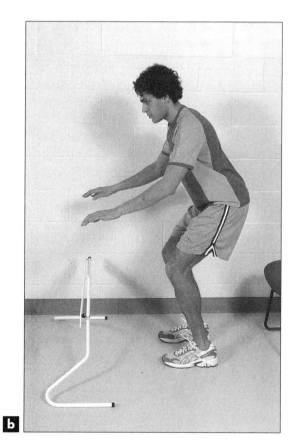

FIGURE 15.25 Leg power drill.

Medicine Ball

This drill helps the swimmer develop speed and specific power for starting. The swimmer assumes the starting position on land, holding a medicine ball. On "Go," the athlete throws the ball to a partner standing 7 m away. This action develops the skill needed to lead with the arms through the start, with the correct head position. After throwing the ball, the swimmer runs forward and tries to beat the ball to the 7 m point.

This same drill can be done off the starting block into the pool. After throwing the ball forward to a partner standing 7 m away, the swimmer dives off the block and tries to beat the ball to the partner. The swimmer can do this with a light basketball to start and progress to using a waterproof medicine ball.

Exercises for Core Strength

Besides having strong legs for good starts and turns, the swimmer must have good core strength, which he or she can improve by incorporating the exercises shown in this chapter. The swimmer completes the following in a circuit, working on each exercise for a predetermined length of time. A group new to this type of work works each exercise for 20 seconds and then increases the time when they can hold the positions and work for that period. Rather than increase the time worked, they may work through the routine twice for the same length of time.

Push-Up Hold

The swimmer holds the push-up position with the shoulder blades together, as shown in figure 15.16 on page 262. This simple exercise requires the swimmer to work through the core to maintain stable body position.

Push-Ups

To perform push-ups, the hands are under the shoulders, the fingers point forward, and the back is straight. The athlete lowers the body to the ground but does not put weight on the ground. Figure 15.26, a through c, shows variations to regular push-ups.

Rotation push-ups. Figure 15.26a shows rotation push-ups. The athlete starts in the push-up start position, rotates to the left, completes a full rotation, and finishes in the start position. The exercise is done with an equal number of rotations left and right, in varied combinations.

Extended-arm push-ups. Figure 15.26b shows extended-arm push-ups. In this exercise the athlete positions the hands as far forward as possible while performing the push-up action. The athlete should start with the hands only slightly forward of the shoulders before progressing to the position shown in figure 15.26b.

Split-arm push-ups. Figure 15.26c shows split-arm push-ups. One arm is in the normal push-up position, and the other is moved backward. The athlete does an equal number of push-ups with the left arm back and with the right arm back.

a

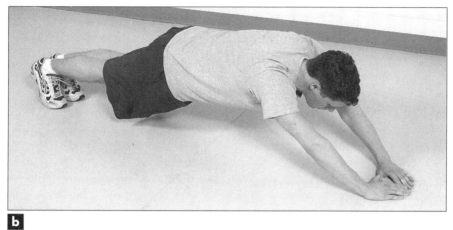

b

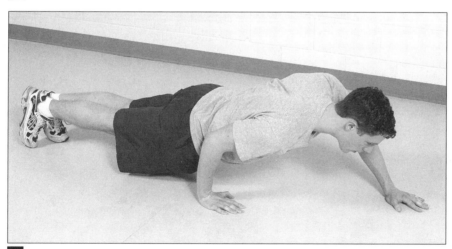

c

FIGURE 15.26 *Push-up variations: (a) rotation push-ups, (b) extended-arm push-ups, and (c) split-arm push-ups.*

Lumbar Hold

The swimmer holds this position for the set period. The start and hold positions are shown in figure 15.17 on page 262. The athlete may perform a set by lifting, holding only for a short period, and lowering back to the start position.

Pull-Ups

Pull-ups should be performed on the elevated bar in the gym. The athlete grips the bar above the head with a wide grip and pulls up to the bar with the back of the head coming up to the bar (lat style, wide grip).

Dips

The ideal way to perform dips is on the dipping station in the gym. Athletes may need to build up to performing dips in this way by going through the exercises outlined in figure 15.27.

If a dipping station is not available, the swimmer can use the triceps dip position shown in figure 15.27, a and b, using steps. The athlete can make the exercise more difficult by extending the foot position farther forward from the position of the hands or by elevating the foot position to a platform in front, as shown in figure 15.27, c and d. The next step is to have the hands platform lower than the foot platform. The athlete then performs the dipping action with the legs elevated above the body.

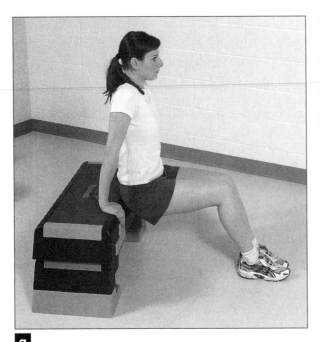
a

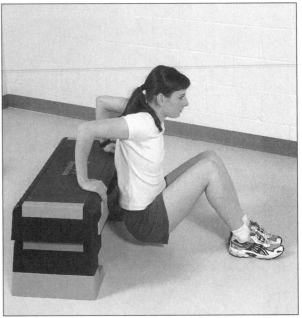
b

(continued)

FIGURE 15.27 Dips.

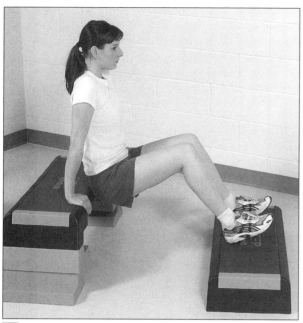

c

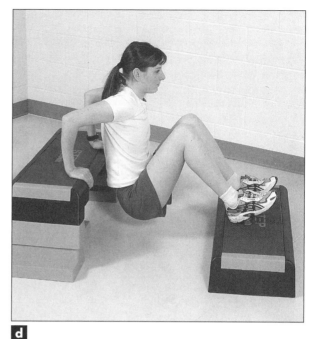

d

FIGURE 15.27   (continued)

Body Pull-Up

The hands are at shoulder-width with three-quarter reach. The swimmer stands at a bar with the hands at three-quarter reach above the head. He or she then presses on the bar above the head, pulls the body off the ground, continues to pull the body past the hands, and then pushes up past the bar. This exercise simulates the pulling action in the water (Atkinson and Sweetenham 1999).

Abdominal Exercises

Abdominal work is important for the swimmer and should be part of a core strength development program. The swimmer can improve abdominal strength by performing exercises in many different ways, as shown in the next section.

Front Abdominal Sit-Ups

The athlete can perform the front abdominal hold shown in figure 15.18 on page 263 in a set by sitting up and then lowering for a predetermined number of repeats.

Crunches

The athlete can perform crunches starting in the position shown in figure 15.28a. From this supine position with the hands at the side of the head, the athlete bends the legs and at the same time sits up, maintaining the position of the hands by the side of the head, as shown in figure 15.28b.

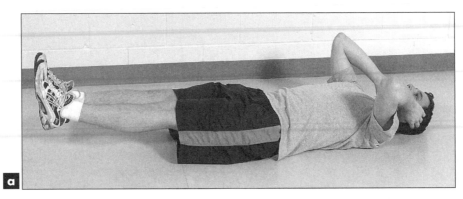

FIGURE 15.28   Crunches.

Bent-Leg Raises

Leg raises are another abdominal exercise. The first leg raise exercise is bent-leg raises. The swimmer starts in the supine position with the arms by the sides and the legs bent, as shown in figure 15.29a. The action is to lift the legs, keeping them bent until a 90-degree angle occurs between the thighs and the torso, as shown in figure 15.29b.

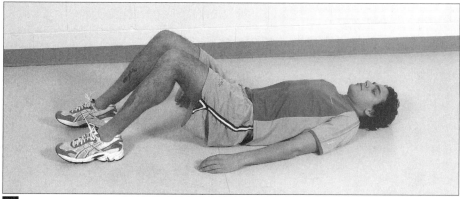

a

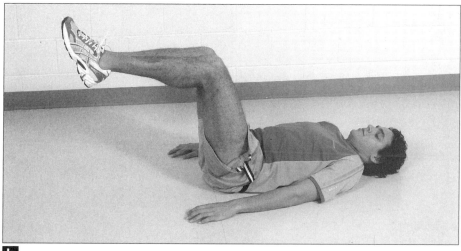

b

FIGURE 15.29   Bent-leg raises.

Advanced Leg Raises

The athlete starts the advanced leg raise exercise in the supine position with the arms out to the sides and palms facing upward. The legs and feet are together, as shown in figure 15.30a. The athlete raises the legs from the floor to a height defined by an angle of 45 to 90 degrees. Figure 15.30b shows a lift to about 45 degrees. The athlete lowers the legs to a position just off the floor and then lifts and lowers them again for a predetermined number of repeats.

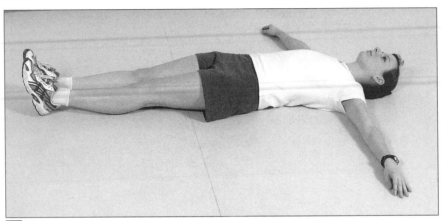
a

b

FIGURE 15.30   Advanced leg raises.

Sit-Ups

The final abdominal exercise shown here is the sit-up exercise, which is similar to the front abdominal hold exercise. The athlete starts in the position shown in figure 15.31a. The legs are bent, the feet are flat on the floor, and the hands are by the sides of the head. The athlete sits up while maintaining the position of the legs and hands, as shown in figure 15.31b. Again, this exercise can be performed for a predetermined number of repeats.

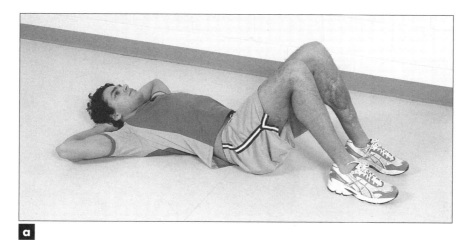

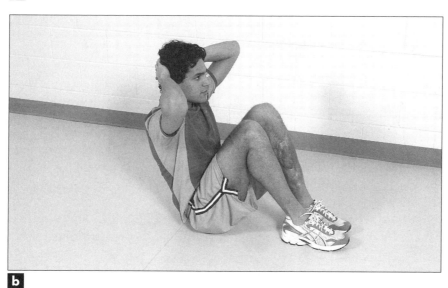

FIGURE 15.31   Sit-ups.

Plank Position

This exercise, shown in figure 15.32, combines abdominal strength along with all-around core body strength. The athlete holds a position with the lower arms on the floor and the hands gripped in a fist. The upper arms stay straight under the shoulders for stability. The head, the back, and the legs stay in a flat position with the toes on the floor. The feet are positioned slightly apart.

The athlete sets the core strength and maintains the hold until significant changes occur in body position and he or she can no longer hold the position. The coach times and records how long the athlete can maintain the position. The swimmer should have a goal of holding the position for one to two minutes.

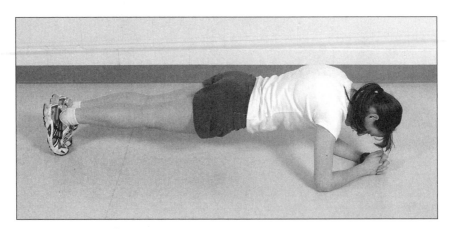

FIGURE 15.32   Plank position.

Dryland training is important in building swimmers' strength and flexibility. Swimmers must take part in a dryland program to complement the work they do in the pool. Dryland sessions should never replace swimming training, but swimmers and coaches can use dryland sessions when they find it difficult to access the pool for training time. A swimmer with improved core strength will have better body position in the water and will therefore have less resistance when swimming. Dryland training can help prevent injury, which is important because swimmers must remain injury free if they are to improve their performance. The information in this chapter is a starting point for a dryland training program that can work alongside the swimming training outlined in this book.

16

Program Evaluation

To aid in the evaluation of his or her swimming program, every swimmer should maintain a training log. The training log should be a record of everything the swimmer does in training sessions and competitions, both good and bad. The swimmer also needs to record anything outside of training that could affect competition results. This documentation will help the swimmer review the previous result and plan for the next major swimming competition. The swimmer is responsible for maintaining the training log, and the coach should review it regularly.

The information contained in the training log is important should the swimmer ever be selected for a representative team. The athlete can then present the log to the person who will be coaching him or her on that team. The more information the swimmer can provide to the coach, the better the coach can prepare the swimmer for competition.

If it's measurable, measure it.
If it's controllable, control it.
Record everything.

What should go into a training log? Both swimmers and coaches commonly ask that question. The log should include several kinds of information, as shown in the following list and examples.

Training Log Checklist

1. The swimmer details recording sheet contains personal information, as shown in figure 16.1.

2. The goal-setting sheet shows short-term, midterm, and long-term goals, verified by the coach, swimmer, and parents, as shown in figure 16.2.

3. Long-course and short-course personal best times should be recorded on a sheet as shown in figure 16.3.

4. Figure 16.4 shows an example of a performance recording log that includes all times from any competitions the swimmer enters, including both good and bad swims.

5. A medical and supplements information sheet includes a record of visits to the doctor, the reason for the visit, any medication prescribed or taken, and any supplements taken. On national teams the information recorded should be presented to the team doctor.

6. A record should be kept of any visits to the physiotherapist, the reason for the visit, and any treatment undertaken.

7. The swimmer should record the prerace warm-up and postrace swim-down procedure for his or her main events.

8. A sheet should show the swimmer's best-ever training sets, including date, set conducted, and any relevant information.

9. The training log should include a sheet summarizing weekly training volume, showing meters for the week, the running total, and the average weekly volume, as shown in figure 16.5.

10. The athlete also completes a weekly recording sheet that shows the main emphasis for each training session, daily resting heart rate, and daily volume along with scores of fatigue, muscle soreness, stress, sleep, and appetite. Height and weight can also be included on this sheet. The sheet should have a section where the coach can add comments for the swimmer. A sample sheet is shown in figure 16.6.

11. Benchmark test-set recording sheets shown in chapter 2 should be included for the test sets that the swimmer completes regularly.

12. Any other tests conducted, such as the core body strength tests outlined in chapter 15, are shown in the training log.

13. Dryland training can also be recorded in the training log so that the coach is aware of the swimmer's entire training program.

Looking back on the season allows both the coach and swimmer to learn from successes and failures how to alter training to improve future competition performance.

14. A training log can be an effective way to communicate with the coach about sensitive issues. For example, a female athlete may signal her male coach that she is having a menstrual cycle by placing the letter *M* in the boxes of the weekly recording sheet and handing her training log to the coach.

15. The swimmer can file handouts from the coach in the training log so that all information is available in one place for the entire swimming season.

SWIMMER DETAILS RECORDING SHEET

Name	
Date of birth	
Parents' names	
Home address	
Home telephone number	
Parents' cell and work telephone numbers	
E-mail address	
Main event(s)	
Most current results	
Best swimming experience	
Club	
Training program	
Coach	
Coach's telephone numbers	
Coach's e-mail address	

FIGURE 16.1 *Swimmer details recording sheet.*

GOAL-SETTING RECORDING SHEET

Short-term (this cycle)	
Midterm (the coming season)	
Long-term (major ambition)	
Signed by swimmer	
Signed by coach	
Date of goal-setting exercise	

FIGURE 16.2   Goal-setting recording sheet.

PERSONAL BEST TIMES RECORDING SHEET

Insert current personal best times along with splits, stroke counts, stroke rates, and date of swim. Separate sheets can be used for short-course and long-course times.

Long-course/short-course				
	50	**100**	**200**	**400**	**800/1500**
Butterfly					
Backstroke					
Breaststroke					
Freestyle					
Individual medley					

FIGURE 16.3   Personal best times recording sheet.

PERFORMANCE RECORDING LOG

Date	Meet	SC/LC	Event	Time	Splits	Rates	Counts	Comments

FIGURE 16.4   Performance recording log.

WEEKLY VOLUME RECORDING SHEET

Week	Week commencing	Weekly volume	Running volume totals	Average weekly volume
Example	1/1/01	45	45	45
Example	8/1/01	35	80	40
1				
2				
3				
4				
5				
6				
7				
8				
9				
10				
11				
12				
13				
14				
15				
16				
17				
18				
19				
20				
21				

FIGURE 16.5 *Weekly volume recording sheet.*

WEEKLY MONITORING SHEET

Week commencing _____

	Monday	Tuesday	Wednesday	Thursday	Friday	Saturday	Sunday
AM (insert each session's emphasis and total volume)							
PM							
Daily volume							
Resting HR							
Weight							
Height							
Scores							
Fatigue	1 2 3 4 5 6 7	1 2 3 4 5 6 7	1 2 3 4 5 6 7	1 2 3 4 5 6 7	1 2 3 4 5 6 7	1 2 3 4 5 6 7	1 2 3 4 5 6 7
Muscle soreness	1 2 3 4 5 6 7	1 2 3 4 5 6 7	1 2 3 4 5 6 7	1 2 3 4 5 6 7	1 2 3 4 5 6 7	1 2 3 4 5 6 7	1 2 3 4 5 6 7
Stress	1 2 3 4 5 6 7	1 2 3 4 5 6 7	1 2 3 4 5 6 7	1 2 3 4 5 6 7	1 2 3 4 5 6 7	1 2 3 4 5 6 7	1 2 3 4 5 6 7
Sleep	1 2 3 4 5 6 7	1 2 3 4 5 6 7	1 2 3 4 5 6 7	1 2 3 4 5 6 7	1 2 3 4 5 6 7	1 2 3 4 5 6 7	1 2 3 4 5 6 7
Appetite	1 2 3 4 5 6 7	1 2 3 4 5 6 7	1 2 3 4 5 6 7	1 2 3 4 5 6 7	1 2 3 4 5 6 7	1 2 3 4 5 6 7	1 2 3 4 5 6 7

Weekly volume _____   Home coach's comments:

FIGURE 16.6 Weekly monitoring sheet.

Competitive Swimmer's
Self-Evaluation Questionnaire

Swimmers can use the following questionnaire to evaluate the way in which they train. Under each point is a section for them to make comments.

Swimmer's name _____

Home program _____

Home coach _____

Camp coach _____

1. Maintain correct stroke technique throughout the training session.
   _____

2. Start each workout with a correct racing start.
   _____

3. Take at least two strokes out of every start or turn before breathing on butterfly and freestyle, regardless of the intensity of the set.
   _____

4. Finish each repeat as if it were a finish in a race, regardless of the intensity of the set.
   _____

5. Concentrate at all times while doing stroke drills.
   _____

6. Execute perfection in all stroke drills, concentrating on taking fewer strokes but gaining maximum propulsion on all pulls.
   _____

7. Work on streamlining on every start, push-off, and turn.
   _____

8. Leave on the correct time for all training repeats.
   _____

9. Look at the clock for the time on all repeats after the finish, not during the finish. Take heart rate following all repeats and record it.
   _____

10. Do you always do legal turns on butterfly and breaststroke training, including the touch and the underwater pullout in breaststroke?
    _____

11. Do you always start on alternate arms in backstroke sets so that you develop turns on both arms?
    _____

12. When asked, do you work on controlled breathing patterns, such as every three strokes in butterfly?
    _____

13. Do you keep a neat, accurate logbook?
    _____

14. Do you record all your competition times in your logbook?

15. Do you ask your coaches how they think you are doing?

16. Do you always approach your training with a positive attitude?

17. Do you believe that a champion has to try to work hard even if he or she does not feel like it?

18. Would you say that you contribute to a positive training environment, either through your work rate or your attitude?

19. Would you intentionally miss laps or lengths during workouts if the opportunity were available?

20. Does it worry you if someone with a slower personal best time constantly beats you in workouts?

21. To get an efficiency rating, add the number of strokes it takes to do a certain repeat to the time required for that repeat. For example, 30 seconds for 50 m done in 30 strokes produces a rating of 60. The lower the rating, the better the repeat.

22. Do you concentrate on hand speed at the back end of each stroke without slipping?

23. Do you time yourself on every repeat in training, including drills, kick, pull, and swim? If so, do you record these times in your logbook?

24. Do you work on improving proficiency at stroke extremities during dryland training?

25. Do you perform core-stability exercises every day, either at training or at home before bed?

26. What dryland training do you perform in your club program? How often and for how long?

27. Do you practice turning both ways on all strokes?

28. Do you count your strokes down and back in pools to check maintenance of stroke efficiency?

29. Can you perform to your absolute best in the worst possible conditions?

30. Is the successful swimmer the most talented or the best-prepared talent?

    _____

31. Is the successful swimmer the person with the will to win or the person with the will to prepare to win?

    _____

32. Are successful swimmers confident of giving their best in competition because they have always been consistent in giving their best in practice?

    _____

33. Do not rely on God-given talent. Add self-discipline to create a greater total athlete. What are you prepared to do to take the next step in your swimming?

    _____

To progress in everything we do, we need to evaluate the results that we have attained. Each season the swimmer and coach should undertake this process and review the year in detail. Throughout the season, they should regularly assess the progress being made. The information in this chapter will help the coach and swimmer review issues and take things forward in the next season.

Glossary

adaptation training week—A week of training placed at an appropriate time in the training macrocycle, as and when required by the athlete or as planned by the coach. An adaptation week maintains training volume (distance covered) but is of lower intensity, thereby helping the swimmer recover from previous training.

aerobic training—Training at a prescribed level, described as doing the greatest amount of work in the shortest possible time with the least amount of rest. Each of the three types of aerobic training has a slightly different emphasis, as explained in the glossary. The swimmer may have one aerobic system, but it can be trained at different levels. The body requires oxygen when training aerobically. This type of training is also referred to as the swimmer's aerobic base training.

aerobic 1 (A1)—Training at a heart rate of 50 to 70 beats below the swimmer's maximum heart rate. This low-intensity training (recovery work) complements training done at higher levels, such as race-pace and speed training. This training is not recommended for a female, unless she is a heavily built sprinter.

aerobic 2 (A2)—Training at a heart rate of 40 to 50 beats below the swimmer's maximum heart rate. This training, which can be described as aerobic maintenance training, will maintain current aerobic fitness but will not improve it. A2 training is more important for recovery training for females than A1 is.

aerobic 3 (A3)—Training at a heart rate of 30 to 40 beats below the swimmer's maximum heart rate. This training, which can be described as aerobic development training, will improve the aerobic fitness of the swimmer.

age-group swimmer—Term used for swimmers about 11 to 13 years old for females and 11 to 14 years old for males.

anaerobic threshold training—Training at a heart rate of 20 to 30 beats below the swimmer's maximum heart rate. Anaerobic threshold is defined as the speed at which a swimmer can train without significant buildup of lactic acid.

anaerobic zone training—Working at high intensity levels normally associated with race-pace training. Because the body produces extremely high levels of lactic acid when doing this type of training, it can be described as lactate training.

bands—Normally made from inner tubes. The inner tube is cut into bands that are used to hold the legs together for pull training.

broken swims—Training repeats with more than one break, such as the following: 200 m with 10 seconds at 50 m and 100 m; or 200 m with 10 seconds at 50 m and 150 m; or 200 m with 10 seconds at 50 m, 100 m, and 150 m.

build swims—Swims during which the swimmer increases speed throughout the distance being performed. In performing a 400 m freestyle swim, the swimmer might split the swim by recording these times on each 50 m of the swim: 39, 38, 37, 36, 35, 34, 33, 32. The swimmer does the first 50 m in 39 seconds and the final 50 m in 32 seconds. Because speed and effort builds through the swim, this type of swim is called a build swim

critical speed training—High-intensity endurance swimming training. Repeat times for training are established using the method described in chapter 1. The heart rate will be 10 to

20 beats below the swimmer's maximum heart rate on 50 m to 200 m repeats. Holding the critical speed training time is the swimmer's goal when doing this type of work.

descending sets—Sometimes referred to as reducing sets. The athlete performs each swim within a set faster. An example is 4 × 100 m FS, descending the time on the swims from 66 to 65 to 64 to 63.

distance per stroke—Performing a race or training repeat with the minimum number of arm strokes, thereby having great distance per stroke and efficiency.

endurance training week—A week of training placed at an appropriate time in the training macrocycle. This type of week has the highest volume in the macrocycle and emphasizes all types of endurance training.

even split—Swimming the same time on the first half and second half of a race or training repeat. For example, if the total time for a 400 m FS were 4:10.00, the splits would be 2:05.00 and 2:05.00.

finger paddles—Worn in training, finger paddles fit underneath the fingers and are designed so that the swimmer pulls with correct technique at the start of the arm stroke. The swimmer does this by applying pressure under the fingertips when starting the pull and keeping the wrist high.

finishes—How the swimmer touches the wall at the end of a race or training repeat. The swimmer should practice finishes as outlined in chapter 10.

hand paddles—Worn on the hands in training sets, hand paddles are generally slightly larger than the swimmer's hand and are designed to increase resistance felt by the swimmer. Each of the many types of paddles available serves a specific need. The one to use depends on the type of result the swimmer is pursuing. The coach should evaluate the strengths and weaknesses of the athlete, determine the desired outcome, and then select the appropriate type of hand paddle. The coach should choose hand paddles for swimmers based on individual needs or may consider designing and making suitable paddles.

heart rate—Many sets in training are controlled by the use of heart-rate levels. Swimmers can take their own heart rates by measuring beats per minute or by using heart-rate monitors.

heart-rate drift—Occurs through some long sets such as 20 × 100 m FS. A swimmer's heart rate may be 146 beats per minute (bpm) after the 3rd 100 m and drop to a 120 bpm before the swimmer starts the 4th 100 m. The difference is 26 bpm. Will the heart rate be the same after the 18th swim going into the 19th? The heart rate after the 18th swim may be higher because of heart-rate drift. If it were, the swimmer would be performing a similar workload at a slightly higher heart rate because of the time of the workload. After the 18th 100 m, the heart rate may be 156 bpm and fall to 130 bpm before the 19th.

high-performance endurance (HPE)—Training in which the swimmer works at a high level of intensity in endurance training, such as sets up to 3000 m with the heart rate at 10 to 20 beats below maximum. Critical speed, lactate removal, and $M\dot{V}O_2$ training fall within this type of training.

high-velocity overloads—Swims conducted at faster than 50 m racing speed over distances shorter than 50 m.

junior swimmer—Term generally used for swimmers 10 years old and younger.

kick training—Training by using just the legs, with the arms positioned in a nonpropulsive position or on a kickboard.

lactate-removal training—Endurance training at high intensity, thereby making the body more efficient at removing lactate through the training set. The set is based primarily on a heart rate of 10 to 20 beats below maximum.

lactic acid—A by-product of exercise produced by swimming at any intensity level. The intensity of training determines the quantity produced. Low-intensity aerobic swimming produces low levels of lactic acid, whereas race-pace training produces high levels of lactic acid. Lactic acid is sometimes referred to as lactate.

macrocycle—Each seasonal plan is broken down into smaller macrocycles. Normally, macrocycles are 15 to 24 weeks long and have a goal for the end of the cycle. Within each macrocycle are smaller periods called mesocycles. For example, a 15-week macrocycle may be broken down into five mesocycles of three weeks each.

main set—The primary training objective conducted during a training session.

main stroke—Sometimes referred to as best stroke or number-one stroke.

masters swimming—Competition in age categories above the age of 19. For example, in Great Britain the youngest age band is 19 to 24 years old. Categories continue in 5-year age bands through to the oldest possible age band of 95 to 99 years old.

maturation—Phase of a child's development in which the body undergoes a series of physiological and biological changes toward becoming a fully developed adult. This normally occurs between the ages of 11 and 16.

mesocycle—Period of one to six weeks that usually has its own training emphasis, such as endurance, speed, or race-pace training. Mesocycles fit into a macrocycle.

microcycle—Training week with a specific training emphasis, such as preparation, endurance, quality, mixed, adaptation, specifics, or taper. Some coaches use microcycles shorter than one week.

mixed training week—A week of combined endurance and quality training placed at an appropriate time in the training macrocycle.

M$\dot{V}O_2$ training—Training in the heart-rate range of 10 beats below maximum heart rate to maximum heart rate. M$\dot{V}O_2$ training is swimming at speeds close to maximum for approximately 300 m to 500 m.

negative split—Performing the second half of a race or training repeat faster than the first half of the swim, normally on repeats of 200 m or farther in training. For example, a 400 m FS with a total time of 4:10.00 and splits of 2:06.00 and 2:04.00 is a negative split. The coach should specify to the swimmer what negative is needed (1, 2, 3, or 4 seconds, etc.).

personal best time—Fastest time recorded for a swimming event by a swimmer.

pool lengths—Although the book refers to all training distances in meters, swimmers can perform each set and distance in yards pools as well as meters pools. Training repeat times may have to be adjusted.

preparation training week—A week of training placed at an appropriate time in the training macrocycle. Because the preparation training week is an introductory week of training to ease the swimmer back into work, it generally occurs at the beginning of the macrocycle. Refer to chapter 12 for more details.

pull buoys—Flotation devices that the swimmer uses when performing certain types of pull training. The swimmer holds them between the thighs to support the legs in a more suitable position.

pull training—Any form of swimming training in which the swimmer uses only the arms.

relay teams—Generally, a team of four swimmers who combine to race against other teams of four swimmers. Each swimmer completes a segment of the event with a finish at the wall. The next swimmer takes over from the previous swimmer to complete the next section of the event.

quality training week—A week of training placed at an appropriate time in the training macrocycle. This very intensive training week exposes the swimmer to high-performance endurance training sets. Refer to chapter 12 for more details.

quality training—Race-pace training is crucial to the swimmer's development in all events and to determining individual race strategy. Race-pace training can be used in a variety of ways. We suggest that any set done at 400 m pace or faster be an anaerobic-based (quality) training set.

overdistance training—Long repeats, either in sets or as one long swim, longer than racing distance. Any distance longer than the race distance of the swimmer can be overdistance swimming.

race-pace training—Training based on the goal racing pace of the swimmer.

race profiling—Contains starting time, turning time, stroke rate, stroke counts, split times, and finishing times for a swimmer's goal time. All swimmers should do race profiling to plan how they will swim their event.

rating of perceived exertion—Rating given to any form of training so that the coach has an indication of how the swimmer feels when performing at a certain level.

sculling—Putting the hands and arms in the correct position to maximize propulsion in the water. Swimmers of all ages should practice this skill in training to learn and improve their feel for the water.

seasonal plan—Each swimming year is planned and broken down into smaller cycles of work. The season is split into smaller macrocycles. Two or three macrocycles will normally be conducted in a swimming seasonal plan. The seasonal plan is also called the annual plan or yearly plan. The major competition for the swimming year or season occurs at the end of the seasonal plan.

secondary set—The second main objective of the training session after completion of the main set.

specifics training week—A week of training placed at an appropriate time in the training macrocycle. This type of training week is more specific for the swimmer and contains speed and sprint work as well as more training at race pace. The overall volume of training tends to be lower than that in endurance and quality training weeks. Refer to chapter 12 for more details.

speed training—Training at maximum speed, which is different from training at maximum effort. In speed training, swimmers swim at a faster speed than they do in a 50 m race.

split swims—Training repeats with one break, for example, 200 m with 10 seconds at 100 m.

sprinter—Swimmer whose primary events are sprints, that is, 50 m races.

sprint training—Training at faster than race pace. For the 1500 m swimmer, sprint training may be a set of 50 m repeats; for the 50 m or 100 m swimmer, it may be 15 m repeats.

starts—To start a race, the swimmer performs a start from a diving block. Start variations include the grab start and track start, as outlined in chapter 10.

streamlining position—From the start and turn, the swimmer must assume a streamlined position off the push. The swimmer extends the arms hand over hand and places the head between the arms.

stroke count—Number of arm strokes performed on each lap or length of the pool.

stroke rate—A useful tool for assessing efficiency, measured by using a stopwatch with a stroke-rate function. The coach times three complete stroke cycles. For freestyle and backstroke, the watch starts as one hand enters the water. This first entry, termed 0, is the starting point for the three cycles. The second entry is 1, the third entry is 2, and the fourth entry is 3. As the swimmer makes the fourth entry, the watch stops to mark the completion of the third stroke cycle. In butterfly, the watch starts as both hands enter the water. The sequence is the same as that used for the freestyle and backstroke sequence—0 for start, 1, 2, and 3 for stop. With breaststroke, the starting and stopping point of the three-stroke sequence is when the head breaks the surface or when the hands are at full extension.

swim-down—Performed to aid recovery following a hard training set or a competition performance. The purpose of the swim-down is to remove the lactic acid that builds up in the body. The swim-down can also be referred to as the cool-down.

Swiss ball training—Also referred to as fit ball training or physio ball training. The swimmer uses the ball to perform beneficial stretching exercises.

taper training weeks—One or several weeks of training placed at an appropriate time in the training macrocycle. Taper weeks prepare the swimmer for optimum performance at the upcoming competition. Training focuses on final race preparation, and volume declines gradually as the swimmer prepares to swim fast. Refer to chapter 14 for more details.

torpedo position—Same as streamlining position.

training session—The length of time and the training sets that a swimmer completes at the pool. The training session contains several elements, such as the warm-up, main set, secondary set, and swim-down.

turns—Performed at the end of each lap or length, turns allow the swimmer to change direction during races and in training.

stroke technique—The way in which a swimmer performs the stroke or drill, as requested by the coach. For example, butterfly technique is how the swimmer performs butterfly. Each coach has a model for the optimum way to swim each stroke.

underwater swimming—Performing a kicking or swimming drill under the surface of the water. The amount of underwater swimming depends on the skill and maturation level of the athlete. The coach carefully monitors underwater swimming, and the swimmer builds up this type of work over the season so that he or she does not push too far too soon. The coach and swimmer must use caution for this type of work and be sure that the swimmer has sufficient rest.

youth swimmer—Term used for swimmers 14 to 17 years old for females and 15 to 18 years old for males.

warm-up—Swimming set conducted before the main set of the training session, or a land-based series of exercises performed before the swimming warm-up, or what the swimmer does in the buildup before a race at a competition.

References

Atkinson, J.D. 1992. The Norwich age group programme. *Swimming Coach* (Journal of British Swimming Coaches Association) 10(3):16-18.

Atkinson, J.D. 1998a. The state of our turns. *Australian Swim Coach* (Journal of the Australian Swimming Coaches and Teachers Association) 14(5):32-33.

Atkinson, J.D. 1998b. Plans for developing junior swimmers. *Australian Swim Coach* (Journal of the Australian Swimming Coaches and Teachers Association) 14(6):19-26.

Atkinson, J.D., and W.F. Sweetenham. 1999. *Bill Sweetenham's test sets for age and youth level swimmers.* Lavington, NSW, Australia: Australian Swimming Coaches and Teachers Association.

Balyi, I. 2002. Models of long-term athlete development and training requirements of different sports. *New Zealand Coach* 10(3) (autumn): 6-9.

Blanch, P. 1997. *The swimming machine—make the most of every stroke by being flexible and strong.* Dickson, ACT, Australia: Australian Swimming Inc.

Burke, L., D. Pyne, and R. Telford. 1996. Effect of oral creatine supplementation on single effort sprint performance in elite swimmers. *International Journal of Sports Nutrition* 6(3):222-237.

Carew, J., and D. Pyne. 1999. How much huff and puff?—training endurance swimming. *Australian Swim Coach* (Journal of the Australian Swimming Coaches and Teachers Association) 15(3):37-40.

Costill, D., D. Hinrichs, W.J. Fink, and D. Hoopes. 1988. Muscle glycogen depletion during swimming interval training. *Journal of Swimming Research* 4(1):15-18.

Friden, J., J. Seger, and B. Ekblom. 1989. Topographical localization of muscle glycogen: An ultrahistochemical study in the human vastus lateralis. *Acta Physiologica Scandinavia* 135:171-174.

Maglischo, E.W. 1993. *Swimming even faster.* Mountain View, CA: Mayfield.

Miyashita, M. 1996. Key factors in success of altitude training for swimming. *Research Quarterly for Exercise and Sport* 67 (Supplement no. 3).

Nelson B. 1994-1997. Individualising medley. *Coaches guide.* Vol. 1, 9-17. Lavington, NSW, Australia: Australian Swimming Coaches and Teachers Association (ASCTA).

Olbrecht, J. 2000. *The science of winning—planning, periodizing and optimizing swim training.* Kersenbomenlaan, 37, 3090 Overijse, Belgium: J. Olbrecht.

Pyne, D. 1995. The specificity of training—a fresh look at an old principle: Using aerobic training to improve both aerobic and anaerobic fitness. *Australian Swim Coach* (Journal of the Australian Swimming Coaches Association) 11(7):27-30.

Pyne, D. 1999a. Integrating all aspects of training into a single 6000 m workout. *Coaches guide.* Vol. 3, 28-39. Lavington, NSW, Australia: Australian Swimming Coaches and Teachers Association (ASCTA).

Pyne, D. 1999b. Training for positive outcomes. *ASCTA 1999 conference presentations*, 109-114. Lavington, NSW, Australia: Australian Swimming Coaches and Teachers Association.

Pyne, D., and W. Goldsmith. 1996. The top ten training tips. *Australian Swim Coach* (Journal of the Australian Swimming Coaches and Teachers Association) 12(2).

Richards, R. 1995. Future directions in coaching. *Australian Swim Coach* (Journal of the Australian Swimming Coaches and Teachers Association) 11(12):6-11.

Richards, R. 1996. *Coaching swimmers—an introductory manual.* Dickson, ACT, Australia: Australian Swimming Inc.

Richards, R. 1999. Building conceptual models: Linking scientific principles to coaching practice. *Australian Swim Coach* (Journal of the Australian Swimming Coaches and Teachers Association) 15(2):14-25.

Richards, R., D. Pyne, B. Sweetenham, and W. Goldsmith. 1996. 1990-1995 age group performance comparisons. *Australian Swim Coach* (Journal of the Australian Swimming Coaches and Teachers Association)

Sweetenham, B. 1990. *Australian Institute of Sport Swimming Manual 1990.* Belconnen, ACT, Australia.

Sweetenham, B. 1994-1997. Coaching in a training camp environment. *Coaches guide.* Vol. 1, 29-31. Lavington, NSW, Australia: Australian Swimming Coaches and Teachers Association (ASCTA).

Sweetenham, B. 1996a. Progression stroke drills for national tip top squad members. *Australian Swim Coach* (Journal of the Australian Swimming Coaches and Teachers Association) 12(4).

Sweetenham, B. 1996b. Turning skills for national tip top squad—freestyle and backstroke and national drills for tip top squad members. *Australian Swim Coach* (Journal of the Australian Swimming Coaches and Teachers Association) 12(2).

Sweetenham, B. 1996c. A personal view of Australian age group swimming. *Australian Swim Coach* (Journal of the Australian Swimming Coaches and Teachers Association) 12(1).

Sweetenham, B. 1997a. Feel the stroke drill. *Tip Top Times* (Newsletter of Australian Swimming Tip Top Squad Members) 2(2):2.

Sweetenham, B. 1997b. Swim in, swim up, swim down, swim out for age group and youth swimmers. *Tip Top Times* (Newsletter of Australian Swimming Tip Top Squad Members) 2(4):2-3.

Sweetenham, B. 1998-1999. Coaches self evaluation. *Coaches guide.* Vol. 2, 88-89. Lavington, NSW, Australia: Australian Swimming Coaches and Teachers Association (ASCTA).

Sweetenham, B. 1998a. Preparing pre-maturation female endurance athletes. *Australian Swim Coach* (Journal of the Australian Swimming Coaches and Teachers Association) 14(5):14-18.

Sweetenham, B. 1998b. Coaching and parenting for age group youth level swimmers. *Australian Swim Coach* (Journal of the Australian Swimming Coaches and Teachers Association) 14(5):11-14.

Sweetenham, B. 1998c. Coaching philosophies and strategies for working with talented age group and youth swimmers. *Australian Swim Coach* (Journal of the Australian Swimming Coaches and Teachers Association) 14(4):9-11.

Sweetenham, B. 1998d. *21st century swimming—volume 1 freestyle* (Video). Lavington, NSW, Australia: Australian Swimming Coaches and Teachers Association and JOBEN Media Productions.

Sweetenham, B. 1998e. *21st century swimming—volume 2 backstroke* (Video). Lavington, NSW, Australia: Australian Swimming Coaches and Teachers Association and JOBEN Media Productions.

Sweetenham, B. 1998f. *21st century swimming—volume 3 breaststroke* (Video). Lavington, NSW, Australia: Australian Swimming Coaches and Teachers Association and JOBEN Media Productions.

Sweetenham, B. 1998g. *21st century swimming—volume 4 butterfly* (Video). Lavington, NSW, Australia: Australian Swimming Coaches and Teachers Association and JOBEN Media Productions.

Sweetenham, B. 1998h. *21st century swimming—volume 5 individual medley* (Video). Lavington, NSW, Australia: Australian Swimming Coaches and Teachers Association and JOBEN Media Productions.

Sweetenham, B. 1998i. *21st century swimming—volume 6 starts, turns and finishes* (Video). Lavington, NSW, Australia: Australian Swimming Coaches and Teachers Association and JOBEN Media Productions.

Sweetenham, B. 1998j. *21st century swimming—volume 7 advanced drills* (Video). Lavington, NSW, Australia: Australian Swimming Coaches and Teachers Association and JOBEN Media Productions.

Sweetenham, B. 1998k. *21st century swimming—volume 8 mini squad/junior squad* (Video). Lavington, NSW, Australia: Australian Swimming Coaches and Teachers Association and JOBEN Media Productions.

Sweetenham, B. 1998l. *21st century swimming—volume 9 coaching hints* (Video). Lavington, NSW, Australia: Australian Swimming Coaches and Teachers Association and JOBEN Media Productions.

Sweetenham, B. 1999a. Preparing pre-maturation female endurance athletes. *Coaches guide.* Vol. 3, 20-23. Lavington, NSW, Australia: Australian Swimming Coaches and Teachers Association (ASCTA).

Sweetenham, B. 1999b. Age group development—coaching philosophies and strategies for working with talented age group and youth swimmers. *Coaches guide.* Vol. 3, 102-104. Lavington, NSW, Australia: Australian Swimming Coaches and Teachers Association (ASCTA).

Sweetenham, B. 1999c. Drills, short term goals, etc. *Coaches guide.* Vol. 3, 112-116. Lavington, NSW, Australia: Australian Swimming Coaches and Teachers Association (ASCTA).

Sweetenham, B. 1999d. Break point volume. *Australian Swim Coach* (Journal of the Australian Swimming Coaches and Teachers Association) 15(4):26-29.

Sweetenham, B., and W. Goldsmith. 1997. The missing link: Linking drills to main sets for faster swimming. *Australian Swim Coach* (Journal of the Australian Swimming Coaches and Teachers Association) 13(2).

Sweetenham, B., and W. Goldsmith. 1998. Developing a successful age group swimming program. *Australian Swim Coach* (Journal of the Australian Swimming Coaches and Teachers Association) 14(5):7-10.

Treffene, B. 1992. Heart rate sets: What are they? *Australian Swim Coach* (Journal of the Australian Swimming Coaches and Teachers Association) Nov.

Treffene, B. 1994-1997. Glycogen replacement rate and its use in program design. *Coaches guide.* Vol. 1, 127-131. Lavington, NSW, Australia: Australian Swimming Coaches and Teachers Association (ASCTA).

Volkers, S. 1994. Stroke drills and speed drills. *Australian Swim Coach* (Journal of the Australian Swimming Coaches and Teachers Association) 11(6)

Index

Note: The italicized *f* and *t* following page numbers refer to figures and tables, respectively.

A

abdominal exercises
    advanced leg raises 276, 276*f*
    bent-leg raises 275, 275*f*
    crunches 274, 274*f*
    front abdominal sit-ups 263*f*, 273
    plank position 278, 278*f*
    sit-ups 277, 277*f*
aerobic base and endurance swimming
    about 12-13
    males *vs.* females 13
    optimal adaptation 15
    progression examples 13-15
    training volume 15
aerobic training (zone 1)
    blank training log 213, 215*f*
    coaching 213, 214
    completed training log 213, 214*f*
    double-up training sets 219-221
    explained 213
    overdistance and continuous training sets 215-217
    short-rest training sets 217-218
    types 5-6
    varied-pace training sets 218-219
age-group swimmers
    age-group basic 24-week macrocycle 175, 176, 176*f*
    age-group varied 24-week macrocycle with ascending loading sequence 176, 177, 178*f*
    macrocycles, mesocycles, and microcycles 175
anaerobic (race-pace training) (zone 4)
    competition time 10
    explained 9-10
    lactate production 10
    lactate tolerance 11
    lactate training, types of 9
    peak lactate 11
    peak lactate training sets 11, 233
    progression from production to tolerance training 233
    race-pace lactate-production sets 10, 229-230
    race-pace lactate tolerance sets 11, 231-233
    split and broken swims 10
anaerobic threshold (zone 2)
    explained 6-7
    sample sets 221-222
annual plan 174

B

backstroke
    advantages of 73
    backstroke checklist 81-82
    backstroke technique stroke analysis 81
    backstroke technique stroke analysis sheet 83-84
backstroke drill progressions
    arm scull drill 77
    bent-arm sculling drills 77-78
    crossover kick with rotation 78-79
    end-of-stroke drill 79
    feel-the-stroke drill 79
    fists and paddles 76-77
    hip, shoulder, and trunk rotation 75-76

    junior squad backstroke drill progression 80
    lateral side kick rotation 77
    overreaching correction 79
    rotation scull feel 76
    scull catch 74-75
backstroke stroke technique 73-74, 74*f*
breaststroke
    about 85
    breaststroke stroke technique 85, 86*f*
    checklist 97-98
breaststroke drill progressions
    breaststroke 89
    distance per stroke breaststroke (lane ropes) 89
    feel-the-stroke drill 92
    fists and paddles 86
    junior squad breaststroke drill progression 92-93
    kick and pull 88-89
    kick and scull-pull 90
    kick drill and timing development 87
    pull and timing drill 87-88
    sample breaststroke progression 8 90-91
    speed drill 88
    strong kick development 91
    tennis balls and sinkers for pull development 92
breaststroke technique stroke analysis
    about 93
    sheet 94-96
butterfly, backstroke, and freestyle starts and turns
    backstroke start drill 143
    backstroke start progression 144
    freestyle start and turn drill 145
butterfly drill progressions
    Biondi drill 63
    breathing and timing (with or without fins) 65-66
    breathing, timing, and kicking 62-63
    feel-the-stroke drill 66
    fists and paddles 64
    junior squad butterfly drill progression 67-68
    kick development 65
    power kick and timing drill 64-65
butterfly technique stroke analysis
    about 68
    checklist 71-72
    sheet 69-70

C

club (squad system). *See* squads
cold-swim test 34-35
competition, frequency of
    described 172-173
    less dedicated *vs.* dedicated swimmers 173, 174*f*
    levels 173
    per month 173
core strength, exercises for
    abdominal exercises 273-278
    body pull-up 273
    dips 272, 272*f*-273*f*
    lumbar hold 262*f*, 272
    pull-ups 272
    push-up hold 262*f*, 270
    push-ups 270, 271*f*

core strength tests
  advanced core strength bench test 263, 264, 264*f*
  front abdominal hold 263, 263*f*
  lumbar hold 262, 262*f*
  push-up position hold test 261, 261*f*, 262
  push-up test with shoulder blades together 262, 262*f*
  swim bench test 263

D
double-distance 400-meter test 25-26
double-up training sets
  explained 221
  sample 219
drilling
  specific drill progressions 59
  stroke-efficiency progressions 55-59
dryland conditioning
  core strength tests 261-264
  exercises for core strength 270-278
  exercises for starts and turns 264-270
  flexibility tests 264
dryland conditioning, warm-up and stretching
  adductor stretch 256, 256*f*
  alternate arm crossing 255, 255*f*
  arm crossing swinging 255, 255*f*
  arm swinging, backward and forward 254
  combined internal rotation elevation stretch 256, 256*f*
  double-arm skiing 254, 254*f*
  explained 253-254
  external rotators stretch 258, 258*f*
  hamstring stretch 259, 259*f*
  internal rotators stretch 258, 258*f*
  latissimus stretch 260, 260*f*
  pectoral stretch 260, 260*f*
  skipping rope 254
  supine stretch 261, 261*f*
  teres stretch 257, 257*f*
  triceps stretch 259, 259*f*
  upper trapezius stretch 257, 257*f*

E
endurance training progression for maturation-- elite-level age groupers
  aerobic and skill training base 207-208
  benefits 208
  goal 208
  summary points for coaches 208

F
finishes
  backstroke finish 157, 157*f*
  breaststroke finish 158, 158*f*
  butterfly and breaststroke finishing drill 159
  butterfly finish 156, 156*f*, 157
  checklists for finish of each stroke 156-159
  freestyle finish 158, 158*f*
  start, turn, and finish drill 159
flexibility tests 264, 265*f*
freestyle drill progressions
  feel-the-stroke drill 105
  fists and hand paddles 104
  front lateral kick with hip rotation 104-105
  high elbow recovery and rotation 102-103
  hip, shoulder, and trunk rotation 101-102
  junior squad freestyle drill progression 106
  rotation scull feel 103
  scull catch 100
  touch-the-kickboard drill 105
  weak-arm, strong-arm hand paddle rotation drill 103-104
freestyle stroke technique 99, 100*f*
freestyle technique stroke analysis
  about 106
  distance-swimming checklist 110-111

sheet 107-108
sprint checklist 109-110

H
heart-rate test, maximum
  achieving 30
  double-distance 400-meter test recording sheet 27*f*
  recording sheet for 200 m and farther swimmers 28*f*
  recording sheet for 50 m & 100 m swimmers 29*f*
  test set 26, 27, 29-30
  warm-up 26
heats, semifinals, and finals 248
high-performance endurance test-set progression
  explained 35, 36
  prescribing training repeat times 37
  sample 3000 and 2000-meter time trials 37
  40 × 100 m freestyle recording sheet 36*f*
high performance endurance (zone 3)
  critical speed (CS) 7-8, 222-223
  lactate removal 8-9, 223-224
  M$\dot{V}O_2$ 9, 224-225
  sets and sessions 225-228
  training sets, adjusting 223

I
IM, high-performance endurance sets
  critical speed 124-125
  M$\dot{V}O_2$ 123-124
IM and form stroke count efficiency test for age- group swimmers 13 years and younger
  about 46
  form test 48
  100-meter IM 47
  200-meter IM 48
  400-meter IM 48
  recording sheet 48, 49*f*
IM checklist 125-126
IM pace test progression
  blank IM strengths and weaknesses chart 40*f*
  completed IM strengths and weaknesses chart 39*f*
  using 38
  10 × 100 m and 1 × 200 m IM pace test recording sheet 41*f*
  6 × 200 m IM pace test recording sheet 42*f*
IM sets
  aerobic 118-122
  anaerobic training zone sets (including race- pace training) 122-123
  butterfly sets for IM swimmer 118
  high-performance endurance sets 123-125
  100-meter 115-116
  switch training and sample sets 116-118
individual checking speed (ICS) tests
  efficiency 50, 51
  explained 50
  fitness 52
  psychological 52
  recording sheet 50, 51*f*
  speed 50
  stroke rate 51
  technical and tactical 52
  using 50
individual medley (IM)
  about 113
  checklist 125-126
  drill progressions 114
  planning 113-114, 115*t*
  sets 115-125

K
kick and pull training
  pull training 165-167
  swimming with hand paddles 167

kick test sets
  comparing 43
  recording sheet 44*f*
  test protocol 43
kick training
  about 161
  conditioning legs 162
  kickboards 162
  kicking with flippers 163
  kick sets 162, 163-165
M
macrocycle 174
masters swimmers
  15-week macrocycle 186, 186*f*, 187
  15-week macrocycle with descending
    mesocycles 187, 187*f*
maximum heart rate test. *See* heart-rate test,
    maximum
mesocycle 174
microcycles, sample (training weeks)
  adaptation training week 198
  endurance training week 189, 190*t*
  mixed training week 191, 192, 192*t*
  preparation training week 189, 190*t*
  quality training week 189, 191, 191*t*
  specifics training week 192, 193*t*, 194*t*
  specifics training week with heat, semifinal,
    and final progression 192, 193, 193*t*
  taper training week 1 194, 195, 195*t*
  taper training week 2 195, 196-197, 196*t*
  taper training week 3 197, 197*t*, 198
P
planning development of junior swimmer
  club squad system 198-207
  philosophy 198
  talent identification 198
program evaluation
  competitive swimmer's self-evaluation
    questionnaire 286-288
  goal-setting recording sheet 279, 282*f*
  performance recording log 279, 283*f*
  personal best times recording sheet 279, 282*f*
  swimmer details recording sheet 279, 281*f*
  training log checklist 279-280, 281
  weekly monitoring sheet 279, 285*f*
  weekly volume recording log 279, 284*f*
program planning
  developing junior swimmer 198-207
  early training parameters 171
  endurance training progression for
    maturation—elite-level age groupers 207-208
  frequency of competition 172-174
  microcycles (training weeks) 189-198
  tapering 172
  training cycles 174
  training models 174-189
  training phases 209-212
  triathletes 171, 172
  winter swimming 212
pull tests 45, 45*f*
pull training
  about 165
  sample pull sets 165-167
R
recovery and swimming down
  about 249
  calculating when swimmer is recovered 249-250
  competitive swimmer's competition checklist
    251-252
  individual checking speed test, using 250
relay swimming, drills 159-160
S
sculling
  flat wrist 127, 127*f*

  midpoint 127, 127*f*, 128
  wrist down 127, 127*f*
  wrist up 127, 127*f*
sculling for core strength
  explained 131
  progression 1: introduction level 131-132
  progression 2: intermediate level 132-134
  progression 3: advanced level 134-136
sculling progressions
  backstroke 128, 128*f*, 129*f*
  breaststroke 129, 129*f*
  butterfly 128
  butterfly and breaststroke combination scull
    130
  freestyle 129-130
  IM mixture 130
seasonal plan 174
speed tests
  areas of 45-46
  explained 46
  recording sheet 46, 47*f*
sprint (zone 5)
  explained 11
  high-velocity overloads (HVO) 11
  speed training pace, calculating 12
  training sets 234-236
squads
  clubs 198, 199
  level 1 199-200, 200*t*, 201
  level 2 201-202, 202*t*
  level 3 203, 204*t*-205*t*, 206-207
  structure 198, 199, 199*t*
starts
  about 137
  backstroke start underwater 141, 141*f*
  breaststroke underwater 142, 142*f*
  butterfly, backstroke, and freestyle starts and
    turns 143-145
  checklists for start of each stroke 140-143, 141*f*,
    142*f*
  flight and entry following grab start 139, 139*f*
  grab start 138, 139, 139*f*
  grab start position 138, 139*f*
  grab start position using handles 138, 139*f*
  hoop dives 140
  track start 139-140, 140*f*
starts, turns, finishes, and relay takeovers
  finishes 156-159
  relay swimming 159-160
  starts 137-145
  turns 145-155
starts and turns, exercises for
  about 264
  leg power drill 269, 269*f*
  lunges 266, 266*f*
  medicine ball 270
  plyometric jump 267, 268*f*
  squat jumps 266, 266*f*-267*f*
stroke-efficiency progressions
  about 55
  achieving 55-56
  drill progression to improve whole stroke 57,
    58-59
  progression example 57
  progression of skill acquisition, factors in 56
  stroke-drill progression program 56
Sweetenham, Bill 8
swimming down and recovery. *See* recovery and
    swimming down
T
taper, planning
  about 237
  carbohydrate intake 246
  chart model 238, 238*f*, 239-240

taper, planning *(continued)*
  developing model 237-238
  dual-peaking situation 246-247
  flat spots 239
  four to five weeks from competition 240-241
  intensity 238
  monthly mesocycle 238, 239*t*
  one week from competition 243
  resting for midseason meets 247
  tapering principles 238, 239
  tapering volumes 244, 244*f*, 245, 245*f*
  three weeks from competition 241-242, 243*t*
  training log 239
  two weeks from competition 243
  warm-up and swim-down rehearsal 245-246
tapering for competition
  coping with heats, semifinals, and finals 248
  explained 237
  planning the taper 237-247
  swimming down and recovery 249-252
test sets
  about 17
  cold-swim test 34-35
  double-distance 400-meter test 25-26
  high-performance endurance test-set
    progression 35-37
  IM and form stroke count efficiency test (age-
    group swimmers 13 years and younger) 46-49
  individual checking speed tests 50-52
  individual medley pace test progression 38-42
  kick test sets 43-44
  maximum heart-rate test 26-30
  pull tests 45, 45*f*
  recording results 17-18
  speed tests 45-46
  8 × 50 meter efficiency test 30-34
  7 × 200 meter step test 19-25
test sets, planning use of
  IM pace set 54
  individual checking speed tests and IM and
    form-stroke efficiency test 54
  testing pattern 52-54
training models
  about 174-175
  age-group swimmers 175-178
  masters swimmers 186-187
  triathletes 188-189
  youth and senior swimmers 178-185
training phases
  breakpoint volume 210
  improvement at and after maturation 211-212
  learning-to-achieve 209-210
  learning-to-swim 209
  learning-to-train 209
  long-term development program 210-211
training systems. *See also* training zones
  aerobic training zone 213-221
  anaerobic base and endurance swimming 12-15
  anaerobic (race-pace training) 229-233
  anaerobic threshold 221-222
  categories 3
  high-performance endurance 222-228
  how to individualize 4-5
  monitoring 3
  sprint 234-236
  total training volume, percentage of 3, 4*t*
training zones
  aerobic 5, 6, 213-221
  anaerobic (race-pace training) 9-11, 229-233
  anaerobic threshold 6-7, 221-222
  high-performance endurance 7-9, 222-228
  sprint 11-12, 234-236

triathletes, 24-week macrocycle 188, 188*f*, 189
turning drills for freestyle and backstroke
  about 148
  backstroke lane rope turning progression 151,
    151*f*
  freestyle and backstroke jump turns 153, 153*f*
  freestyle and backstroke midpool turns 152
  freestyle kickboard turns 154
  freestyle lane rope turns advanced progression
    150
  freestyle lane rope turns introductory
    progression 149
  freestyle midpool turning tests 152-153
  lane line 149
  midpool turns 152
  rotation speed for freestyle and backstroke
    turns 152
  stationary midpool turns 152
  target times 151
turns
  about 145
  checklists for turn of each stroke 146-148
  freestyle lane rope turns introductory
    progression 149-154
  habits 146
  IM turns 148
  incorrect turns 146
  practicing turns 146
  turning drills for butterfly and breaststroke
    154-155

W
winter swimming 212

X
8 × 50 meter efficiency test
  explained 30, 32
  manipulating 32
  recording sheet 33*f*
  sample test set results, time *vs.* stroke count 31*t*
  sample test set results, time *vs.* stroke rate 31*t*
  stroke count *vs.* velocity graph 31*f*
  stroke rate *vs.* velocity graph 32*f*
  using over eight-week period 32, 34
7 × 200 meter step test
  age-group and youth test set 19
  assessment of 18-19
  conducting 18
  heart rate *vs.* velocity graph 21*f*
  for IM swimmers 23, 24, 25*f*
  lactate *vs.* velocity graph 21*f*
  rate of perceived exertion *vs.* velocity graph 23*f*
  recording information 20-23
  recording sheet 24*f*
  sample test-set results for senior 21*t*
  senior test set 19-20
  stroke count *vs.* velocity graph 22*f*
  stroke rate *vs.* velocity graph 22*f*
  swim-down 23
  warm-up 19

Y
youth and senior swimmers
  distance swimmers' varied 24-week macrocycle
    181, 182, 182*f*
  early season 15-week macrocycle 178-179, 179*f*
  midseason 15-week macrocycle 179, 180*f*
  senior sprinters' 15-week macrocycle with
    reverse periodization 184-185, 185*f*
  sprinters' varied 15-week macrocycle 183, 184,
    184*f*
  sprinters' 15-week macrocycle 182, 183, 183*f*
  varied 15-week macrocycle 180, 181*f*

Z
zones. *See* training zones

About the Authors

Bill Sweetenham was the coaching force behind Australia's success at the Olympic and Commonwealth Games. He was voted Australian Coach of the Year three times and has coached 63 swimmers in international competitions to 27 medals in four Olympics and seven World Championships. He spent more than 20 years coaching Australian swimmers to success before accepting the position of head coach of the Hong Kong Sports Institute (1991 to 1994). He then returned to Australia as the national youth coach to prepare up-and-coming swimmers for the 2000 Olympics. To date, he says he's most proud of placing nine swimmers on the 1989 Australian Pan Pacific Team who scored a 100 percent strike rate for improved heats to final performances and a 100 percent personal best strike rate.

Sweetenham was named Great Britain's national performance director in November 2000, a position he currently holds. The rebuilding of Great Britain's team didn't take long: They posted their best results since 1975 at the 2001 World Championships in Japan.

In addition to taking national teams to the height of international success, Sweetenham continues to lecture, publish, and conduct clinics all over the world.

John Atkinson returned to his homeland and joined Sweetenham in Great Britain as the national youth coach with British Swimming in November 2000. Born in the United Kingdom, where he swam competitively before starting a coaching career in 1985, Atkinson was a team coach at the national and club level in Australia from 1995 to 2000. While in Australia, he coached at the Elizabeth Aquatic Club; was team coach with the Australian team at the Oceania Championships in 1997; national youth camp coach in 1997; and head coach for the successful Tip Top program in 1998, where he first had the opportunity to work with Sweetenham.

Atkinson has worked with teams from Australia, Japan, India, and the Republic of South Africa national youth team. He currently resides in Lancashire, England, with his wife, Victoria.

The best coaching in swimming

In *Breakthrough Swimming*, legendary coach Cecil Colwin provides a rich perspective on the development of competitive swimming and teaches the optimal techniques for each stroke. Accompanied by detailed illustrations, this engaging text is one of the most thorough and insightful technical presentations ever made in swimming. It combines history with the latest breakthroughs to provide a complete perspective on the past, present, and future of competitive swimming.

ISBN 0-7360-3777-2 • 262 pages

Ernest Maglischo reveals the science behind the training principles that led his teams to 13 NCAA Division II national championships. *Swimming Fastest*'s detailed technique analysis of the four primary strokes includes more than 500 photographs and illustrations showing exactly how to execute each phase of each stroke. Complementing the technical instruction is a thorough explanation of the physiology behind the most effective training methods, with detailed sample workouts and training programs for each event.

ISBN 0-7360-3180-4 • 800 pages

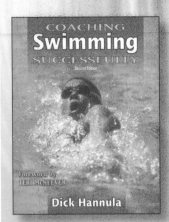

In *Coaching Swimming Successfully*, coaching legend Dick Hannula covers the full range of responsibilities every successful swim coach strives to master.

Every stroke is taught in this comprehensive guide, as are new underwater kicking techniques. It is packed full of information on how to develop a coaching philosophy, schedule and conduct effective practices, prepare for competitions, and evaluate swimmers' performances.

ISBN 0-7360-4519-8 • 192 pages

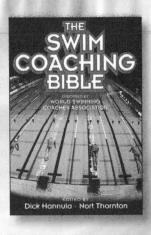

The *Swim Coaching Bible* provides 25 of the world's top experts in the sport, sharing their insights for swimming success. This superb how-to-book offers teaching techniques for every stroke and training programs for every event. From program administration to running an effective practice, the world's top coaches give you the competitive edge.

ISBN 0-7360-3646-6 • 376 pages

HUMAN KINETICS
The Premier Publisher for Sports & Fitness
P.O. Box 5076, Champaign, IL 61825-5076
www.HumanKinetics.com

2335

To place your order, U.S. customers call

1-800-747-4457

In Canada call **1-800-465-7301**
In Australia call **08 8277 1555**
In New Zealand call **09-523-3462**
In Europe call **+44 (0) 113 255 5665**